Ling Bao Tong Z

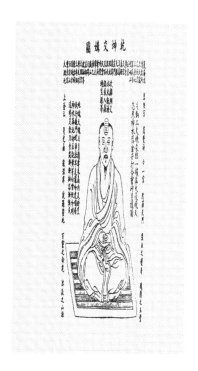

Wang Li Ping
Translated by Richard Liao

1

Library of Congress Cataloging-in-Publication Data

ISBN-13: 978-1470174545

ISBN-10: 1470174545

Contents

Translator's introduction

When I was about thirteen years old, living with my parents in Guangzhou, China, I read martial art novels that started me dreaming about the day that I could have such powers and become a hero. I started to look for a Qi Gong Master who could guide me to that level. I found a meditation and health book written by an acupuncturist and traditional Chinese medicine doctor, published in 1962. I began to study the book and follow the meditation practices it described. I focused on the Lower Dantian, practicing ½ to a few hours each day. Months and years passed by, and then an interesting thing happened: I was meditating one day and my Lower Dantian started pulsing, and became warm and powerful, and I knew that next step was to focus on the Life Gate, located between Lumbar 2 and 3 and there was warm sensation and power push from the exterior, and lastly one focus the perineum. The body can be the source of many unusual experiences and some of these are miracles. But what is the next step, why is it happening? How can I cultivate my practice to the immortal level?

I was keeping my eyes open, until in 1987, I was visiting China, and my high school classmate told me Master Wang Liping was teaching the Taoist meditation of Ling Bao Tong Zhi Neng Nei Gong Shu. I asked him what is the big deal about this Master Wang? He told me that Master Wang taught his students how to practice with trees. I said, I have already seen several books with different method for that, and he said, well, Master Wang told us do not record at this moment in the class, but we have still turned on the recording mode under the table, whenever, the machine didn't have the power to record his words. What he said opened my eyes; this was the power I had been looking for all of my life! Years later I found that the tape where my high school classmate talked about Master Wang lecture the spirit of each organ was blank.

Finally, in 1995, I was in Fushun City in Liaoning Province, China, where Master Wang grew up. I was staying in Master Wang's student's house hoping to find him, but he was in Dalian, about five hundred miles away. I spoke to him for about fifteen seconds on the phone that night, and he said he could not come to Fushun at that time. The next morning I awoke at 7 a.m. and was lying in bed when I felt two flies walking on my left forearm. The feeling was both clear and vivid. I opened my eyes and looked at my arm and there were no flies; I closed my eyes and felt them again, even more strongly, and I looked again and there were no flies and I was somewhat afraid and then I asked myself "What did you come here for?" The answer came: " Looking for Master Wang and miracles" and then I relaxed and allowed the sensation to persist and I knew these sensations were Master Wang's empowerment especially for my self and I was not enough to this level. Yet, as soon as I gave permission one hundred invisible prickles bloomed all over on my left forearm and even under my skin. Not much happened on my right forearm and the feelings continued as natural as oxygen and sunshine, evenly and gently for two hours, after which I had to get up for an appointment. This sensation has continued for years and I still have it if I am practicing the Master's teaching.

From that time, lying in bed in Fushun, I knew Master Wang was a genuine Master and that he was the person I could learn from. In later years when I began to translate this book, I found Master Wang's method of blending himself with the natural world matched the Taoism text book more than a thousand years old that came straight from the ancient Taoist Masters Zhong, Liquan and Lu, Dongbin, who had written about one thousand and thirteen hundreds years ago and had founded the lineage of Wang, Chongyang and which had led to the Dragon Gate branch of Qiu, Chuji about eight hundred years before the present time.

After becoming Master Wang's student, I asked him, how old his grand Master Zhang, Hedao was when he passed away from his human level? Master Wang told me he had been 140 years old! Where? He was the mountain. What was the reason Master Zhang, Hedao had to leave his human body? He told me his Yang Shen of physic eye would be not enough able to travel back and forth for miles distant. And he gave his human physical body into within and out of immortal level.

Please read *Opening the Dragon Gate* by Chen Kaiguo and Zheng Shunchao, translated by Thomas Cleary. This book tells the story of Master Wang Liping's training from childhood on and deals with a great deal of Taoist theory.

If you read the three Taoist text books cited here without already understanding the theory, you will gain a great knowledge in spite of yourself and come to understand that Taoism is based upon what happens in the natural world and the way in which it mirrors the universe. The text Zhong Lu Chuan Dao Ji (Zhong and Lu Deliver Tao Series) describes the basic theory which came from those who followed the Jin Dan path of the internal golden pill. The Wu Pian Ling Wen (Five Ling (soul) Articles) text is about experiences derived from this practice and offers guidelines and the Tai Yi Jin Hua Zhong Zhi (Min version), is a different version a practice known as the secret of golden flower text and emphasizes how to practice and seek the power from the soul and the light experience. All the Taoist practices and meditations are from purpose into no purpose, from no purpose into within and out, from within and out into achievement.

This book has been written with Master Wang's guidance, and all the copyrights belong to Master Wang, Li Ping and Richard Liao.

A special thank you to Suzanne Portero, the spiritual lady who has very patiently edited my English and thanks also to Amy Lee, Betsy Punch, Buffy Laurer, Christopher Liao, Daniel Tao, Denise Ng, Frederick Winslow, Geneviere Le Goft, Jeannette Ho, Jon Fellman, Michael Esposito, Michelle Hrish, Michi Pringle, Pamela Zhang, Patty Lee, Rachel Sun, Ron Elkayam, Ted Marshell and Tim Kurtz. Without them, I could not have finished this book.

Respectfully,

Richard Liao, Acupuncturist and Traditional Chinese Medicine Practitioner and Master Wang authorized instructor. San Francisco Bay Area, U.S.A.

Face book at Tao pathway and email: taopathway@gmail.com

Master Wang Liping's recommendation letter

Acupuncturist and Traditional Chinese Medicine Practitioner and healer Richard Y. Liao has been my student and my friend for more than twenty years, studying with myself the Tai Shang (Upper infinite) pathway to enlightenment gained through understanding the Dan of the golden pill. He uses the teachings and theories of the golden pill in his continuing practice of Traditional Chinese Medicine, using the Xian of immortality to assist in his treatment of his patients. He practices the precepts of Taoism with a sincere heart.

China has one of the worlds' oldest and richest cultures. The Xian of immortality and the Dan of the golden pill methods form the root of Chinese Taoism, refining the Xing Ming of nature self and life, for healing and for the general benefit of mankind.

At a few years ago, Richard asked my permission to embark upon an English translation of the methods I have been taught of the Dragon Gate sect of Taoism from my grand Master Zhang, Hedao and Master Wang, Jiaoming and Jia, Jiaoyi and the golden pill pathway texts of Zhong Lu Chuan Dao Ji, Wu Pian Ling Wen and Tai Yi Jin Hua Zhong Zhi.

Our endeavor is to provide those who perhaps have not the opportunity to learn the disciplines of a Chinese Taoist practitioner and are interested in the mysteries of the pathway to the internal medicine of the golden pill.

This is the first book to be completed in our series.

Congratulations and my deepest gratitude to Richard for his dedication to this project, and also to those who have assisted him in his fine accomplishment.

To those who will read this book I send greetings and wishes for your health and good fortune.

Wang Li Ping
Dalian, China

Lao Zi Academy's letter

Master Wang Liping was first introduced to the West as a modern Taoist master in Thomas Cleary's translation of his book *Opening the Dragon Gate*: The Making of a Modern Taoist Wizard. This biographical novel tells the story of how Master Wang was taught and trained by three Taoist hermits. The first was Zhang Hedao, a 16th generation master. Wang Jiaoming and Master Jia Jiaoyi, both 17th generation transmitters of the Dragon Gate branch of the Complete Reality tradition which originated at Mount Lao in Shandong Province, were also his teachers.

This new book by Master Wang, Ling Bao Tong Zhi Neng Nei Gong Shu represents a practical guide to Taoist health cultivation and meditation and a distillation of over thirty years of teaching both the philosophy and practical methods of Taoism. In the 1980's, we learned of Master Wang and, realizing the many health benefits of the practices he was teaching, began studying with him. Throughout the 1980's and 90's, we participated in many retreats taught by Master Wang, and forged a close bond with him. On the final day of the 1995 annual Jinhua Temple retreat, Master Wang quietly approached and sat down beside Dr. Li. Master Wang asked me for a piece of paper, on which he wrote his phone number and address. It was on this day that we knew that we had a special mission to help spread the tradition of Taoism. Later, I realized that this would be his last retreat before he took a twelve year sabbatical from teaching publicly. During this period, both of us left China to pursue graduate studies abroad.

By 2006, we had both completed our studies (Dr. Kathy Li is a Western medical doctor and Dr. Kevin Sun holds a Ph.D. in physics) and received a message from Master Wang inviting us to China to meet with him. Some years earlier,

Master Wang conceived the idea of establishing a school for the purpose of helping people by bringing the traditions, practices and secrets of Taoism to the West. He called the school the Lao Zi Academy, and is a nonprofit organization co-funded by Mr. Wang Liping, Mr. Kevin Sun, Mrs. Kathy Li and Mr. Richard Liao. Named after Taoism's primordial ancestor, Lao Zi (also written "Lao-Tse" or "老子" in Chinese). Master Wang expressed that he wanted us to help him bring the traditions and practices of Taoism to Westerners by helping him establish the Lao Zi Academy. During this time, Master Wang transmitted several special practices to us and then prepared documents certifying us as his disciples and authorized us to teach overseas.

Soon after this meeting, in 2008, we met Richard Liao; a practitioner of Chinese Medicine based in California, and began working together with him to establish the Lao Zi Academy. We saw ourselves as a team whose mission was to build a cultural bridge for communication between East and West. To inspire us in our new endeavor, Master Wang presented us with a banner for the new academy, which had written in beautiful Chinese calligraphy. Richard Liao also began the important work of translating this book into English.

During the past several years, we, along with Richard Liao, have brought many seekers of wisdom to China to learn from Master Wang. All of the students who experienced this traditional practice firsthand have been impressed by this treasure of the East.

As Western scientists from China, we regard the Taoist health cultivation and meditation techniques in this book as a type of "Eastern science." This Eastern science emphasizes the "dual cultivation of body and mind" that is central to Taoist thinking. Modern Western scientists have started to explore how this type of cultivation and meditation affects human physiology and psychology. In recent years, through the use of modern scientific research methods, science has indeed proven the benefit of these practices and has helped us to more comprehensively understand the physiological mechanisms of the ancient Taoism culture and science.

In 2011, researchers at Yale University, supported by grants from National Institute on Drug Abuse and the U.S. Veterans Affairs New England Illness Research Education and Clinical Center, published a paper, entitled "Meditation experience is associated with differences in default mode network activity and connectivity" in the Proceedings of the National Academy of Sciences about the effects of meditation. Their research showed that, compared with novice meditators, experienced meditators had significant deactivation in parts of the brain associated with what is called the "Default Mode Network" (DMN), i.e., areas linked with attentional lapses and anxiety. Practiced meditators also reported less mind-wandering during meditation than did their less-experienced counterparts. Conversely, mindfulness training has been shown to benefit certain conditions, such as pain, substance abuse disorders, anxiety, and depression.

Aside from its association with attention lapses and anxiety, the DMN has also been associated with certain conditions, including Attention Deficit Hyperactivity Disorder (ADHD) and Alzheimer's disease. The researchers concluded that the findings may have a host of clinical implications, including the use of meditation in the treatment of these conditions.

Taoist health cultivation is part of Taoism, which is China's aboriginal religion. Because it incorporates numerous physical cultivation practices, it is somewhat different from other religions. With physical culture and fitness becoming more popular these days, it has great appeal to modern Western seekers. However, one must keep in mind that body cultivation is just half of the complete Taoist health cultivation system. The other half is mind cultivation, which should never be, and cannot be, separated from body cultivation.

The practice of health cultivation, then, is analogous to its agricultural counterpart in the natural world, in which one first works the soil, sows the seed, supports and nurtures it, keep predators and weeds away, allows it to grow, and gradually raises it to full bloom. Eventually the seed will become a completely grown plant, and cultivation will no longer be a separate practice but become one with life itself.

The aim of the Lao Zi Academy is to help teach this ancient process of health cultivation and promote a dialogue between East and West, and thus benefit all of humankind. It is our belief that Taoist culture is a treasure of humanity that is irreplaceable and critical to the preservation of wellness and balance in the world.

Finally, we would like to express our deep appreciation to Richard Liao for the time and effort he has devoted to make this English version book available for us.

We sincerely hope you enjoy this book of Taoist health cultivation written by a true Master.

Kevin Sun and Kathy Li

For more information about the Laozi Academy, please visit the website (www.laoziacademy.us) or send an email to: mail@laoziacademy.us.

A Note on Sacred Texts in Taoism

I first met Dr. Liao when he provided acupuncture treatment for a sprained wrist. From friends I had heard about how respected he was in the Chinese medicine community, and how he's been a mentor to many practitioners over the years. Later, when I heard of his book project, I was eager to learn more about the Taoist practices he had learned from his teacher Master Wang Liping.

Taoism is one of the world's great religions, and people all over the planet are inspired and enlightened by its teachings. Many are drawn to Taoism's insights into the balance of life, and it's observation that every aspect of our existence is in a constant state of flux. As water always trickles back to the sea, or air always rises back into the atmosphere, Taoism posits that our human experiences, emotions, thoughts, and very lives also have an elegant rhythm and flow. The famous Yin/Yang symbol, called the Tai Chi, is the visual representation of this philosophy, showing that the stronger anything gets, the closer it comes to its zenith, and that as soon as any trend fully subsides, it is that much closer to getting back on the track to prominence. By careful observation of nature, the ancient Taoists of China developed a way of life that recognizes the inherent ups and downs of things as they are, and shows how one can immerse oneself deeply in this experience, to fulfill our human heritage as a participant in the cosmic flow of life's interchanging energies and activities.

Although many of us are fascinated by the world of Taoist philosophy, there is a distinct lack of practical instruction available. Like all Chinese religious traditions, Taoism has many branches, many of which have mystical and transformative teachings within them. However, these teachings are often taught only an expert to his disciples, and are very difficult to understand from the outside. These experiential training programs require a great amount of time and effort to truly master, so that only the initiated are able to understand the fullness of Taoist teachings.

After a century of difficulty and challenge, some among the Taoist community have chosen to open up their teaching to the outside world. Because these training methods have been developed over many years, they contain amazing and effective ways to directly experience what the philosophical books only hint at. By making these transmissions available, teachers like the esteemed Wang Li Ping have given all of us the opportunity to more directly understand Taoism, and the value that its day to day practices have for improving our health, emotions and thoughts. Whereas in the past we were able to gain inspiration from the Tao Teh Ching and other books, we are now able to study and train in the daily exercises that open up our lives to the inner workings of the Tao. As with all Chinese classical arts and sciences, Taoist teachings take time, work, and persistence to unravel and embody. However, gradual and careful effort results in direct, personal knowledge of what Taoist philosophers have been pointing to for centuries – how humankind can find a more natural, effortless and satisfying experience of life here on Earth.

Readers of this book will be very interested in the biography of the man who inspired the creation of this text, Wang Li Ping. In the book *Opening the Dragon Gate*, translated by Thomas Cleary, we learn of Wang's extraordinary life history and his experiences as an apprentice to three Taoist masters who were trained in a previous, almost pre-modern, era. Wang learns esoteric practices directly from oral instruction, as well as the traditional textbooks of the Dragon Gate sect. We are lucky to have access to his teachings, as he is able to draw on a very deep well of both his personal experience,

and the transmitted knowledge of his Taoist lineage.
The translations presented here form a powerful concentration
of Taoist knowledge, and a potent source of information for
future generations of seekers. The first text was written by
Wang Li Ping and details the step by step training and
exercises used in the Dragon Gate sect for cultivating the
various aspects of Taoist practice. The three texts following it
are all books that Mr. Wang studied during his time as a
student, and are considered to be part of a crucial body of
literary knowledge passed down from ancestors during the
past thousand years. Taoist alchemical practices require that
the practitioner be steeped in both the written aspects of the
training, as well as the oral tradition, for they both support
each other and achievement is not possible with book learning
alone.

The texts are expertly translated, but remain abstruse and
challenging for even the most experienced scholars. The
Western reader especially will struggle to understand and
make sense of the metaphors and constructs that these books
offer. Keep in mind, however, that even native readers of
Chinese will also be challenged and confused by these dense
and complicated writings. However, this is not a fault of the
reader, nor even the author. Old religious writings,
particularly from the Taoist tradition, are written specifically
this way so that the reader is forced to struggle and labor with
the reading. They must digest it and make it their own, on an
experiential rather than intellectual level. The ancients were
well aware that information easily obtained is easily forgotten,
but that which is hard won can change a person's life in a
deep and meaningful way. Thus these texts are designed to
confuse the reader on the surface, and lead them to grapple
with concepts and ideas that expand their mind and lead them
to a deeper and more fulfilling understanding than could be
had if the instructions were more explicit and simplified.

By combining the ancient texts, written in metaphor, with a straightforward and easy to follow instructional method of physically exercising the principles, Wang Liping has given readers a unique opportunity to delve deeply into Taoist practice on both an intellectual and experiential level. Each step of the process is profound, and if carefully investigated, applied and savored over time, will lead the reader ever closer to a deep and meaningful understanding of Tao, the path of life that all sentient beings walk on together.

Jess O' Brien
Berkeley, California U.S.A.

Chapter One: Yin Xian Fa

Yin Xian Fa teaches basic Taoist skills and is the first stepping stone to the practice that leads to reaching the Xian of the immortal level. There are twelve techniques, all are basic skills. You can practice one technique or one to twelve techniques at the same time. All these practices lead to the same end and more complex practices will be mixed Yin Xian Fa techniques.

1. Reverse the Mind to Return to Self

Find a quiet place, close your eyes, lips are lightly closed and teeth are touching each other with the tip of tongue on the soft palate and behind the front teeth. Sit with legs crossed on the floor and place your palms on your knees. Sit on a chair, if you have pain. Guide mind, vision, and hearing, smell return inside the body, relax and let go of thought, tension and the physical body until you are within and out, simultaneously as big as nature and as small as a dust mote.

2. Regulate the Posture

Sit on the floor and straighten the spine, neck and head. Remain cross legged on the floor; you can stretch or move your upper body, not your legs. Insure that lips together and teeth are each touching, with tip of tongue remaining on the soft palate and behind the front teeth. Holding the above position, cross leg as character as fetal position and relax the mind; match Mother Nature's five elements and space of four directions that are the mirror of different human organs. As
the human body came from the earth, the natural rhythm of the earth will serve to modify organs in the body. The Heart fire character acting as the sun will go down to warm the
Kidney water character embodied by the ocean. Within the human body, South representing Heart fire and Kidney water

in the North of the natural world in the North of the natural world communicate with each other to achieve balance between the upper and lower. The Liver is embodied by the trees of nature communicate with each other to achieve balance between the upper and lower. The Liver is embodied by the trees of nature and represented by the wood character and the direction East; the Lungs are represented by the metal character and the direction West. Together the Liver and the Lungs form a middle bridge of communication assisting in the regulation of the upper Heart fire and lower Kidney water. The Spleen is represented as earth character and in the Middle. Keep the body and extremities still and relaxed so that Spleen Qi does not leak. The Spleen will serve as the axis on which the harmonization of left, right, and up and down movements occur.

3. Not Seeing and Listening

Return all senses, the mind, vision, hearing, and smell inside the body. Relax and let go of thought, tension and the physical body until you are feeling peaceful and relaxed and strong. Eyes are closed and looking within; the eyes are the window to the Liver, the Hun of decision making, the Liver spirit resides in the Liver. The Kidney's opening ear listens within the body, the Zhi of confidence, the Kidney spirit resides in the Kidney. As the nose does not smell outside; the Lung's opening nose smells within the body, the Po of courage, the Lung spirit resides in the Lung. Silence; the tongue is not moving and the Heart becomes calm: Heart, in which the Shen of spirit, the Heart spirit resides. As the body and its extremities are not moving that is their connection to the Spleen is made, where the Yi of intention, the Spleen spirit resides. The Heart spirit, the Shen of activity, Kidney spirit, the Zhi of confidence, Liver spirit, the Hun of decision, Lung spirit, the Po of courage, and Spleen spirit, the Yi of intention: all combine and harmonize all combine and harmonize within the body; the Qi starts to move the five organ elements: Urinary Bladder water nourishes Liver wood, Liver wood nourishes Heart fire, Heart fire supports the Spleen and Stomach earth, Spleen and Stomach earth create metal Lung, and metal Lung turns into Kidney water, Kidney water moves back down to Urinary Bladder. This state is similar to what happened at the beginning of Mother Nature; and is similar to the Qi moment when life began. At this point, you reproduce the original state of being and begin to heal yourself.

4. Returning Vision and Hearing Back within the Body.

The vision and hearing can relax and pay attention to the movement of Qi in the body. Listen to yourself, your heartbeat and blood's movement through your blood vessels, organs and your entire body. Pay attention to the sights and sounds of the entire body, especially the skin, the feeling of inhaling natural Qi into the skin within the body exchange of nutrition and Qi energy and exhaling from the skin to radiate out and mix with natural air, which becomes a different power of Qi energy. Listen to space, the universe; while listening to space or the universe you need to establish that you are the controller, and that whatever you hear or see must have a peaceful face.

5. Regulating Human Breathing

Regulate nasal breathing until becomes regular: take even, deep and long breaths. Watch your breathing until it establishes a rhythm, in and out, moving the breath through the whole body, until the mind and the body are breathing through the skin of the body as in fetal breathing, and you proceed to the state of reverse healing from the beginning.

6. Calming and Strengthening Shen (mind) in a Three Step Technique

The first step is to place the tongue on the soft palate and behind the front teeth, and keep it there. The tongue is the doorway of the Heart, and the Heart is the house of Shen. Stabilizing the Shen will calm and strengthen the Shen, which is mind and spirit. The second step is to close your eyes, and look toward the inside of the body. The eyes are the window for delivering and reversing Shen. While the eyes look inside of the body, the Shen will be generated. The third step is to listen to the inside of the body, to reverse and seal the Shen.

The first is stabilization, the second is generation, and the third step is sealing so there will be no leaking of vital Qi.

7. Regulate the True Breathing

True breathing is internal original Qi breathing. There are three levels to practicing true breathing:

1. First level: the Lower and Middle Dantian communication.

Use nose breathing to guide true the Middle and Lower Dantian breathing. When you are inhaling, the lower abdomen moves in the Lower Dantian is located one third
below the navel between the navel and the pelvic bone; interior connects to the Duan line and Qi from the Middle
Dantian. Where the center sternum between sixth and seventh ribs is located, the interior connects to the Duan line; and moves down to the Lower Dantian. The Duan line runs from the scalp through the pituitary gland down to the perineum. When you exhale, the lower abdomen moves out, and Qi moves up along the Duan line to the Middle Dantian.

2. Second level: The Lower and Middle Dantian and skin breathing with body and nature communicating.

Inhale the natural Qi through the skin of the whole body into the

Lower Dantian and the Qi from Middle Dantian through the Duan line into the Lower Dantian. Exhale, the Qi from the Lower Dantian along the Duan line goes up to the Middle Dantian, and the Qi from the Lower Dantian expands through the whole skin and out to nature. After you are accustomed to the second level use your imagination to envision yourself inside a ball; the edge of the ball is as big as the edge of the universe: inhale from the edge of the ball to the Lower Dantian and exhale from the Lower Dantian back to the edge of the ball.

3. The third level is fetal breathing: when you no longer have to consciously regulate breathing through the nose, there is another automatic breathing that takes place in the body naturally; follow it.

Glossary:

The Duan Line practice is the Upper Shen, Middle Heart and Lower Kidney Dantian communication. The Middle Dantian Heart and the Lower Dantian Kidney are fire and water communication. The human body acts as a symbol or representation of the planet. The Heart character is the sun and fire and the Kidney and reproductive organs are water and the ocean. The heat of the Heart's sun goes down to warm the Kidney's ocean; and in turn, the Kidney's ocean water ascends to nourish the fire of the Heart. This communication creates life in the earth and is the source of Qi in the human body.

The purpose of fetal breathing is to guide you back to the fetal state; which is a source of Qi movement, anti-aging, and adjusting and reorganizing the Qi to exist again as it did in the beginning.

8. Practicing Preventing Leaking

The eyes are closed and focused on watching inside, the ears are listening to sounds inside the body, the nose smells the scents inside, and the tongue is on the soft palate and behind the front teeth, body is still. The Shen is looking inside; the body is still while sitting on a towel against the perineum as a seal to prevent the essential Kidney Jing from leaking. Concentrate the Shen on the skin of the whole body until the Shen is stable and still.

It is during this time the spirit of the Live Hun of decision is not leaking out from your eyes. The Kidney spirit Zhi of confidence stays in the Kidney and is not leaking out from the ears. The Lung spirit Po of courage stays in the lungs and is not leaking out from the nose. The Heart spirit Shen stays in the Heart and does not leave from the tongue and mouth. The Spleen spirit Yi of intention remains in the extremities and does not leak out from the muscles. The Qi and spirits are not spent and leaking; they move internally in the original fetal condition.

9. Watching and Listening Inside

After Shen and the body are still, start to listen and watch for the Qi and spirit movement of the five elements. The first one is the Urinary Bladder, then the Liver, the Heart, the Spleen and Stomach, the Lung, the Kidney, and back to the Urinary Bladder; until this cycle completes itself.

10. Concentrate, Brighten and Still the Body

After the Qi and spirit move through the five organs, the essences generated from the five organs are ready to journey to the Lower Dantian to make a Jin Dan (golden pill). The Shen brings concentration, brightness and stillness to the Lower Dantian and the skin of the whole body. There will be a considerable amount of Qi and Jing of essential movement in the body. Insure you are at a peaceful and relaxing place to be ready for this.

11. Listening and Following the Breath

Using the true breathing technique listen and follow your breaths; feel the Middle Dantian as the natural sun within as it communicates with the Lower Dantian and the earth and water in Nature. Feel the true fire from the Heart and the true water from the Kidneys as they communicate, paralleling the communication between the sun and the ocean. It is only when these elements are combined, timeless, empty, and still, that they will they bind to the Jin Dan (golden pill).

12. Caring for the Shen while Taking an Invisible Shower

Care and concentrate emptiness into the Lower Dantian; watch and enjoy the Yuan (source); which at the first beginning of the embryo and the in synchronic beginning of Qi formed the universe. Yuan Shen, Yuan Jing of essence and Qi start to combine and move. After reaching this stage, you are stepping into the Xian of Heaven's door, looking for the next level, San Xian Gong.

Chapter Two: Zhi Neng Gong

Zhi indicates intelligence, Neng indicates power and Gong indicates capacity.

Zhi Neng Gong is the method for training the Shen of mind and Ling of soul to use Heaven's eye to deliver Xin and Ling of information and the soul, understanding of the meaning of life and death, and training the uncontrollable thought Yin Shen of emotion, dreams and worry and the controllable thought Yang Shen immortal body. This training can be at the beginning of practice or whenever Xin and Ling of information and the soul enter the practitioner or the practitioner needs to clear emotions and activate the Shen of mind and Ling of soul.

Zhi Neng Gong training is to train the mind mentally. It requires discipline and if there is an instance of mental illness, this training may need to be approached with great caution.

There are three levels in this section, and each level is divided into three exercises:

A. First level:

The first level is training the Shen of mind and Ling of soul to use Heaven's eye to exchange and deliver Xin and Ling of information and the soul with human, time, space and universe.

1. Reverting to the state of infancy.
2. Clarify true or false
3. Shen of spirit and Zhi of clear intelligence.

B. Second level:

The second level is training directed towards understanding the meaning of life and death and the Yin Shen of uncontrollable thought to be controllable through of the practice of Yang Shen.

1. Knowing my future.
2. Surviving with fasting.
3. Dress in new clothes.

C. Third level.

The third level is training the Yang Shen; thought is subject to control and human's immortal body movement.

1. Understanding the secret code of nature.
2. Encircling the world and universe.
3. Watching and stepping into the moon.

Introduction to the first level practice:

1. Reverse the Memory back to Infancy (Hui Ying Yi Wang))

This section is practicing reversing memory:
 Remember-forget and remember again.

Sit on the floor, naturally cross your legs, straighten the spine and place your hands on your knees, your tongue against the soft palate and behind the front teeth.

Open your eyes and straight look forward as far as you can; let the Shen Guang (mind and light) slowly move back to between the eyebrows, close your eyes gently.

Remember matters from the morning until now, every detail you can, from getting up in the morning, cleaning your teeth and washing your face…until you sit down to practice this moment. If in between something is forgotten, try to remember again. Past memories will be as fresh as when you were a new born baby; look at each of them carefully. It may come with matter: flower, tree, color, bird, animal… look at each memory carefully and let it bloom, after totally blooming; the memories will be less frequent and disappear. Let positive memories bloom and let go of negative memories.

2. Clarify true or false (Zhen Jia Fen Ming)

This section's practice is about making decisions:
Deciding, changing the mind, and deciding again.

Continuing reverse memories, what is right or wrong? If it is wrong; how do I correct the error? If it is right; what do I do about it? Is the correction perfect or any decision better than this one? If I am seeing objects; are they making sense or nonsense? Why? For example, I have hiked mountain trials, which one is best for me? For example, as I was writing an article, what sentence or word worked? For example, when I am seeing my internal organ, is it the right color and shape compared to the illustrations in an anatomy textbook? If not, practice again until there is a complete match.

3. Shen of Spirit and Zhi of Intelligence Clarified (Shen Zhi Qing Qing)

This section's practice predicts what will happen and what the consequence may be:

One sets up the object, makes a decision, and sets up the object again.

Continued practicing clarifies true or false. After a decision has been made; what will happen? Refining the decision:

For example, after having finished this political article, what will the effect be? Or, after having decided to go the party tomorrow night, who is the first person I will see? After that, is it the right or wrong one? Was I peaceful enough to predict it or was it just a logical guess?

Glossary:

There are three types of vision: The first is the normal vision that we all share. The second is a practitioner opens his eyes and looks into the distance, as far as he can, using the vision in his right eye. The third is the practitioner closes his eyes and looks as far as is possible for him, using his Shen Gang (mind and light).

Chapter Three: San Xian Gong

San Xian Gong has three levels of practice, leading to immortality. San indicates three. Xian indicates immortality. Gong indicates capacity and power.

San Xian Gong came originally from the renowned grand master Zhong Liquan and his student Liu Dongbin; both wrote the book and called it "Ling Bao Bi Fa" about thirteen hundred years ago. The Taoist lineage was passed along by these great teachers and eventually to Wang, Chongyang, and about eight hundred years ago, he changed the name to San Xian Gong. Wang, Chongyang's student Qiu, Chuji opened the Dragon Gate branch of Taoism

San Xian Gong is discovering in your practice how the natural universe and the human body relate to each other, how they affect each other including the sun, moon, stars and earth separately and in various combinations. It is divided into three levels; the Ren Xian Gong translates as the human immortal level. Di Xian Gong translates as the earth immortal level and Tian Xian Gong translates as the Heaven level. There are ten techniques and forty five sections. A full time practitioner needs to practice nine years, graduates in ten years.

San Xian Gong is the central methodology of the Dragon Gate Taoist sect. All other trainings as described in this book relate to San Xian Gong, which may be practiced by itself or with any of the other methods in Jin Dan of golden pill pathway's text.

San Xian Gong detail:

A. Ren Xian Gong-health, anti ageing and enjoyment

1. Matching Yin and Yang.

(1) Yin Yang exchange: Yang fetus and Yin breathing.
(2) Yin Yang match: True fetal breathing.
(3) Yin Yang back into source: Matching Kan (water) and Li (fire).

2. Gathering and vaporizing water and fire

(1) Original infinite Tai Yi embraces true Qi.
(2) Refining the body at the first level.
(3) Heavenly boy and Heavenly elder.

3. Dragon and tiger interaction

(1) Collecting and strengthening the Jing and Qi back to the Dan (golden pill).
(2) Caring for Xian (immortal) fetus.
(3) Water and fire harmonize.
(4) True husband and wife meet.
(5) Qi connected without shape.

4. Cooking Dan and medicine

(1) Optimal fire temperature.
(2) Xiao Zhou Tian (microcosmic orbit).
(3) Zhou Tian optimal fire temperature.
(4) Gathering Shen and nourishing the Qi.
(5) Gathering Qi and nourishing the Shen.
(6) Refining the Yang and nourishing the Shen.

B. Di Xian Gong: refine life and avoid death

5. Zhou Hou Fei Jin Jing (Behind the elbows the golden crystal flies through Xiao Zhu Tian of microcosmic orbit circulation)

(1) The Jing of body essence flows up to nourish the brain.
(2) Starting the He Che, a vehicle flowing in the river.
(3) Connecting the dragon and tiger.
(4) Drawing up lead and adding mercury.
(5) Returning to the state of a child.

6. Jade fluid returns to the Dan

(1) Jade fluid refining body Fu (symbol has substance).
(2) Bathe the immortal fetus.
(3) Small return path to the Dan.
(4) Great return path to the Dan.
(5) Returning to the Dan seven times.
(6) Nine circles to the Dan.

7. Jin (golden) fluid returning to the Dan

(1) Jin fluid practicing body Fu (symbol has substance).
(2) Starting fire to refine burn the body.
(3) Golden flower Jade nectar.
(4) Grand harmony.
(5) Yellow and white technique.

C. Tian Xian Gong: Heaven level.

8. Pilgrimage to the Source (Yuan) and refining the Qi

(1) Beyond the Nei Yuan (Upper Dantian in the brain).
(2) Refining the Qi into Shape.
(3) Purple Jin Dan.
(4) Firing Yang Shen.
(5) Gathering three flowers at the crown of the head.

9. Seeing internal exchange

(1) Gathering Yang Shen.

(2) Connecting Heavenly fire.

(3) Exchanging Xian (immortal) and mortal form.

(4) Human and Heavenly realm.

10. High form leaves the human body and changes into a different Shape

(1) Moving in and out to different shapes.

(2) Shen Xian (immortal spirit) sheds previous mortal body.

(3) Mortal moves into immortal realm.

An explanation three levels of San Xian Gong:

1. Ren Xian Gong

The first level is Ren Xian Gong: Ren indicates humanity, Xian indicates immortality, Gong indicates capacity and power. The first level is refining the human body to attain the immortal level. There are four sections and seventeen techniques. It is refining for strengthening health and mind; which uses the human body as a furnace, and the body's Qi as medicine. The Heart is fire, the Kidney is water, refining the Dan nine times circle and seven times back, Kan water and Li fire connected, metal Lung mother fluid given to the Jin Dan of golden pill. For male going into original infinite Tai Yi embraces true Qi practice method; Female goes to Niu Dan Xin Fa of female golden pill capacity method with San Xiao Gong practice.

Using the body as a furnace, the body is divided into two halves, upper and lower, the upper is the Heart fire; lower is the Kidney water; the fire of Li goes down to bond with the Kidney water Kan to create Jin Dan. During this processing, the Jin Dan will seven times back and circle nine times forward, Kan water bonds with Li fire, water steaming up until metal Lung fluid flows to the Jin Dan.

2. Di Xian Gong

Di indicates earth. Di Xian Gong is practicing changing into earth immortal level.

The middle level is Di Xian Gong. It has three sections and fifteen techniques. Starting from Ren Xian Gong level, the Qi flows through the Xiao Zhou Tian; which is the Qi moving in a circle from the spine of Du and a center line in front body of Ren channel. It may also be called the microcosmic orbit. Xiao indicates little, Zhou indicates circle, and Tian indicates sky. There are two movements in Xiao Zhou Tian: one is human body Du and Ren channel movement, and another is the natural moon cycle, the natural monthly movement's effect on human Du and Ren channels bonded with natural movement of the moon.

The Xiao Zhou Tian practice enables Qi, Jing (essence) and Yang to nourish the Shen of mind and brain, gathering Shen to nourish the Qi and Yang as a circle. The Du and Ren channel Qi movement into a pipe. In this level, the left dragon and right tiger will connect. After this, it is necessary to practice with capturning moon's light and capturning sun's Jing technique. The Xiao Huan Dan of the five element movement technique: five organs' Qi gathering in the Lower Dantian to feed the immortal baby is the beginning of nine circles back and forward of the Jin Dan movement.

Di Xian Gong uses Shen as furnace, Qi as medicine, sun as fire, moon as water, finding treasure in the bottom of the ocean, walking into emptiness and watching the moon. Yin water will be upward and Yang fire will be downward as they bond and harmonize.

3. Tian Xian Gong

Tian indicates sky or Heaven. Xian is a person on the mountain who is practicing to attain the immortal level.

Last level is Tian Xian Gong; there are three sections and eleven techniques. Shen is a furnace. Xing (true self) is medicine, Xing turns into Ling (soul); Ding is water and stability. Hui (intelligence) is fire. One self crown of the head Jiu Gong of nine magic squares and the eight directions with Heaven's nine squares and space are bond.

Introduction to the first section of the Ren Xian Gong practice:

1. Exchanging Yin and Yang of Yang Fetus and Yin Breathing (Yin Yang Jiao Huan)

After practicing Yin Xian Fa from the first section of the book, remain sitting on the floor, cross your legs, straighten the spine and place your palms on your knees, your tongue against the soft palate and behind the front teeth; the breath and the mind are quiet, and you are starting to exchange Yin and Yang:

Inhale; the Yi and Nian guide the natural universal Qi from every direction, pressing into the pores of whole body of the edge of the human body's universe, depositing Qi into the Lower Dantian; feel the strength of Li.

Exhale; let the human body's internal Qi expand through its pores into the natural universe.

After you are used to Yin Yang exchange breathing, combine with this, inhale; the inner Qi from the Middle Dantian to the Lower Dantian. Exhale; the Qi is moving from the Lower Dantian to the Middle Dantian through the Duan line. The Duan Line is located between the eyebrows, straight into the brain about the length of your index, middle and ring fingers; to find the location of Heaven's eye and the Upper Dantian; draw a vertical line from the scalp down to the perineum. This line connects Shen, Heart and Kidney and Upper, Middle and Lower Dantian. The next step is to inhale for one minute or more and exhale for one minute or more. The Ling Bao Bi Fa textbook requires six thousand breaths each practice.

Glossary:

A. Three different kinds of Qi:

1. Primordial Qi; everyone needs to have this Qi for life.

2. The body's internal Qi, which is combined with primordial Qi to sustain life and enable healing.

3. Magical Qi; the capacity of the human body's internal Qi to radiate out and combine with primordial Qi for healing and connecting.

B. Jin Dan:

Jin Dan is the golden pill that one creates inside the body; the pill is an internal medicine and power factory that heals and controls life and death.

C.Yi, Nian and Li:

Yi is intention in the universe with movement and direction.

Nian is thought in the universe without direction or movement.

Li is strength in the human body.

D. Breathing:

San Xian Gong breathing is inhaling with the area of the lower abdomen at the Lower Dantian moving in; when exhaling this area moves out. During the inhale and the exhale, the emphasis of the abdominal movement takes place below the navel. The breathing speed is stable, long, slow, even and natural. The inhale is longer than the exhale in the morning. The exhale is longer than the inhale in the afternoon.

E. Three Dantian locations:

Dantian is the field where is it possible to create the Jin Dan (golden pill). Upper Dantian: The Upper Dantian is from between eyebrows three fingers length into the brain. Middle Dantian: The Middle Dantian is the space between the sixth and seventh ribs and three fingers length into the chest. Lower Dantian: The Lower Dantian is located three fingers below the navel and three fingers into the lower abdomen.

F. Yin and Yang exchange:

The exchange of Yin and Yang is the exchange of nature and human Qi and Heart fire and Kidney water.

G. Yang fetus and Yin breathing:

The Yang fetus is physical human body and this fetus is breathing in the Yin uterus as its natural environment to exchanges invisible Qi through Yin breathing.

2. Yin and Yang matching of True Fetus Breathing (Yin Yang Pi Pei)

The Yi and Nian create you are in the center of a ball; the ball can be as small in length as your arm and as big as the edge of the universe.

Inhale; the Yi and Nian guide natural Qi from the edge of the ball through the body pores, into the Lower Dantian to exchange body Qi, and feeling the strength of Li.

Exhale; the Yi and Nian guide the Lower Dantian internal Qi radiates to the edge of ball.

Glossary:

A. Yin and Yang matching: True fetal breathing.

After the Yin and Yang exchange the next step is matching; matching the Yin and Yang to exchange equal amounts and within and out is no different; in this level the true fetal breathing will be starting. Fetal breathing is when the practitioner feels a second breathing directly through the pores to the body, when the practitioner experiences it; just follow it, in and out through the skin. Practitioner is as fetus breathing through the skin surrounded by the ball that is the uterus in Mother Nature.

The benefit of fetal breathing is reversing back to the fetal state with pre-natal and original Qi, which can help reverse aging and realign and adjust the body back to an empty stage where one can begin again. The pre-natal Qi is the equivalent of nuclear power; the post-natal Qi is the equivalent of electrical power.

3. Yin and Yang Return into Original Position of the Kan and Li Bonded (Yin Yang Gui Wei)

Bend the thumbs; four fingers curl over to cover the thumb, as stable Spleen and Stomach hand form.

Illustration of stable of Spleen and Stomach's hand form:

Inhale; let the Yi and Nian guide the Qi from the ball at edge of the universe, through the pores into the Lower Dantian and exchange body Qi, turn into internal Qi and feel the strength and power of Li.

Hold the breath for a while for five element movements.

Exhale; let internal Qi from the Lower Dantian expand through pores to the edge of universe ball.

Repeat again.

Five elements movement:

Practicing for a period of time and get used to, inhaling and holding the breath, moving the internal Qi from the Lower Dantian to Urinary Bladder, from Urinary Bladder to Liver, Liver to Heart, Heart to Spleen and Stomach, Spleen and Stomach to Lungs, Lungs to Kidneys, Kidneys to Urinary Bladder, Urinary Bladder to Lower Dantian.

Glossary:

A. Bend the thumb, four fingers curl over and cover it.

Thumb covered by four fingers indicates a stable Spleen and Stomach.

B. Five elements movement.

The five elements movement represents the five elements of the natural world as represented by the internal organs. After the practitioner exchanges natural Qi in the Lower Dantian; the Qi needs to move and channel into the five organs and return to Lower Dantian. The path through the five organs starts at mother water Urinary Bladder nourishing Liver wood, mother wood Liver nourishes fire Heart, mother fire Heart nourishes Spleen and Stomach earth, mother earth Spleen and Stomach nourishes metal Lung, mother metal Lung nourishes water Kidney and water Kidney nourishes the water Urinary Bladder.

C. Holding the breath.

Holding the breath is necessary for transforming and dissolving Qi. Hold the breath as long as it is comfortable to do so.

D. Kan and Li bonded.

Yin and Yang return to the original position and the Kan (Taoism's Kan water) and Li (Taoism's Li fire) bonding practice is exchanging inner Qi and native natural Qi and Lower Dantian water and Middle Dantian fire communication.

Chapter Four: Tai Yi Jin Hua Zhong Zhi

Tai Yi Jin Hua Zhong Zhi is the practice for Ling of soul. Tai Yi indicates original infinity; Jin Hua indicates bright golden light. Zhong Zhi indicates the vital order of the universe.

This method of practice comes from the Tai Yi Jin Hua Zhong Zhi textbook and emphasizes the practice Tai Yi Jin Hua, the original light of infinity, which can be combined with and within the human body to create the Jin Dan of the golden pill and match the self with nature. All other methods are within this practice, and it can be practiced singularly or after and before other training.

In order to practice Tai Yi Jin Hua Zhong Zhi one needs to understand the synchronicity of the Tao and be taught by a Master with an understanding of this discipline.

Introduction to the first four sections, twelve techniques in Tai Yi Jin Hua Zhong Zhi:

1. Li of strength opens Heaven's eye, brightens Heart and seeing reveals the Xing of true self.

A. Yi transforms Shen and Guang (light).
B. Li of strength opens Heaven's eye.
C. Kan of water and Li of fire connect.
D. Three lights automatically gather together.

2. Setting the Shen in the ancestral orifice of An Shen Zu Qiao, moving the light and concentrating the Ling of soul.

A. Returning the light and concentrating Ling.
B. Circling and moving the sun and moon.
C. Sun and moon together.

D. Ling gathering Xuan Qiao (orifice) of entering emptiness, one finds substance.

3. Concentrate the Shen into the Qi point; invisible shower of optimal caring.

A. Dropping eye lids, and returning the light.
B. Medicine created in the Kun (Lower Dantian) palace.
C. Regulating breathing and an invisible shower of carring.
D. Light gathering into the Su bead.

4. Returning, watching and brightening the interior, moving and dissolving the five elements.

A. Shen leading the Su bead.
B. Moving and dissolving five elements.
C. Shen and Ling combined as one.
D. Warming and caring for the dragon bead.

Illustration lines of body:

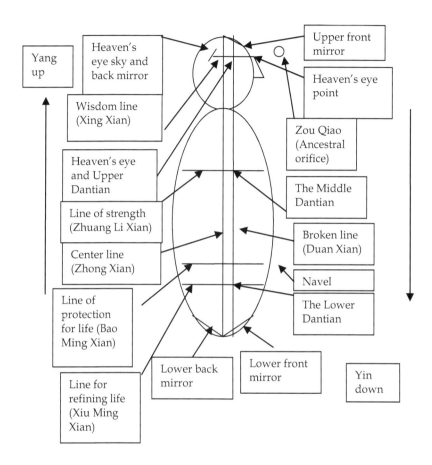

Tai Yi Jin Hua Zhong Zhi first four sections practice:

The Four sections should be performed in order.

1. Li of strength opens Heaven's eye and brightens Heart, seeing Xing of original self (Li Kai Tian Mu and Ming Xin Jian Xing).

A. Yi transforms Shen and Shen and Guang (light) (Yi Yuan Shen Guang).

(1). Returning the mind to original self.

Sit with legs crossed, hands on knees; shoulder, upper arms, elbows, wrists and hands relaxed; straight spine, lips are together, teeth are together and tongue is on the soft palate behind the front teeth. Open your eyes look straight forward as far as you can and let the Shen Guang (mind and light) move slowly back to between the eyebrows where Heaven's eye point is, then lightly close your eyes. Sit quietly and practice Zhi Neng Gong to purify the Shen of mind and Ling of soul.

(2). Human breathing guides true breathing.

Keep the body straight and relaxed. Concentrate on breathing through the nose with small, long and even breaths. Let the concentrated Yi and Nian go down to the Lower Dantian.

Inhale; the lower abdomen starting to move in, short and small movements. Exhale; the lower abdomen is moving out, gradually increase the depth and strength of the breathing as you move the lower abdomen in and out. As soon as the lower abdomen movement is deep enough and you are feeling the movement in the genital region, feel the genitals, the perineum and anus follow the lower abdomen moving up and down.

Inhale; the Yi and Nian guide the natural universal Qi from every direction, pressing into whole body pores of the edge of the human body universe, depositing into the Lower Dantian and feeling the strength of Li. Exhale; the Yi and Nian of the Lower Dantian Qi flow through the pores back to the natural universe.

During this time the Lower Dantian will feel warm or hot. Move the Duan Line when inhaling; move the duality of Yi and Nian from the Middle Dantian down to your Lower Dantian, and exhale from the Lower Dantian back up to the Middle Dantian. After feeling the pores are sealed, slowly decrease the speed of breathing, slow down the movement of the lower abdomen, and decrease the strength of activity in the lower abdomen, until you return to natural breathing.

Glossary:

1. Sealing three Yins: Concentrating, breathing, contracting and relaxing the genitals, perineum and anus with a series of movements until the area is sealed and is stable.

2. Set up the furnace and Ding (three legged tripod pot for cooking the Dan of golden pill): The furnace for the Ding is located below the navel. When there is warm sensation below the navel, exercise the Duan line through the Middle and Lower Dantian to set up the furnace alignment. The Ding is the body and the Ding's cover is the head. Use breathing through the pores to stabilize the skin of the Ding's body

3. Sealing the furnace is obtained by exercising the Duan line of the Middle and Lower Dantian communication, below the navel, and breathing through the pores to seal the skin.

4. Human and true breathing: Basic human breathing is through the nose; true breathing is the Middle and Lower Dantian communication and skin breathing. This section's practice involves nose breathing and Duan line of Middle and Lower Dantian breathing and breathing through the pores at the same time. The lower abdomen movement is from short to deep and from deep to short again.

B. Li of strength opens Heaven's eye (Li Kai Tian Mu).

After even breathing, eyes remain closed, head is up and looking forward, seeing as far as you can and straight ahead. Look into the distance and then reverse your gaze from the far away Shen Guang slowly bring back to the location of Heaven's point between the eyebrows; keep going, continue three fingers length into the brain; which is Heaven's eye and the Upper Dantian, and continue straight back into the mirror of Heaven; which is in the area of the pineal gland, and notice the light, shape, size and color of the mirror. Guide the Shen Guang from Heaven's mirror through the Heaven's eye and Heaven's point; speed forward as far as possible and repeat this process twice.

C. Kan and Li connected (Kan Li Jiao Hui).

Let the Shen Guang from the Heavenly mirror travel down to the spine and into the Hui Yin on perineum; observe the Hui Yin on perineum's shape, color and size; let the Shen Guang follow the center channel from the Hui Yin straight up to the brain, seeing the Bai Hui in top of the skull and the brain's size, color and shape; go down back to the Hui Yin, repeat the exercise twice and concentrate the flow into the Hui Yin, head up, eyes closed looking forward as far as you can, seeing the line from the Hui Yin angle up and Heaven's point Xing Xian of wisdom line straight ahead combine into one point. Please see the illustration of Kan and Li connection.

Illustration: Kan and Li connection:

Kan of water from the perineum at about a forty five degree angle up, and Li of fire from the forehead straight forward connect, to make the external Kan and Li connection.

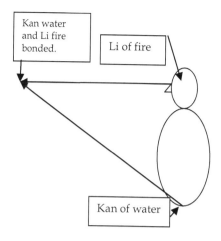

D. Three lights automatically gathering together (San Guang Zi Ju).

(1). Practice three light gathering.

Let the Shen Guang from the Kan and Li connection point back into Heaven eye's point; between the eyebrows, the left eye is sunlight, the right eye is moonlight and Heaven eye's light looking at Heaven eye's point's light; these are the three lights gathering together. Concentrate on nose breathing; to regulate breathing long, gentle and even, follow the breathing, direct the concentrated Yi and Nian down to the Lower Dantian. First inhale and exhale letting below the navel respond slowly and for a short distance moving in and out. Second, slowly with shallow breaths, the Lower Dantian follows the same rhythm, moving in and out, longer and stronger, and now contracts the anus, perineum and the genital region up and down at the same time.

(2). Practicing the Duan Line:

Practice finding the Duan Line by hand; the Duan Line is

located between the eyebrows, straight into the brain about the length of your index, middle and ring fingers; to find the location of Heaven's eye and the Upper Dantian; draw a vertical line from the scalp down to the perineum. This line connects Heart and Kidney and Upper, Middle and Lower Dantian. Lift the hands up from the knees, place them level on the Middle Dantian with one hand is on the top of the other. The palms face the body and are angled down towards the Middle Dantian. Inhale; the hands go down to the Lower Dantian and the concentrated Yi and Nian from the Middle Dantian to the Lower Dantian. Exhale; palms are face up and move from the Lower Dantian and Middle Dantian and the concentrated Yi and Nian from the Lower Dantian to the Middle Dantian and repeat this process several times.

(3). Moving the five elements by hand.

Lower Dantian:
One hand is on the top of the other, above the Lower Dantian, moving, squeezing, and a pulling out the inhalation and pushing back the exhalation motion and the concentrated Yi and Nian in the Lower Dantian. Repeat several times.

Urinary Bladder:
Exhale; the palms angled down move to above Urinary Bladder and relax and while inhaling and exhaling, the concentrated Yi and Nian are in the Urinary Bladder and the hands are moving, squeezing, and a pulling out the inhalation and pushing back the exhalation above the Urinary Bladder. Repeat several times.

Liver:
Inhale with palms up above the Liver, relax, and while inhaling and exhaling, the concentrated Yi and Nian and the hands are moving, squeezing, and a pulling out the inhalation and pushing back the exhalation above the Liver. Repeat

several times.

Heart:
Inhale, the palms angled up moving above the Heart, the concentrated Yi and Nian and the hands are moving, squeezing, and pulling in the inhalation and pushing back the exhalation. Repeat several times.

Spleen and Stomach:
Exhale; the palms angled down above the Spleen and Stomach, the concentrated Yi and Nian and the hands are moving, squeezing, and pulling out the inhalation and pushing back the exhalation. Repeat several times.

Lung:
Inhale; the palms angled up and separate above the Lungs, the concentrated Yi and Nian and hands are moving, squeezing, and pulling out the inhalation and pushing back the exhalation. Repeat several times.

Kidney:
Exhale; the palms angle down to above the Kidneys, a hand on each Kidney, the concentrated Yi and Nian, the hands are moving, squeezing, and pulling out the inhalation and pushing back the exhalation. Repeat several times.

Urinary Bladder:
Exhale; the palms angle down, one hand on top of the other, above the Urinary Bladder, the concentrated Yi and Nian in the Urinary Bladder and the hands are moving, squeezing, and pulling out the inhalation and pushing back the exhalation motion. Repeat several times.

Repeat the five element movement six times.

4). Lower Dantian and refining the Xiu Ming Xian (life line):

Inhale; the palms angle up move from the Urinary Bladder to above the Lower Dantian, relax and move the hands above the Lower Dantian and concentrated Yi and Nian in the Lower Dantian. Inhaling; lower abdomen moving in, the hands pull out above the Lower Dantian, and concentrated Yi and Nian from the spine through the refined Xiu Ming Xian to the hands. Exhaling; the hands push back and the Yi and Nian from the hands move into the spine. Repeat several times.

After the life line exercise, place hands on knees, adjust the body; sit up straight with lips closed and teeth touching. The tongue is against the soft palate and behind the front teeth. Relax the shoulders, arms, elbows, wrists and hands and focus on breathing through the nose with regular breaths until the breath is long, even, and deep. Let the Yi and Nian go down to the Lower Dantian; inhale, the Lower Dantian moves in, and exhale, the Lower Dantian moves out; the breathing and Lower Dantian movement are even, move the lower abdomen a short distance, watching it; is there any change and is there a space in the Lower Dantain? Keeping the lower abdomen movements small, in and out and paying more attention to concentrating on the Lower Dantian, and slowing the breathing and lower abdomen movement until you return to natural breathing.

2. Set the Shen into the ancestral orifices (An Shen Zu Qiao); backing up the light and concentrating the Ling of soul (An Shen Zu Qiao and Hui Guang Shou Ling).

A. Back up the light and concentrate the Ling using the hand form Tian Gang Ba Gua Zi Wu (Hui Guang Shou Ling).

Concentrating into Lower Dantian, relaxed and quiet, one hand's thumb and middle finger tip touches the other hand's base with its fourth finger; the other middle finger touches the tip of its opposite thumb. Either hand over the other is fine.

This is Tian Gang Ba Gua Zi Wu hand form. Recheck shoulders, arms, elbows, wrists and hands and check that the whole body is relaxed, spine is straight, upper and lower lips are touching, and teeth are touching each other; the tongue is against the soft palate behind the front teeth; breathing is through the nose.

The concentrated Yi and Nian are still in the Lower Dantian. Inhale natural air through the whole body's pores, and exhale back from the pores out to nature. Practice several times and when you feel the skin has been sealed, slow down the breathing until there is a return to natural breathing. Concentrate on the pores of the whole body.

Eyes closed, look forward as far as you can and straight ahead. Look into the distance and then reverse your gaze from the far away Shen Guang (mind and light); slowly back up the Sheng Guang and move them into the Zu Qiao (ancestral orifice); located an index finger's length in front of Heaven's eye point between the eyebrows. Left sunlight and right moonlight eyes look at the ancestral orifice, watching the Shen Guang, shape and image. The forehead needs to be open and relaxed. In this stage, whatever happens, you are the controller.

B. Moving the sun and moon (Zhuan Dong Ri Yue).

If you are not seeing the Shen Guang, with both eyes closed, move your eyes clockwise and counterclockwise. If the light is seen, then bring the light back to the Xing Xian (wisdom line) in front of Heaven's eye point. The Xing Xian is the line from nature straight into the Heaven's eye point between the eyebrows; continuing to Heaven's eye of the Upper Dantian located by the length of index finger, middle finger and ring finger, into Heaven's mirror under the occipital. Please see illustration line of body.

C. Sun and moon together (Ri Yue Ge Bi).

Relax the left and right eye, move the Shen Guang forward in the Xing Xian and slowly back into the Zu Qiao of ancestral orifice and left eye's sunlight, right eye's moonlight focus and the Heaven eye's light gather the lights into the Zu Qiao.

D. Ling of soul gathering in the Xuan Guan (Ling Ju Xuan Qiao of entering ancestral orifices, one finds substance).

Relax the whole body, open the forehead and observe the Zu Qiao, enjoy without effort, but still concentrate the Shen Guang, circle the eyes to regulate the distance of the Shen Guang from Heaven's eye point, move the Shen Guang back and forth through the Xing Xian (wisdom line) until it lines up with and enters the Zu Qiao. The Shen Guang is gathered and condensed to the size of a grain of millet in the Xuan Guan (gate of emptiness or different name of Zu Qiao).

3. Concentrate the Shen into the Qi Point, Invisible Shower of Optimal Caring (Ning Shen Qi Xue and Wen Wu Lin Yu).

A. Dropping the Eyelids and Returning the Light (Chui Lian Hui Guang).

Watching the external medicine of bright millet, inhale; move the Shen Guang from the Upper Dantian, the eyes look down and move the mind to the tip of the nose, continuing to Middle Dantian, the Middle Dantian looks down to the Lower Dantian, the Shen Guang travels through the Duan line from Upper Dantian to Middle and Lower Dantain. Inhale; lower abdomen is moving in a short distance and small movement. Exhale; the lower abdomen is moving out, seeing and feeling that the Shen Guang is in the Lower Dantian yet, if you are not sure, repeat motion above, and then concentrate the millet size light into the Lower Dantian.

B. Medicine Created in the Kun Palace of Lower Dantian Region (Yao Chan Kun Gong).

Concentrate Shen Guang in the Lower Dantian. Inhale; the lower abdomen is moving in. Exhale; the lower abdomen is moving out. Slowly increase the lower abdomen movement going deeper for a longer distance, concentrated Yi and Nian go from the Middle Dantian down to the Lower Dantian with the inhale and with the exhale communication begins between the Lower Dantian and the Middle Dantian. Continue until the Lower Dantian is warm; add natural Qi through the pores into the Lower Dantian with the inhale. Exhale; internal Qi expands from the Lower Dantian through the pores to the natural world. At this moment, the lower abdomen is bright.

C. Regulating Breathing and an Invisible Shower of Caring (Diao Xi Lin Yu).

Inhale; let the Shen Guang into the lower abdomen with a slow, mild movement. Exhale; the lower abdomen is moving out. Breathing until the breath is even, long, gentle and gradually slow it down, until there is a return to natural breathing. Concentrate on and care for the Lower Dantian.

D. Gathering Light into the Su Bead (Guang Ju Su Zhu).

Concentrate on Lower Dantian, lift the head up, close eyes and look straight forward as far as you can, the concentrated Yi and Nian will travel far away to see the Shen Guang.

If Shen Guang is not bright enough; let the concentrated Yi and Nian stay where they are and let the Shen Guang travel slowly back to in front of eyes into the Zu Qiao with both eyes paying attention into Zu Qiao. If you still did not see the light, slowly move eyes clockwise or counterclockwise to see where the light is and let the light come back into the Xing Xian

(Wisdom line) in the Zu Qiao.

Relax the body and mind and push the Shen Guang further and further, slowly back into the Zu Qiao; let the Shen Guang condense to the size of a grain of millet, the Su bead. If the bright Su bead wants to move, follow it and push it gently. If it is moving too fast, push it further and bring it back. Su bead indicates that the Ling of soul has been activated.

4. Return watching and Brightening Interior, Moving and Dissolving the Five Elements (Fan Guan Nei Zhao and Yu Hua Wu Hang).

A. Shen Leading the Su Bead (Shen Ling Su Zhu).

Gathering Shen Guang as the grain of millet size Su bead slowly let it return. Inhale; eyes look down to the tip of the nose, from there look down to the Middle Dantian, from the Middle Dantian look down to Lower Dantian. At the same time, the Su bead reverts back to the Upper Dantian, down to Middle and Lower Dantian. Inhale and the lower abdomen is moving in, and with the exhale, the lower abdomen is moving out. Gradually increase the movement of the lower abdomen, going deeper and stronger and feeling a warm sensation in the Lower Dantian, and adding the concentrated Yi and Nian from nature through the pores into Lower Dantian with the inhale. Exhale from the Lower Dantian through the pores back to nature, until the Lower Dantian is bright and warm, and then slow the abdominal movement until there is a return to the rhythm of natural breathing. This is the method for transforming enchanted stones into gold.

B. Moving and Dissolving Five Elements (Yun Hua Wu Hang).

Concentrate more into the Lower Dantian and inhale, the

lower abdomen moves in; exhale, the abdomen moves out; repeat several times. During the five elements movement the entire organ system's Shen Guang expands to the boundary of the universe that is within the human body and this universe can simultaneously be as large as all of nature and as small as a dust mote.

Urinary Bladder:
Exhale; the concentrated Yi and Nian push the Shen Guang from the Lower Dantian down to Urinary Bladder. Exhale; the Shen Guang and the Urinary Bladder are expanding in the human body universe. Inhale; the Urinary Bladder is contracting and the Shen Guang is in the Urination Bladder. Repeat several times.

Liver:
Inhale; the Shen Guang moves from the Urinary Bladder to the Liver. Exhale; the Shen Guang and the Liver are expanding in the human body universe. Inhale; Shen Guang moves into the Liver and the Liver is contracting. Repeat several times.

Heart:
Inhale; the Shen Guang moves from the Liver to the Heart. Exhale; the Shen Guang and Heart are expanding in the human body universe. Inhale; the Shen Guang flows into the Heart and Heart is contracting. Repeat several times.

Spleen and Stomach:
Exhale; the Shen Guang from Heart is moving down to the Spleen and Stomach. Inhale; the Shen Guang moves into the Spleen and the Spleen and Stomach are contracting. Exhale; the Shen Guang and Spleen and Stomach are expanding in the human body universe. Repeat several times.

Lungs:

Inhale; move the Shen Guang from Spleen and Stomach to the Lungs. Exhale; the Shen Guang and Lungs are expanding in the human body universe. Inhale; the Shen Guang is in the Lungs and the Lungs are contracting. Repeat several times.

Kidneys:
Exhale; the Shen Guang goes from the Lungs down to the Kidneys. Inhale; the Shen Guang is in the Kidneys and Kidneys are contracting. Exhale; the Shen Guang and Kidneys are expanding in the human body universe. Inhale; the Shen Guang is in the Kidneys and Kidneys are contracting. Repeat several times.

Urinary Bladder:
Exhale; the Shen Guang goes from the Kidneys to the Urinary Bladder. Inhale; the Shen Guang is in the Urinary Bladder and Urinary Bladder is contracting. Exhale; the Shen Guang and the Urinary Bladder are expanding in the human body universe. Inhale; the Shen Guang and the Urinary Bladder are contracting. Repeat several times.

Lower Dantian:
Inhale; move the Shen Guang from the Urinary Bladder to the Lower Dantian. Exhale; the Shen Guang and Lower Dantian are expanding in the human body universe. Inhale; the Shen Guang is in the Lower Dantian and the Lower Dantian is moving in. Repeat several times.

Circle the five elements in this manner several times.

C. Shen and Soul Combined as One (Shen Ling Ge Yi).

Finally, when inhaling the Shen Guang moves back in to Lower Dantian, the five organs' Qi is deposited into the Lower

Dantian, and when inhaling, the lower abdomen is moving in and Lower Dantian is contracting, and when exhaling, the lower abdomen is moving out and the Lower Dantian is contracting with a gradual strong, deep movement; repeat a few times, slowly decreasing the frequency and movement of the lower abdomen, until the lower abdomen breaths with small movement, add pores breathing to inhale natural Qi and Shen Guang moving in the Lower Dantian and exhaling, the Shen Guang opens to nature until you return to natural breathing. Concentrate on caring for the Lower Dantian, where there is movement and feeling, and bright golden light Jin Dan (golden pill) forms the Ling of soul and Qi, the Jing of essence having now been condensed into the Lower Dantian. This is first refining the Dan and as small return to the Dan.

D. Warming and Caring for the Dragon Bead (Wen Yang Long Zhu).

Concentrate on Lower Dantian and watching and caring for the dragon bead as a hen cares for and sits on her egg to wait for the chick to be born. Wait until the lower abdomen and the Lower Dantian have movement by themselves; place hands on knees, relax the whole body, relax the shoulders, arms, elbows, wrists and hands, straighten the spine, close the lips, teeth touch each other, tongue is on the soft palate behind the front teeth. Inhale; pores take in the natural Qi and the body is contracting. Exhale; internal Qi flows through pores back to nature and the body is open. Slowly increase breathing speed until the body is warm and bright, and then slowly decreases speed until you return to natural breathing.

Slowly increase breathing speed until the body is warm and bright, and then slowly decreases speed until you return to natural breathing. You are feeling and caring for the Jin Dan or the dragon bead and watching the pores of the whole body moving and changing.

Chapter Five: Nu Dan Xin Fa

This training is for females who would cultivate the method of the inner Jin Dan (golden pill).

Female training branches off into Nu Dan Xi Fan (female's golden pill guide line) after a woman has finished the first three sections of Yin Xian Fa, Zhi Neng Gong, Tai Yi Jin Hua Zhong Zhi and the first three sections of San Xian Gong, which after she becomes adept, all the practices can be mixed.

Nu Dan Xi Fan can bring a woman back to the state of childhood before puberty; therefore caution must be observed if the female student still menstruates and wants to become pregnant.

Nu Dan Xin Fa has ten sections and fourteen techniques.

1. Golden mother watching the Heart.
2. Practicing to regulate menstruation.
3. Stopping dragon secret technique.
4. Reversing menstruation technique.
5. Su Nu of virgin practicing and regulating menstruation.
6. Practicing to reverse breast development.
7. Setting up Ding (a three legged pot that represents the cooking and processing of our internal medicine and awakened awareness) creating immortal fetus of section one and dissolving essence into Jin Dan as described in section two.
8. Movement of fetal breathing.
9. Practicing Yang Shen.
10. Yang Shen moving into brightness and fullness.

Introducing Golden Mother Watching the Heart (Jin Mu Guan Xin)

1. Golden mother watching the Heart (Jin Mu Guan Xin) I.
2. Swallow flying and fire pushing metal movement (Jin Mu Guan Xin) II.

1. Golden Mother Watching the Heart (Jin Mu Guan Xin):

Sit up straight, lips slightly touching and teeth touching, and tongue against the soft palate and behind the front teeth, the thumb and middle finger touching the other hand's fourth finger at the base and that hand's thumb and middle finger tip are touching each other are relaxed and touching each other. One hand is over the other. This is the Tian Guan Zi Wu hand form.

Concentrate into the Zu Qiao (ancestral orifices); letting the Shen Guang (mind and light) go down to the Lower Dantian. After the Lower Dantian starts to move, put the hands and palms up with fingertips against each other and almost touching in front of the Lower Dantian and exhale; The lower abdomen is moving out, the hands are going up to the Ru Xi which is located between the sixth and seventh rib on the sternum with palms facing the Ru Xi, inhale, as the lower abdomen is moving in, the hands out, concentrated Yi and Nian flows from the Ru Xi to the palms. Stabilize the hands and arms in a circular position in front of the chest in the Golden mother watching the Heart form. With palms facing the Ru Xi, feel the Ru Xi, the Lower Dantian, breasts and uterus. Focus on the Ru Xi, Lower Dantian, breasts and uterus until either one or more has Qi movement or is cool or warm.

Illustration Jin Mu Gua Xin of golden mother watching the Heart hand form:

Exhale; palms push back to the front of Ru Xi. Turn the palms face down. Inhale; palms push the Qi from the Ru Xi down to the Lower Dantian. Exhale; and with palms face up push the Qi up to Ru Xi. Repeat the breath cycle three, six, twelve, twenty four or thirty six times depending upon the Qi movement inside the body.

If the uterus or genital region has Qi or Shen Guang, inhale; palms face down push the Qi from Ru Xi to the Lower Dantian, inhale again, and push the Qi to the uterus. Exhale; turn the palms face up and push the Qi from the uterus to the Lower Dantian, exhale again, palms face up push the Qi up to Ru Xi. Inhale; turn the palms face down and push the Qi to the Lower Dantian, inhale again, push the Qi to uterus. Repeat above three, six, twelve, twenty four or thirty six times, according to your inner feeling.

The last hands movement from the Lower Dantian back up to Ru Xi, palms facing the Ru Xi, inhale; pull the Qi from Ru Xi to the palms and stabilize the hands and arms in a circle in front the chest for Golden mother watching the Heart form. The eyes remain closed, watching the Ru Xi, the Lower Dantian, breasts and uterus until their Qi is moving.

Exhale; palms facing the Ru Xi and push the Qi in front of the Ru Xi. Palms facing down; inhale and push the Qi down to the Lower Dantian. Turn palms face up, one hand on another; the thumbs' tips touch each other and represent Heaven, humankind and earth in the form of human hands. Remain quiet and still no matter how strongly the Qi is moving in the body, and continue to sit peacefully.

Illustration Tian Di Ren of Heaven, human and earth hand form:

2. Swallow Flying, Fire Pushes Metal Moving II (Jin Mu Guan Xin of Shuang Fei Yang and Huo Bi Jing Hang)

Continue the above practice if the Qi flowing to the Lower Dantian is not strong. Keep the body still while sitting on a towel which is pressed against the perineum as a seal to prevent the essential Kidney Qi and Jing from any leaking and to increase pressure in the Lower Dantian.

Palms are face up with fingertips facing each other and almost touching. Exhale and push the Qi from the Lower Dantian to

Ru Xi, turn the palms to face Ru Xi. Inhale; pull the Qi from the Ru Xi to the palms, and stabilize the palms, arms form a circle in front of the chest as Jin Mu Guan Xin (Golden mother watching the Heart) form until the Qi starts to move.

Exhale; the lower abdomen moves out, palms push back towards Ru Xi; turn palms face down and inhale, the lower abdomen moves in, pushing the Qi from Ru Xi down to the Lower Dantian. Repeat three, six, twelve, twenty four or thirty six times.

Continue concentrating on the Ru Xi until the Qi is moving. Palms facing down, inhale; push the Qi from the Ru Xi to the Lower Dantian; inhale again, push the Qi to the uterus, let the side of your hands press on the groin region and hold there. Exhale; focus on the uterus. Inhale; the side of hands still pressing on the groin region, four fingers angled up and moving up to guide the uterus Qi to the Lower Dantian. Inhale; the hands still press on the groin region, thumbs facing each other and moving down, push the Qi back down to the uterus. Repeat three, six, twelve, twenty four and thirty six times.

Place one hand on the other, palms facing up and above the uterus. Inhale; push the Qi from the uterus to the Lower Dantian, the concentrated Yi and Nian in the Lower Dantian and the hands facing the Lower Dantian. The hands are moving, squeezing, and pulling out above the Lower Dantian, pulling out the inhalation and pushing back exhalation from the Lower Dantian. Repeat several times and starting moves the five elements.

Urinary Bladder:
Exhale; the palms are relaxed and angled down moving to above the Urinary Bladder, relax and while inhaling and exhaling. The concentrated Yi and Nian are in the Urinary

Bladder and the hands are moving, squeezing, and pulling out the inhalation and pushing back the exhalation above the Urinary Bladder. Repeat these motions several times.

Liver:
Inhale and angle the palms up to above the Liver, relax, and while inhaling and exhaling. The concentrated Yi and Nian and the hands are moving, squeezing, and pulling out the inhalation and pushing back the exhalation above the Liver. Repeat several times.

Heart:
Inhale; the palms facing upwards and moving above the Heart. The concentrated Yi and Nian and the hands are moving, squeezing, and pulling out the inhalation and pushing back the exhalation. Repeat these motions several times.

Lungs:
Inhale; the palms open up to separate above the Lungs. The concentrated Yi and Nian from the Heart to the Ru Xi and to the Lungs and the hands are moving, squeezing, and pulling out the inhalation and pushing back the exhalation like the form flying swallow. This is the form of fire pushing metal. Repeat the series several times.

Kidneys:
Exhale the palms angle down to above the Kidneys with a hand over each Kidney. The concentrated Yi and Nian and the hands are moving, squeezing, and pulling out the inhalation and pushing back exhalation. Repeat this series of movements several times.

Urinary Bladder:
Exhale; the palms angled down, one hand on top of the other above the Urinary Bladder. The concentrated Yi and Nian in

the Urinary Bladder and the hands are moving, squeezing, and pulling out the inhalation and pushing back the exhalation. Repeat the series several times.

Lower Dantian:
Inhale; palms angle up to Lower Dantian. Exhale; palms moving down to the uterus, press the lateral side of hands on the groin region and hold on. Inhale; the hands continue to press on the groin region, and thumbs face and moving down, push the Qi down to the uterus. Exhale; the hands still pressing on the groin region, four fingers angle up and moving up, push the uterus Qi up to Lower Dantian. Repeat three, six, twelve, twenty four or thirty six times.

Place one hand put on top of the other above the uterus, inhale, concentrate on the uterus; exhale, palms angled and moving up, push the Qi from the uterus to the Ru Xi, palms facing the Ru Xi; inhale, pull the Qi from the Ru Xi to the palms, the arms forming a circle on the chest for the Jin Mu Guan Xin of Golden Mother watching the Heart form. Relax the mind and body until the Qi is moving.

Exhale; push the palms back to Ru Xi, inhale, palms angled and moving down, and push the Qi to the Lower Dantian.

Change the position of the top and bottom hands, palms are facing up, the thumbs touching each other representing Tian Di Ren of Heaven, human and earth in the form of human hands. Relax and feel the Qi moving for as long as you remain comfortable.

Chapter Six: Shui Gong

Shui Gong of sleep meditation is the practice of relaxing the physical body and brain of Shen and enables the practitioner is not asleep while meditation but is somewhere in between waking and sleeping to heal and train the Qi and Shen, exchanging Xin of information and Ling of soul with nature.

There are three levels:

1. Healing the physical body.
2. Exchanging Xin of information and Ling of soul to understand life and death and the secret code of nature and healing.
3. Using the Ling of soul to healing another person.

Introduction to the first nine techniques:

These nine practice techniques can be connected to each other or you can practice them individually, one or more times a day.

1. Calming the Shen form (An Shen Shi) is for stable the Qi, Shen and Jing.
2. Descending blood flow form (Tiao Ya Shi) is descending blood flow strengthens Jing.
3. Strengthen the Jing and enriching the blood form (Bao Jing Fu Xue Shi) is strengthening the Jing and blood are needed to reverse the Yang.
4. Reversing the Yang, strengthen Qi and Yang power form (Huan Yang Zhuang Li Shi) is reversing the Yang is needed to strengthen physical deficiencies.
5. Strengthen weakness and returning the Yang position form (Bu Xu Huan Yang Shi is strengthening weaknesses is necessary to regulate Qi.

6. Regulating the Qi form (Tiao Qi Fu Xin Shi) is regulating the Qi is necessary to strengthen the Liver.
7. Strengthen the Liver and brightness Gall Bladder form (Bao Gan Ming Dan Shi) is strengthening the Liver is necessary to strengthen the Spleen.
8. Balance and harmony Spleen and Stomach form (Fu Pi Jian Wei Shi) is balancing and harmonizing the organs into a state of joy.
9. Joyfulness Form (An Le Shi) is opening the Heaven's eye and into a state of joy.

1. Calm the Shen Form (An Shen Shi)

This practice can calm the mind, release fatigue and nourish Jing of essence. The body may feel itself expanding or flying as the Qi moves.

Body, breathing and mind:

Lie flat, adjust your pillow and stretch your body until you are comfortable. The hands should be next to the body with palms face down. Open your eyes, lips pressed lightly together and upper and lower teeth are touching each other. Tongue is against the soft palate and behind the front teeth, and the body and mind are relaxed.

Keep the eyes open and look out in front of forehead. Bring back the Shen Guang (mind and light) to Heaven eye's point, located between the eyebrows and close your eyes; look down to the end of the nose and from there look down to the Lower Dantian.

Inhale; the concentrated Yi and Nian from natural universe Qi presses though the body pores into the Lower Dantian. Exhale; the Yi and Nian guide the Lower Dantian's internal Qi flows through the whole body's pores into Nature. Breathing needs to be deep, long and even. Repeat twenty four times and then return to natural breathing.

2. Descending Blood Flow Form (Tiao Ya Shi)

This practice is also calming to descend the Qi for lower high blood pressure and strengthens the legs. The body may experience the flow of Qi as a sensation of growing bigger or smaller.

Body, breathing and mind:

Lie face up, adjust your pillow and stretch your body until you are comfortable, place the hands next to the body with palms down. Open your eyes, lips touch and teeth touch each other, place tongue on soft palate and behind the front teeth and relax the body and mind.

Look in front of forehead for while with eyes opened and bring up the Shen Guang to Heaven eye's point between the eyebrows and close your eyes, eyes look at the tip of nose and from the nose look down into the Yong Quan, the point on the sole of the foot one third of the distance from the base of the second toe to the back of the heel.

Inhale; the concentrated Yi and Nian from the bottom of the feet's Qi to the Lower Dantian. Exhale; the Yi and Nian and Qi from the Lower Dantian back down to the bottom of the feet. Breathing needs to be deep, long and even. Repeat twenty four times and return to natural breathing.

3. Strengthen the Jing and Enriching the Blood Form (Bao Jing Fu Xue Shi)

This practice is strengthens Jing of hormone, urinary bladder, ovary and uterus or testicles. The body may experience warmth and Qi movement in the lower abdomen and genital region.

Body, breathing and mind:

Lie face up, adjust your pillow and stretch your body until you are comfortable, place both hands above the pubic bone with palms down. Open your eyes, lips lightly pressed together, top and bottom teeth gently touching, tongue on soft palate and behind the front teeth and body and mind are relaxed.

Keep the eyes opened. Look outward in front of forehead and bring up Shen Guang to Heaven eye's point located between the eyebrows and close your eyes; the eyes look down to the tip of the nose and from the nose, down to where the palms down are resting about one inch above the pelvic bone where Zhong Ji point is.

Inhale; the concentrated Yi and Nian and natural Qi from everywhere presses the body pores into the Zhong Ji point and closed your eyes. Exhale; the Yi and Nian guide internal Qi from Zhong Ji point through the whole body and out through the pores into Nature. Breathing needs to be deep, long and even. Repeat twenty four times and return to natural breathing.

4. Reversing the Yang, Strengthen Qi and Yang Power Form (Huan Yang Zhuang Li Shi)

This practice is directed towards strengthening the Lower Dantian, intestines and sexual organs. The body may experience warmth and moving in the Lower Dantian and Qi movement and sound from the abdomen.

Body, breathing and mind:

Lie face up, adjust your pillow and stretch your body until you are comfortable. Place the hands on the Qi Hai where about one inch below the navel with palms down. Open your eyes, lips lightly pressed together, top and bottom teeth gently touching, tongue on soft palate and behind the front teeth and body and mind are relaxed.

Keep the eyes opened and look outward in front of forehead and bring back the Shen Guang to the Heaven eye's point between the eyebrows and close your eyes. Look down to the tip of the nose and from there gaze downward to the Qi Hai.

Inhale; the concentrated Yi and Nian and natural Qi from everywhere is pressing body pores into the Qi Hai. Exhale; the Yi and Nian guide internal Qi from the Qi Hai flows through the whole body and out through the pores and expand into Nature. Breathing needs to be deep, long and even. Take twenty four of these breaths and return to natural breathing.

5. Strengthen Weakness and Returning to Yang position Form (Bu Xu Huan Yang Shi)

This practice is reversing ageing and returning to the state of fetal energy. The body may experience Qi movement, warmth and sound in the abdomen.

Body, breathing and mind:

Lie face up, adjust your pillow and stretch your body until you are comfortable. Place hands face down on the navel where Shen Jue point is. Open your eyes, lips pressed lightly together and upper and lower teeth are touching each other. Tongue is against the soft palate and behind the front teeth, and the body and mind are relaxed.

Keep the eyes opened and look out in front of forehead. Bring back the Shen Guang to Heaven eye's point, located between the eyebrows and close your eyes; look down to the end of the nose and from there look down into the Shen Jue.

Inhale; the concentrated Yi and Nian and natural Qi from everywhere is pressing body pores into the Shen Jue. Exhale; the Yi and Nian and the Shen Jue's internal Qi flow through the whole body and through the pores and expand out into Nature. Breathing needs to be deep, long and even. Repeat twenty four times and return to natural breathing.

6. Regulating the Qi and Strengthen the Heart Form (Tiao Qi Fu Xin Shi)

This practice is strengthening the Middle Dantian: the chest, Stomach, Lung, and Heart's Qi and regulating and smoothing menstruation. The body may experience Qi movement in the chest and feel stronger or bigger during this exercise.

Body, breathing and mind:

Lie face up, adjust your pillow and stretch your body until you are comfortable. Place palms face down on the Middle Dantian where Shan Zhong point is, on the sternum between the fifth and sixth ribs. Open your eyes, lips pressed lightly together and upper and lower teeth are touching each other. Tongue is against the soft palate and behind the front teeth, and the body and mind are relaxed.

Keep the eyes opened and look out in front of forehead. Bring back the Shen Guang to Heaven eye's point, located between the eyebrows and close your eyes; look down to the end of the nose and from there look down into the Shan Zhong.

Inhale; the concentrated Yi and Nian and natural Qi from everywhere presses body pores into the Shan Zhong. Exhale; the Yi and Nian and the Shan Guang's internal Qi expand through the pores into Nature. Breathing needs to be deep, long and even and repeated twenty four times before returning to natural breathing.

7. Strengthen the Liver and Brightness Gall Bladder Form (Bao Gan Ming Dan Shi)

This practice is regulating and strengthening the Qi in the Liver and in the Gall Bladder. The body may experience Qi movement and jumping in the Liver and Gall Bladder.

Body, breathing and mind:

Lie face up, adjust your pillow and stretch your body until you are comfortable. Place the palms face down on the region of the Liver and Gall Bladder. Open your eyes, lips pressed lightly together and upper and lower teeth are touching each other. Tongue is against the soft palate and behind the front teeth, and the body and mind are relaxed.

Keep the eyes opened and look out in front of your forehead and bring back the Shen Guang to Heaven eye's point between the eyebrows and close your eyes; look down to the tip of the nose and from the tip of the nose look into the Liver and Gall Bladder.

Inhale; the concentrated Yi and Nian and natural Qi from everywhere presses body pores into the Liver and Gall

Bladder. Exhale; the Yi and Nian and the Liver and Gall Bladder internal Qi flows through the whole body and the pores are open to expand the Qi out into Nature. Breathing needs to be deep, long and even and repeated twenty four times. Return to natural breathing.

8. Strengthen Spleen and Stomach Form (Fu Pi Jian Wei Shi)

This practice is focused on healing and strengthening the Spleen and the Stomach. The body may experience intestinal movement, Qi movement, and warm sensations in the Spleen, Stomach and abdomen.

Body, breathing and mind:

Lie face up, adjust your pillow and stretch your body until you are comfortable, place the palms face down on the Spleen and Stomach region. With your eyes open, lips touching and teeth touching each other, place the tongue on the soft palate and behind the front teeth and relax the body and mind.

Keep the eyes opened and look out in front of the forehead and bring back the Shen Guang to Heaven eye's point between the eyebrows and close your eyes, look down to the tip of the nose and from the tip of the nose look into the Spleen and Stomach.

Inhale; concentrated Yi and Nian and natural Qi from the universe are pressing body pores into the Spleen and Stomach. Exhale; the Yi and Nian and Spleen and Stomach internal Qi flows through the whole body and the pores are open to expand the Qi out into Nature. Breathing needs to be deep, long and even and repeated twenty four times, and return to natural breathing.

9. Joyfulness Form (An Le Shi)

This practice is exchanging Xing of secret code and Ling of soul with nature. The practitioner may see light, image and feel electricity.

Body, breathing and mind:

Lie face up, adjust your pillow and stretch your body until you are comfortable, place your hands next to the body with palms face up. Open your eyes with your lips lightly pressed together and teeth touching each other. Place the tongue against the soft palate and behind the front teeth and relax the body and mind.

Keep the eyes opened and look out in front of forehead and bring back the Shen Guang to Heaven eye's point, located between the eyebrows and closed your eyes.

Inhale; the concentrated Yi and Nian and natural Qi comes from far away in the sky into Heaven eye's point. Exhale; the Yi and Nian in Heaven eye's point radiates back to the far sky. Breathing needs to be deep, long and even. Repeat twenty four times and return to natural breathing.

Chapter Seven: Nei Shi Fa (Inner Vision)

Nei Shi Fa indicates method of inner vision.

The method to reverse vision to look inward has been a secret for thousand years. It is only taught in Taoism and has been lost for the last hundred years. This method uses inner vision to view the inner scene.

We may use inner vision to see our inner view. Inner vision is called inner scene. We may use it to experience outer view, which is called the external scene. There are two books written on this experience: Huang Ting Nei Jing Jing and Huang Ting Wai Jing Jing.

Master Mrs. Wei wrote the Huang Ting Wai Jing Jing and Ling Fei Jing to show techniques for teaching the public. Her technique depends on Eastern Qi for practice. Our inner vision method depends on self only.

Inner vision practice can be individual or within Yin Xiang Fa, Tai Yi Jin Hua Zhong Zhi, San Xian Gong, Nu Dan Xin Fa and Shui Gong.

Body, breathing and mind:

Sit with legs crossed, hands on knees. Shoulder, upper arms, elbows, wrists and hands are relaxed. Keep the spine straight, lips closed and teeth together and tongue on the soft palate behind the front upper teeth.

Use Yin Xian Fa to regulate your body and mind. Let the concentrated Yi and Nian focus on the Lower Dantian. With closed eyes, see the Lower Dantian. Relax the shoulders, arms, wrists and hands, and tuck the chin. Regulate your breathing; breathe slow, long and even breaths.

Stabilize and relax your body. Slow your breathing as you relax your body and mind. Keep your breaths slow and long, inhaling and exhaling evenly.

Continue to relax your body as you slightly raise your head. Let the Qi into your head. Keep your eyes closed and look straight forward, and your concentrated Yi and Nian in front of your eyes. Practice Heaven's eye breathing. In this you inhale from in front the space between your eyebrows into your brain. Follow by exhaling from you brain and through your eyebrows into the in front of you. Inhale with your vision looking into your head and then exhale as you look forward. Take an even and long breath in and look inside your head; exhale and feel your head's pores expand. Inhale and feel the pores contract and let your vision access the cavity in your brain through this meditation. Repeat this process a few times. Let the head pores move as you breathe naturally. Slowly reverse your vision back into the head and look inside your skull; do you see any cavity access in the head? Do you have any brightness inside your head and in front of your eyes? Breathe even and long breaths as you regulate your breathing again. Reverse your vision and look at the crown of head and the Bai Hui (which is located at the highest point on the crow of the head) and the Tian Men (which is the Heaven door and at junction of the frontal and parietal bones). Your brain should be slightly bright. Slightly squeeze your skull and head's pores as you inhale. Exhale and let the pores and skull slightly expand. Inhale and let the pores get smaller and smaller. Exhale and feel the pores getting bigger and bigger.

At this moment, the head should be bright. Inhale and contract the skull then exhale expand the skull. Pay attention to the head's inner cavity. Inhaling contracts the skull and head's cavity and exhaling expands the skull and head's cavity. Pay attention to the degree of brightness in your head's cavity.

Inhale and slightly contract the head's pores and skull, and then exhale to slightly expand the pores and skull. Inhaling contracts the head's inner cavity and makes it smaller and smaller. Exhaling expands the head's cavity and makes it bigger and bigger. Repeat this a few times. Breathe naturally. Reverse your vision to look into the head's cavity. Notice the skull's movement and changes inside your head.

Regulate your breathing with long and even breaths as you use inner vision and your Yi and Nian guide both the Sheng Guang (mind and light) and Qi. Slowly descend from the crown of head to the mouth and swallow the Qi or saliva. Descend to the chest cavity and look at the Lungs and Heart. With your Yi and Nian guide the inner vision look into the Lungs. Slightly contract your Lungs when you inhale and slightly expand the Lungs when you exhale. Inhale the Lungs contract to be smaller and smaller and exhale the Lungs are expand to get bigger and bigger. Slow your breathing, making each breath even and gentle sounding as you pay attention to any changes in your Lungs.

Exhale and notice that the body is more relaxed and Sheng Guang and Qi are descending downward. Make your breaths long and light.

Now as the concentrated Yi and Nian are in the Heart, listen to the Heart beating as both eyes look into it. Inhale and slowly contract the Heart; exhale and slowly expand the Heart in the human body universe.

Your breathing should be slow and even as you Yi and Nian focus on your respirations. Inhale very gently and then exhale very gently several times and then hold your breath for a few seconds while your eyes and ears pay attention to your Heart beating and body inner pulsing.

Let the heartbeats guide gentle breathing. Relax and count on your heartbeats as you follow the Heart's movements. The beating of your Heart should sound louder than your gentle breathing at this time. Pay attention to your heartbeats and let your breaths be slow, even and long as you relax your body.

Reverse your vision to look at the Lungs. As you inhale and exhale the Lungs should move just slightly. Slowly turn the breathing inward naturally. Look at your Lungs, Heart, and chest as you reverse your hearing to listen to the sound of beating from your Heart, Lungs, and chest. Breathe through your nose into your chest with the breaths quieter than the sound of your chest's movement.

Let your chest move naturally. Listen and watch the Heart and Lungs pulse. Looking at the chest, notice that the breath sounds are quieter than the sound of the chest's movement. As you listen and look at changes to the chest, let your breaths be slow and natural.

Use your concentrated Yi and Nian and inner vision and slowly descend from the chest to the abdomen. The Yi and Nian descend first with the Qi and Shen following. Look at your Liver, Gall Bladder, Stomach and Spleen. Then descend down to look at your Large Intestine, Kidneys and Urinary Bladder. See the genital region; this is the prostate, perineum and anus for males and the uterus, ovaries, perineum and anus for females. As you scan through the genital region, prostate, perineum and anus for male, and ovaries, uterus, perineum and anus for female, you're Yi and Nian are at the lowest point on the human body.

For females, inhaling contracts the genital region while exhaling expands it. Inhale contracts your genital area, bringing it up to the Lower Dantian. Exhale expands your genital area. During the inhalation you may experience sensations from the genital area, uterus or ovaries, notice where the sensations come from.

For males, the testicles are contracted on inhalation and on exhalation the testicles expand and drop. Inhale contracts and pulls testicles up. Exhale descends testicles down. Repeat this process a few times. On inhaling as you experience a warm sensation in the testicles, notice where the heat comes from.

For both sexes, during inhalation and exhalation relax the body and let your breathing become natural with even, long and slow respirations.

The Yi and Nian focus in the Lower Dantian. Relax and turn your attention inward the changing of the Lower Dantian; is there brightness in front of your eyes? Reverse this brightness to the Lower Dantian, relax, and then bring the brightness inward. After the brightness arrives in the Lower Dantian, inhale gently and move it to below the navel. Exhale and move the area below the navel outward gently. With focus still on the Lower Dantian, watch it, and notice if there is a pulsing sensation.

Pay close attention to the related actions of the Heart and Lungs with the Lower Dantian. Breathe through your nose a few times. Sense the Lower Dantian's movement and use your breathing to regulate the Lower Dantian's movement. If the Lower Dantian moves too fast, slow down.

As you breathe more quickly through your nose, check to see if your Lower Dantian follows. Inhale and notice the Lower Dantian's contracting; exhale and sense the Lower Dantian expanding. Hold your breath as you listen to the Lower Dantian and watch its movement.

Now let your breathing follow the Lower Dantian's movement. Your breathing sound should be lower than the Lower Dantian movement sound.

Let the Lower Dantian's movement be greater, and let the Lower Dantian's sound be stronger than that of your breathing. Let you're breathing become slow and gentle as you listen to and watch the Lower Dantian's movement.

Let the concentrated Yi and Nian into the Lower Dantian; let the Shen in, too. Inhale and contract the Lower Dantian, then exhale and expand it as you slowly let your breathing become natural.

Now the Shen is in the inner body and Yi and Nian are in the Lower Dantian. Pay attention to the inner change. Your breaths should be long, even and gentle. The Shen is still in the inner body. Inhale gently and focus on the area below your navel. Tighten your genital, perineum and anal areas and then exhale and relax those same areas. Repeat this a few times.

Inhale and contract the three cavities (head, chest and abdominal); exhale and expand the three cavities in the human body universe. This is inner breathing (not outer breathing). Inhaling contracts all the body's cavities and exhaling expands the cavities in the human body universe. Inhale and squeeze the inner cavities; and exhale and expand them. Inhalation squeezes the inner cavities until they are like a thin bottle; exhalation expands the inner cavities into a normal bottle. Inhale and contract the inner body bottle; exhale and expand to the normal bottle. Inhale and contract the inner body bottle into smaller and smaller; exhale and expand the inner body bottle to bigger and bigger. Repeat this a few times. Then let your breathing become natural with long, deep and even respirations as you see the changes in your inner body.

Now your Yi and Nian are in the Lower Dantian. Relax your body; stabilize the Lower Dantian and the three Dantians. Slowly stabilize your mind and body. Breathe naturally. Reverse your vision and sit for while.

Chapter Eight: Jin Yang Huo and Tui Yin Fu (Turning up the Yang Fire and Bringing down the Yin Fu)

After one has become adept at practicing the Yin Xian Fa, Tai Yi Jin Hua Zhong Zhi and the first section of San Xian Gong, before starting turning up the Yang fire and bringing down the Yin Fu (symbol has substance) training and in order to practice turning up the Yang fire and bring down the Yin Fu one needs to understand the synchronicity of the Tao and be taught by a Master with an understanding of this discipline.

One has well basic skills suddenly there will be a strong flow of Qi from the Lower Dantian to the Sheng Si Qiao, the life of death orifice. This orifice in a male is located where urine and sperm exit, and for a female the location is in the cervical region.

Turning up the Yang fire and Yin Fu descending are refining the Qi and Jing (essence) to the Dan (golden pill) and refining the Dan to the Jing and Qi processing, and refine the Jing to nourish the brain, Yu Ye (Jade fluid) returns to the Dan; Jin Ye (golden fluid) returns to the Dan. But if someone without enough Qi and Jing of substance to turn up the Yang fire will burn out the inner pot of Ding.

There are two methods for turning up the Yang fire and bringing down the Yin Fu.

When your Lower Dantian has filled with Qi and Jing and moving downward, take an inhale, below the navel move in and exhale, below the navel move out and push the Qi and Jing to Sheng Si Qiao; inhale the Yi and Nain guide the Qi flow to the sacrum, upwards to the mid back and to the occiput and the crown of the head.

Exhale, from Tian Men (Tian Men of Heaven's door: the

junction of the frontal and parietal bones) to between the eyebrows, nose, mouth, chest to lower abdomen and finally to the Sheng Si Qiao. This is one complete cycle. Repeat this cycle. After you finish this exercise, the Qi and Jing are deposited in the Lower Dantian. The first method is used by a regular practitioner.

Illustration for first method:

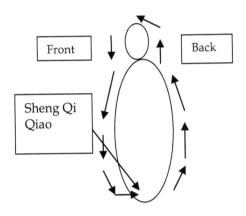

The second method is for one who wishes to reach the immortal level, and is called Duan Ling Gen (stop the sexual lust's root) and is meant for a full time practitioner who stays in the temple and wants to stop sexual lust and reverse the Jing back to the source. This method should be used with caution by anyone who wishes to have children.

When the Lower Dantian has filled with Qi and Jing moving downward, take an inhale, below the navel move in and exhale, below the navel move out and push the Qi and Jing to

Sheng Si Qiao.

Inhale, the Yi and Nian guide the Qi to the sacrum, to the mid back, to occipital region and to the crown of the head. Exhale to the Tian Men, to between the eyebrows, nose, mouth to chest and finally to the level of the Lower Dantian, inhale, the Qi and Jing to the Lower Dantian and exhale, from the Lower Dantian to the Sheng Si Qiao. Inhale, to the sacrum, to the mid back, to occipital region and to the crown of the head. Repeat this cycle. After you finish this exercise, the Qi and Jing have reached the Lower Dantian.

Illustration for the second method:

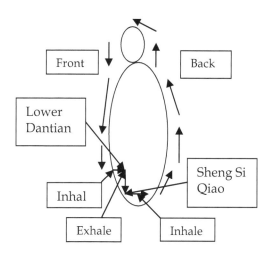

Required eyeball movements:

During this practice one tracks the flow of Qi and Jing with the eyes, looking down and then rotating eyes to look at the sacrum, mid bak, the crown of the head and back down the front of the body to the Lower Dantian and to the Sheng Si

Qiao.

Breathing:

A longer inhale turns the Yang fire; a longer exhale causes the Yin Fu to descend.

Turning up the Yang fire requires a longer inhale and a shorter exhale from 12 a.m. to 12 p.m., and requires nine times of longer inhale with shorter exhale each circle practice, up to thirty six times. Or you can practice turning the Yang fire nine times each and up to four times a day.

Bringing down the Yin Fu requires a longer exhale and a shorter inhale from 12 p.m. to 12 a.m., requires six times of longer exhale with shorter inhale each circle practice. Or you may do this up to twenty four times. Or you can practice bringing down the Yin Fu six times each for up to four times a day.

There are a few ways to practice the Yang fire and the Yin Fu, practice turning up the Yang fire and two hours later practice the bringing down the Yin Fu in either morning or afternoon. Or turning up the Yang fire nine times with bring down the Yin Fu six times. Or turning up the Yang fire thirty six times with bringing down the Yin Fu twenty four times. Or turning up the Yang fire one hundred sixteen times with one hundred forty four times for bring down the Yin Fu. Which depending on the practitioner's inner fire.

All above regulation is not formulaic; it depends on the timing of one's live Zi Shi Qi flow.

Illustration of the flow of Qi in the body:

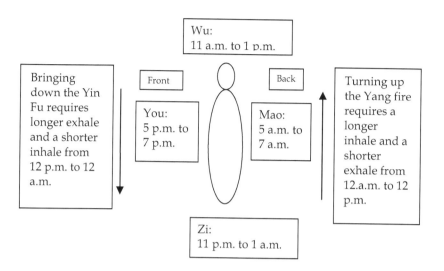

Wu:
11 a.m. to 1 p.m.

Bringing down the Yin Fu requires longer exhale and a shorter inhale from 12 p.m. to 12 a.m.

Front

You:
5 p.m. to 7 p.m.

Back

Mao:
5 a.m. to 7 a.m.

Turning up the Yang fire requires a longer inhale and a shorter exhale from 12.a.m. to 12 p.m.

Zi:
11 p.m. to 1 a.m.

If one practices turning up Yang fire and bring down the Yin Fu use nine longer inhales to turn up the Yang fire and shorter exhale for bringing down the Yin Fu six times. This is the Niu Che (slow ox vehicle). If you have enough Qi and Jing to transform, you do the turning up the Yang fire practice thirty six times and twenty four times for bring down the Yin Fu. This is called Yang Che (the goat vehicle and faster than an ox). And one hundred sixteen times turning up the Yang fire and one hundred forty four times for bringing down the Yin Fu. This is called Lu Che (fast deer vehicle).

If one's Qi flows from the back and is not in a line, or the Qi and Jing falling in front are not in line or are suddenly dropping, that person needs to practice the basics more.

If after turning up the Yang fire and bring down the Yin Fu practice, one's Qi and Jing are stable in the Lower Dantian where the Qi starts to flow again, into either the five elements movement or to the Upper Dantian, it is time for An Shen Zhu Qiao practice.

For a female, if her Qi flowing to the Ru Xi (between the breasts), it is time to practice the Jin Mu Guan Xin (Golden mother watching the Heart) of Niu Dan Xin Fa.

Chapter Nine: Zi Shi Gong

You need a strong foundation in the basic skills of Yin Xian Fa, Tai Yi Jin Hua Zhong Zhi and San Xian Gong before starting Zi Shi Gong training and in order to practice Zhi Shi Gong one needs to understand the synchronicity of the Tao and be taught by a Master with an understanding of this discipline.

"Zi Shi" is the period of time between 11 p.m. and 1 a.m. "Gong" indicates capacity and power.

The Zi Shi Gong method has never been written in a book. It is mentioned in the Tai Yi Jin Hua Zhong Zhi textbook. Zi Shi Gong is taught both by oral instruction and by mental transmission. It is secret in Taoism.

Zi Shi Gong occurs during the night from 11 p.m. to 1 a.m. At this time the natural sun and inner body Yang Qi gather in the Kidney, Urinary Bladder and their channels start to rise. Now is the time to exercise the sprouting Yang Qi.

Wu Shi occurs from 11 a.m. to 1 p.m. as the natural sun and inner body Yang Qi start to descend. This is opposite of Zi Shi Gong.

Mind and body:

Find a quiet place. Close your eyes. Keep your lips lightly closed and let your teeth touch each other. The tip of tongue should rest on the soft palate and behind the front upper teeth. Sit on the floor with your legs crossed and place your palms on your knees.

Practice Yin Xian Fa to regulate your body, mind, five elements, breathing and return the Qi to the Lower Dantian. Keep your eyes close and look forward, straight ahead. Look into the distance and then reverse your gaze from the far away Shen Guang (mind and light) to right in front of your eyes and then continue into your brain.

Look at the crown of your head where the Bai Hui point is located. This is highest point in the human body. Look at the Tian Men, or Heaven's door where is the junction of the frontal and parietal bones. Let your vision guide the Shen Guang and Qi downward, descending slowly, until it reaches the perineum and Hui Yin where is lowest point in the human body and push lower. Inhale and lift one drop of true Yang from the perineum to the Lower Dantian. Use the Shen and true Yang to attend to it. This is the first basic training Zi Shi Gong.

You attend to the one drop of true Yang with gentle breathing and movement of the Lower Dantian. If the Lower Dantian stops, use lower abdominal movement and breathing to activate the Lower Dantian. Here the Qi flows in different directions for a moment. This is the first step of Zi Shi Gong training.

1. If the Qi flows upward and downward continuously. The Qi is in the head and the head's Qi is circulating. This is Jiu Gong (nine magic palaces in Taoism) or Buddhism of the Liu Li space where is a beautiful, crystal and bright environment. The Jiu Gong and Liu Li magical space where have Xin Ling of unlimited inflammation can be found. This space can be changed, which rotated by the rotation of Heaven's eye can control the Jiu Gong rotation.

2. If the Qi flow descends to the Hui Yin, which is the lowest point in the perineum, the Qi may then flow up the spine. This Qi is Yin embracing half Yang and Yang embracing half Yin. The Yang Qi will flow upward and the Yin Qi will descend downward. This activates the three inner cavities

and returns the Jing, which nourishes the brain.

3. If the Qi flows forward and to the genitals, you contract and lift the genitals. Males lift the testicles. For an older male especially this adds oil to support life. Females tighten the genital, too.

4. If the Qi is accompanied by a warm sensation in the Lower Dantian, lift your genitals, perineum and anus and then release while you hold you breathe. Until enough Qi, his body may start to shake, you should let it flow, until the Qi stabilizes, put the Qi into the Lower Dantian for care of inhale the Qi from pores to the Lower Dantian. Exhale and the Qi from the Lower Dantian expands to the all the pores. Repeat this gentle motion for a few minutes and then pause to check the Lower Dantian's movement. If you're Lower Dantian starts to move and follow it. If it does not move, breathe with the Lower Dantian and pores movement again. If the Qi flows up to the head, we practice the An Shen Zhu Qiao.

There is live Zi Shi Gong and it does not require practice only at the midnight. Whenever the practitioner has live inner Qi flow, this is live Zi Shi. For instance, you see lots of money or beautiful girl or handsome man that excited your inner Qi movement. For instant, if you are in peaceful and suddenly have sexual sensation, this is live Zi Shi. Sit cross-legged right the away. For a male, inhale, below the navel and as it moves in, contracts your genital, perineum and anus. Exhale, below the navel and as it moves out, releases the genital, perineum and anus. Repeat this process until the Qi is stable. For a female, inhale below the navel and as it moves in, contracts your genital, vagina, uterus, perineum and anus. Exhale, below the navel and as it moves out, releases your genital, vagina, uterus, perineum and anus. Repeat this process until the Qi is stable.

Chapter Ten: Guan Shi Mo Xiang and Ting Fu Yi Mu (Visualizing Our Master and Memorizing His Image. Listening to and Memorizing Our Parents)

We need to practice visualizing our master and memorizing his image. Also, we need to listen to and memorize the image of our parents and be willing to be open to all these connections and origins. We should seek to see our true selves and brighten our Heart (mind), especially three days before and during the Chinese New Year.

If you practice Yin Xian Fa, Zhi Neng Gong, Tai Yi Jin Hua Zhong Zhi or San Xian Gong or if your Qi and Shen are strong, you can practice these visualizations at any time. The exercises that follow may eliminate Karma and train the Ling (soul) to communicate with others.

Training to visualize our Master and memorize his image and also in listening to and memorizing our parents is training that exercises the mind. It requires discipline. If a would-be practitioner has a history of mental illness, this training may need to be approached with great caution.

1. Listening to and Memorizing Our Parents

Find a quiet place. Close your eyes and close your lips lightly. Your teeth should touch each other as the tip of tongue touches the soft palate behind your upper front teeth. Sit with legs crossed on the floor and place your palms on your knees. If you have pain, sit on a chair.

Regulate your breathing with long and even respirations. Let your Shen expands outward and think about how much space you have in the practice area. What is the shape of space?

Where you are sitting? Are any people around? Slowly reverse your Shen to your inner self. Exercise the pores breathing. Inhale and contract your body's pores and feel your body becoming smaller. Exhale and expand your pores and sense that your body grows larger. This concentrated Yi in the natural universe and Shen in the inner universe is for communicating between the body's inner universe and universe of nature.

When your pores are moving, the edge of your internal universe is connecting the external universe of nature. Reverse your vision to inward and listen to your inner sound. Relax and empty the body; feel the pores moving and communicating outward with nature.

Concentrate and visualize one of your parents. See him or her as young, middle-aged or elderly. Your parent may still be alive or may have passed away. Let your parent's image pass in front of your eye brows and memorize him or her. Ask for first name and last name. Be peaceful and quiet as you think about your parent for awhile. Complete his (or her) image in as much detail as you can. Think about what you learned from your parent during this practice. You may experience emotions such as anger as you communicate with them. Your origin and background influence what you experience. In this moment, you need to decide what is right or wrong. No matter what has happened, we can appreciate that our parent's gave us life and cared for us. When you see your parents in a different space, try to unite with them in a single space. Let the parental image into your Lower Dantian and use our Shen and Yang Qi to care for it.

2. Visualizing Our Master and Memorizing His Image

Find a quiet place and close your eyes. Your lips are lightly closed. Your teeth are touching each other with the tip of tongue on the soft palate and behind the front teeth. Sit with legs crossed on the floor and place your palms on your knees.

Make your breaths long and even. Let your Shen expand outwards and think about how much space you have. What shape is your space while you are practicing? Are any people around in this area? Slowly reverse your Shen inward. Exercise the pores breathing. Inhale and contract all the pores in your body; feel smaller. Exhale and expand the pores; feel bigger. This is concentrated Yi in the natural universe and Shen in the inner self for communicating between your body's universe and the natural universe.

As your pores move, they connect the universe of your body to the universe of nature. Reverse your vision from outward to inward and listen to your inner sound. Relax and empty the body. Feel only the pores moving.

Concentrate and visualize one of your Masters, someone such as Lao Zi, Lu, Dongbin or Buddha. Or see a scene from nature environment, a star, a tree, or an animal... and find the Master you would like to practice on. With humility visualize your Master and let the Master's space match your space until the Master's image and his light appear. Communicate with and listen to him. What can you learn from him? Does his method suit you? Answers to questions. What will be showing is depend on your own origin and background. You establish you are the designer, no matter what that you are the controller. Bring the Master's image and light inward to the Lower Dantian, and use Shen and Yang Qi to give attention to it.

Chapter Eleven: Zi Ran Huan Qi Fa

Zi Ran Huan Qi Fa is the walking practice, exchanging Qi with Nature, and can be practiced when you are walking. In this section the practitioner compresses and expands his Qi and regulates breathing and body movements to exchange Qi and Xin Ling of information of soul with the natural universe until he or she unites body and nature and they become one.

The method for exchanging Qi with Nature was created by Master Lu, Dongbin about thirteen hundred years ago. It is part of Ling Bao Tong Zhi Neng Nei Gong Shu and teaches the practices of body movement, regulating breathing, regulating the body's vital energy Qi with Heart spirit Shen, and includes the Yi and Nian exchange between Nature and soul of Ling of connection, as well as balance, combining different elements and realignment, which establishes movement within the body and mind to create brightening and to strengthen the Ling of soul.

Exchanging Qi with Nature has three sections and nine techniques.

1. Healing and health, longevity and enjoyment.

(1) Walking and breathing.
(2) Walking and holding your breath.
(3) Walking and receiving vital substance.

2. Dissolving the body brings the practitioner to Nature and increases longevity.

(1) Walking expels substance.
(2) Walking creates Qi field.
(3) Walking divides different fields.

3. Jin of longitude and Wei of latitude are exchanged and Heaven and the practitioner are combined.

(1) Walking through channel and closing the door.
(2) Walking delivers soul of Ling.
(3) Walking while is invisible.

There are three types of vision: The first is the normal vision that we all share. The second is a practitioner opens his eyes and looks into the distance, as far as he can, using the vision in his right eye. The third is the practitioner closes his eyes and looks as far as is possible for him, using his Shen Gang (mind and light).

Introduction to the first steps:

1. Three steps walking.

Relax the whole body, open the eyes and look straight forward as far as you can into your far way into the practitioner's gaze, let the Shen Guang (mind and light) travel back in front of the eyes and close the eyes for a while; open the eyes, start to inhale, the concentrated Yi and Nian the Qi from the natural universe enters the body through the pores while you are taking three steps; exhale and take three steps while the Yi and Nian from the whole body pores pour back into the natural universe. Repeat this pattern while continuing to walk and while you are walking imagine you are in the center of surrounding ball.

The smallest size of the ball is of a ball whose circumference, surrounding you is at an arm's length from your body. The largest size of this ball is as big as all of nature. Inhale and bring the natural Qi from the edge of the ball to press into the pores and exhale the body's Qi through the pores back to the edge of the natural ball as you are walking.

If you want to emphasize helping the Liver and Gall Gladder, lead with the right foot; if you want to emphasize helping the Spleen and Stomach, lead with the left foot. You may use this image of being surrounded by a ball for all of the Zi Ran Huan Qi Fa.

2. Six steps walking.

Relax the whole body, open the eyes and look straight forward as far as you can, let the Shen Guang return to the front of the eyes and close the eyes for a while, open the eyes and start to inhale, bringing the concentrated Yi and Nian from universal through the pores and into the body while walking six steps. Exhale and walk another six steps while the Yi and Nian from the body pores pour back to the natural universe. Keep walking using the same pattern.

Image yourself in the center of the ball and inhale the natural Qi from the edge of the ball into the body. Exhale and push the Qi back to the edge of the ball.

If a patient has Liver and Gall Bladder, Spleen and Stomach weakness and menopause syndrome, combine this practice with San Xian Gong.

3. Hold your breath for three steps.

Relax the whole body; open the eyes look straight forward as far as you can. Let the Shen Guang come back in front of the eyes and close the eyes for a while, open the eyes, start to inhale, the Yi and Nian guide the Qi from the universe into your body through the pores while taking three steps, holding your breath while walking three steps, the Yi and Nian in the body as whole small universe.

Exhale; walk three steps while the Yi and Nian leave the body through the pores and return to the natural universe. Keep going walking with the same pattern. Use your mind to place yourself in the center of the ball and inhale the natural Qi from the edge of the ball; follow this by exhaling the Qi back out to the edge of the ball. Inhale natural Qi from the edge of the ball into the body, and exhale the Qi back to the edge of the ball.

4. Holding your breath for six steps.

Relax the whole body, open your eyes and look straight forward as far as you can. Let the Shen Guang travel back to the front of the eyes and close them for a while, open the eyes, start to inhale, the Yi and Nian guide the natural universe's Qi moves through the pores into the body. Hold your breath and take six steps, the Yi and Nian picture in the body as a small whole universe and exhale; walk six more steps while the Yi and Nian guide the Qi from the pores of the whole body send back to the natural universe. Keep walking in the same pattern. Use your mind to place yourself in the center of the ball while you inhale the natural Qi from the edge of the ball into the body and exhale the Qi back to the edge of the ball.

5. Holding your breath for twelve or twenty four steps.

Relax the whole body, open your eyes and look straight forward as far as you can, let the Shen Guang come back up to the front of your eyes. Close them briefly then open them and start to inhale; the Yi and Nian move the Qi from the universe into your body through your pores while you take twelve or twenty four steps.

Hold your breath while walking another twelve or twenty four steps, the Yi and Nian picture in the body as a small whole universe and exhale; walk another twelve or twenty four steps while the Yi and Nian from the body's internal Qi is pushed out through the pores back to the universe.

Keep going walking the same pattern. Picture yourself in the center of a ball; inhale the natural Qi from the edge of the ball into the body and exhale, pushing the Qi back to the edge of the ball.

Chapter Twelve: Ping Heng Gong

Ping Heng Gong is a balance practice, exchanging Qi with trees.

Balance technique is part of Ling Bao Tong Zhi Neng Nei Gong Shu. A practitioner uses balance to exchange Qi; Xin Ling of information and soul with trees, plants, animal, stars, moon, sun and Nature.

Trees have roots spend their lives rooted to the earth; a human is always moving. The tree is Yin and the human is Yang. This section is concerned with practicing the balancing of tree Yin and human Yang, against and in combination with each other to increase the Qi and Xin Ling of information and soul exchange.

A practitioner in good health should exchange Qi with a tree before dawn and/or in the dark of night, daily. If one has health problems, this practice should be done in the daylight.

Table of the five elements:

Five elements	Wood	Fire	Earth	Metal	Water
Organ	Liver	Heart	Spleen and Stomach	Lung	Kidney
Tree	Pine	Paulownia	Willow	Aspen	Cedar
Color	Green	Red	Yellow	White	Black
Direction	East	South	Center	West	North

If the practitioner wants to strengthen and heal the Kidney of urination and hormonal function, he needs to select a cedar tree.

The Liver governs the storage of blood, energy production and regulation of the digestive and emotional systems and requires practicing the exercises with a pine tree to improve these functions.

The Heart governs the circulation of blood and the mind's thought processes, and requires practicing with a paulownia tree.

The Spleen and the Stomach govern the digestive system, store energy and blood and require practicing with a willow tree.

The Lungs perform the function of breathing, encouraging the breath, and stabilizing the flow of Qi downward and require practicing with an aspen tree.

In the five elements, wood Liver is the mother of fire, Heart fire is the mother of earth, earth Spleen and Stomach is the mother of metal, metal Lung is mother of water, Kidney water is the mother of wood.

The practitioner can practice the five trees exercise in a circular order, or if one can not find a particular tree for his to match the five elements organ, he should practice with whatever tree he has access to.

This section is an introduction to the Six Balances tree techniques; one can practice just one or all five, one at a time, in the order above.

At the end of each practice, the internal five elements movements can be practiced once with each of the tree, or practiced all the trees once.

Standing still with body movements:

1. Both hands up and down (Shuang Shou Shang Xia La Dong)

Face the tree, both legs relaxed at shoulder width and knees slightly bent, both hands hanging naturally next to the thighs. Eyes and lips are gently closed and teeth are touching each other, the tongue is on the upper palate and behind the front teeth, and the spine is straight. Stand quietly for a few moments and then lift up both arms, palms facing the tree. The distance from the palms to the tree should be determined by the practitioner feeling the Qi between himself and the tree. Exhale, move both hands down vertically, parallel with the tree while squatting; inhale and bring the hands up parallel with the tree.

The up and down movement of squatting is a strengthening movement, changing with the different heights of the tree.

When the hands are up, the wrists lead up, and when the hands are down, the wrists also lead the movement. Hand movements should be slow and even and the breath long and slow. While the hands and body are moving up and down, concentrate the Yi and Nian picture the color of the hands matching the color of the tree trunk while exchanging, balancing and against the tree's Qi and Xin Ling of information of soul.

After the practitioner has finished hand and body movements in front of the tree, he should move to stand his back is facing the tree; the body's distance from the tree depends on the practitioner feeling the Qi between himself and the tree. Keep the eyes and lips closed and teeth touching each other and the tip of the tongue behind the front teeth, and straighten the spine. Relaxing the body and mind, feel yourself and the tree as one field and begin moving the five elements by hand.

Illustration of both hands up and down:

Moving the five elements by hand:

Lower Dantian:
One hand is on the top of the other hand, above the Lower Dantian, moving, squeezing, and a pulling out the inhalation and pushing back the exhalation motion. The concentrated Yi and Nian are in the Lower Dantian. Repeat several times.

Urinary Bladder:
Exhale; the palms are angled down moving to above the Urinary Bladder. Relax and while inhaling and exhaling. The concentrated Yi and Nian are in the Urinary Bladder and the hands are moving, squeezing, and pulling out the inhalation and pushing back the exhalation motion above the Urination Bladder. Repeat several times.

Liver:
Inhale and angle the palms up to above the Liver, relax, and while inhaling and exhaling. The concentrated Yi and Nian and the hands are moving, squeezing, and pulling out the inhalation and pushing back the exhalation motion above the Liver. Repeat several times.

Heart:
Inhale and the palms angle up moving above the Heart. The concentrated Yi and Nian and the hands are moving, squeezing, and pulling out the inhalation and in a pushing back the exhalation motion. Repeat several times.

Spleen and Stomach:
Exhale and the palms angle down to above the Spleen and Stomach. The concentrated Yi and Nian and the hands are moving, squeezing, and pulling out the inhalation and pushing back the exhalation motion. Repeat several times.

Lungs:
Inhale; the palms angle up and part above the Lungs. The concentrated Yi and Nian and hands are moving, squeezing, and pulling out the inhalation and pushing back the exhalation motion. Repeat several times.

Kidneys:
Exhale and the palms angle down to above the Kidneys, a hand on each Kidney. The concentrated Yi and Nian and the hands are moving, squeezing, and pulling out the inhalation and pushing back the exhalation motion. Repeat several times.

Urinary Bladder:
Exhale and the palms angle down, one hand on top of the other, above the Urinary Bladder. The concentrated Yi and Nian in the Urinary Bladder and the hands are moving, squeezing, and pulling out the inhalation and pushing back

the exhalation motion. Repeat several times.

Lower Dantian:
Inhale; the palms angle up to above the Lower Dantian, moving, squeezing, and a pulling out the inhalation and pushing back the exhalation motion and the concentrated Yi and Nian are in the Lower Dantian. Repeat several times.

Repeat the five element movement six times or more.

Standing and Breathing.

Inhale; the concentrated Yi and Nian guide the universal Qi from every direction entering the whole body through the pores and being deposited into the Lower Dantian and feeling the strength of Li. Exhale; let internal Qi from the Lower Dantian flow through the pores to pour back into the universe. Repeat up to twenty four times or more.

2. Ten fingers vertical crossing (Shi Zhi Zong Hou Qie Ge)

Face the tree, both legs are relaxed and open to shoulder width, with knees slightly bent and both hands relaxed next to the thighs. Close the eyes, lips are closed and teeth are touching each other, and the tongue is on the soft palate and behind the front teeth and the spine is straight. Remain quiet for awhile,

Lift up the arms up, fingers perpendicular to the tree. The fingers' distance from the tree is determined by the Practitioner's feeling the Qi passing between himself and the tree. Exhale and move both hands down and squat; inhale, hands and legs move back up. While moving hands up, the wrist leads and when the hands are moving down, the wrists start down first. The speed and breathing naturally tends to be long, even and stable.

The concentrated Yi and Nian guide the Qi through the fingertips, up and down vertically crossing through the tree, the tree trunk turns into many thin vertical lines to exchange and balance the tree's Qi and Xin Ling of information and soul.

Illustration of ten fingers hand form:

After the practitioner has finished hand and body movements in front of the tree, he turns his back is facing the tree; the body distance from the tree depends on the practitioner feeling the Qi with the tree. Keep the eyes and lips closed and the teeth touching each other and the tip of the tongue on the soft palate and behind the front teeth. The spine is straight. Relax both body and mind, feeling yourself and the tree as one entity, start moving the five elements by hand and pores breathing twenty four times or more.

The instructions for moving the five elements by hand are found under section one both hands up and down of Shuang Shou Shang Xia La Dong. You will use the same methods each time you move the five elements by hand.

3. Ten fingers laterally crossing the tree (Shi Zhi He Xiang Qie Ge)

Face the tree, both legs apart at shoulder width and knees slightly bent, both hands relaxed next to the thighs. Eyes and lips are closed and teeth touching respectively; the tip of the tongue is against the soft palate and behind the front teeth and the spine is straight.

Remain quiet for awhile, lift the arms, palms facing down, and lift the hands to shoulder level. The distance of the fingers from the tree depends on the practitioner's feeling the Qi from the tree to the fingers. Exhale; move the hands to the center, arms stretched out from the body, put one hand on the other, and while holding the breath, pull the hands back to the body, inhale; separate the hands, and move them to the sides and back to shoulder level. Repeat the entire sequence.

Squat down with each inhale and stand up with each exhale; the depth of the squat will depend on the strength of the practitioner's legs. You may mimic the height and width of the tree with the squat.

The concentrated of Yi and Nian from the fingertips move Qi across and through the tree; the tree turns into many different high thin lines as the practitioner exchanges and balances the tree's Qi and Xin Ling of information and soul.

Illustration ten fingers laterally crossing the tree of Shi Zhi He Xiang Qie Ge.

The diagram below demonstrates exhaling and holding the breath:

The diagrams below act of inhaling:

After the practitioner has finished hand and body movements in front of the tree, he turns his back is facing the tree; the body distance from the tree depends on the practitioner feeling the Qi with the tree. Keep the eyes and lips closed and teeth touching each other and the tip of the tongue on the soft palate and behind the front teeth and straighten the spine. Relaxing the body and mind, feel yourself and the tree as one field, and start moving the five elements by hand and the pores breathing twenty four times or more.

The instructions for moving the five elements by hand are found under section one both hands up and down of Shuang Shou Shang Xia La Dong. You will use the same methods each time you move the five elements by hand.

4. Both hands pushing (Shuang Tui Zhang)

Face the tree, legs open to shoulder width and knees bent, hands hanging naturally next to the thighs. Eyes and lips are closed with teeth touching each other, and the tip of the tongue is on the soft palate and behind the front teeth and the spine is straight.

Lift up the arms, palms facing the tree. The distance from the palms to the tree is determined by the practitioner's feeling the Qi between himself and the tree. The fingers of both hands are extended towards the tree. Inhale, the hands pull back to the body with the squat; exhale, hands push towards the tree and the body straightens up from the squat. Inhale again and the hands pull back, squat down; exhale, hands push forward and the legs push up to straight.

The motion should be smooth and flowing, with the concentrated of Yi and Nian, as Qi moving through the hands push and pull against the tree. With the inhale, pull the tree back and straight; exhale and push against the tree bending it to exchange and balance the tree's Qi and the Xin Ling of information and soul.

After the practitioner has finished hand and body movements in front of the tree, he moves to his back is facing the tree. His distance from the tree depends on the practitioner feeling the Qi with the tree. Keep the eyes and lips closed and teeth touching each other and the tip of tongue on the soft palate and behind the front teeth, and straighten the spine. Relaxing the body and mind, feel yourself and the tree as one field and start moving the five elements by hand and pores breathing twenty four times or more.

The illustration below act of exhaling on the left and the illustration below act of inhaling on the right:

5. Sword finger (Jian Zhi) hand form movement

(1) Sword finger moves vertically (Jian Zhi Zong Qie)

Exhale, both hands moving down vertically in the pattern

with tree and squat down; inhale, hands and legs move back up. When the hands are moving up, let the wrists lead, and when the hands move down, let the wrists lead down. The Yi and Nian guide the tips of the index and the middle fingers moves Qi across through the tree; the tree turns into many different thin vertical lines, exchanging and balancing Qi and Xin Ling of information and soul with the human body.

Illustration of two hands sword finger hand form:

After the practitioner has finished hand and body movements in front of the tree, he turns his back is facing the tree; the body distance from the tree depends on the practitioner feeling the Qi with the tree. Keep the eyes and lips closed and teeth touching each other and the tip of the tongue on the soft palate and behind the front teeth and straighten the spine. Relaxing the body and mind, feel yourself and the tree as one field, and start moving the five elements by hand and the pores breathing twenty four times or more.

(2) Sword finger moves laterally (Jian Zhi Heng Qie)

Keep the sword finger form. Exhale, hands from the sides move to the center. Put one hand on the other; while holding the breath, pull the hands back to the body; inhale, separate the hands, the hands from the center opening to the sides and moving forward, exhale, hands from the side to the center and repeat. Inhale, the body up and exhale down.

The concentrated of Yi and Nian from the tips of the index and the middle fingers moves Qi across through the tree; the tree turns into many different thin horizontal thin lines, exchanging and balancing Qi and Xin Ling of information and soul with the human body.

Illustration of single sword finger hand form:

Please see ten fingers lateral crossing the tree of Shi Zhi He Xiang Qie Ge illustration.

After the practitioner has finished hand and body movements in front of the tree, he turns his back is facing the tree; the body distance from the tree depends on the practitioner feeling the Qi with the tree. Keep the eyes and lips closed and teeth touching each other and the tip of the tongue on the soft palate and behind the front teeth and straighten the spine. Relaxing the body and mind, feel yourself and the tree as one field, and start moving the five elements by hand and the pores breathing twenty four times or more.

(3) Sword finger penetrates through the tree (Jian Zhi Chuan Tou)

Inhale, both hands move forward close to the tree; exhale, both hands pull back from to the tree, repeat it over again.

The concentrated of Yi and Nian from Lower Dantian to the tips of the index and the middle fingers move Qi penetrate a dot through the tree as an exhale, the body down, and inhale up, withdraw the Qi from the dot to the Lower Dantian, and to exchange and balance tree Qi and the Xin Ling of information and soul with the Qi from the human body.

Illustration of two hands sword finger hand form:

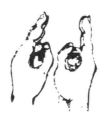

After the practitioner has finished hand and body movements in front of the tree, he turns around so that his back is facing the tree; the body distance from the tree depends on the practitioner feeling the Qi. The eyes and lips are closed with teeth touching each other and the tip of the tongue is on the soft palate and behind the front teeth, and the spine is straight. Relaxing the body and mind, feeling yourself and the tree as one field; start moves the five elements by hand, and pores breathing twenty four times or more.

6. Single chop hand (Dan Pi Zhang)

Face the tree, legs apart at shoulder width and knees slightly bent with both hands resting naturally next to the thighs. Close the eyes and lips, teeth are touching each other and the tip of the tongue is on the soft palate and behind the front teeth and the spine is straight. Stand quietly for awhile.

The distance of the hands from the tree will depend on the practitioner feeling the Qi with the tree.

Begin with the right hand at shoulder level, right palm is facing left, the fingertips pointing at the tree, the left hand at hip level and the left palm is facing the tree. Inhale, the right palm moves down to hip level and is facing the tree, left hand palm is facing right and moves up to shoulder level. Exhale, the right palm faces left and moves up to shoulder level, left palm faces the tree and moves down to hip level.

Holding the breath, turn the palms as if you are holding an invisible ball between your palms; the right palm moves down to hip level and left palm moves up to the shoulder level. The right palm pushes the invisible ball into the tree, while the right palm faces the tree and left hand faces right and fingertips pointing at the tree.

And continuing exercise from left hand leading fist and repeat this entire series several times.

Illustration of single chop movements:

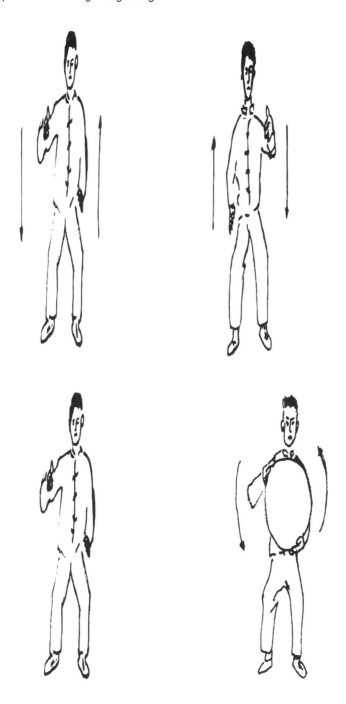

The pattern of the squat follows the rhythm of the breathing; squat down with each inhale and stand up with each exhale; the depth of the squat will depend on the strength of the practitioner's legs. Do not squat when holding the breath.

Using the Yi and Nian, as one palm comes to shoulder level push the tree Qi down, and with the other hand push the Qi up and alternate the hands and repeat the same motions with the next breaths, in and out. Hold the breath with the ball between the palms and push the ball into the tree. The ball is between the palms and being pushed into the tree to align the practitioner's left and right sides, and to exchange and balance tree Qi and the Xin Ling of information and soul with the Qi from the human body.

After the practitioner has finished hand and body movements

in front of the tree, he turns around so that his back is facing the tree and his body's distance from the tree depends on how close he needs to be to feel the Qi from the tree. He keeps his eyes and lips closed and teeth touching each other and the tip of the tongue on the soft palate and behind the front teeth. Spine is straight. Relaxing the body and mind, feeling himself and the tree as one field, he now starts moving the five elements by hand and pores breathing twenty times or more.

Movements of feet, body and arms training:

7. Both hands push (Shuang Tui Zhang)

Face the tree, both legs apart at shoulder width and knees slightly bent, both hands resting naturally next to the thighs. Close the eyes and lips and teeth are touching each other and the tip of the tongue is on the soft palate and behind the front teeth and the spine is straight. Stand quietly for awhile before beginning the exercise.

Lift up both arms, palms facing the tree. The distance of the palms from the tree will depend on the practitioner feeling the Qi from the tree. The fingers of both hands are extended towards the trunk of the tree.

Illustration of both hands push movements:

Illustration of the pattern of the steps:

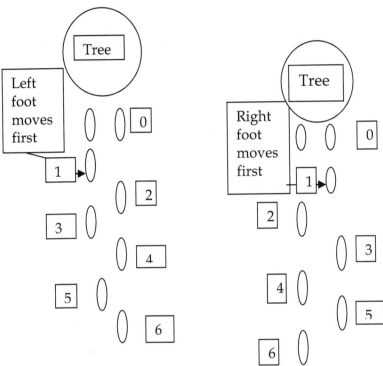

A. Three steps backward:

Stand facing the tree on 0.

Inhale, the palms face down, fingertips facing the tree and as the hands move back to the body. Squat down and move the left leg backward one step on 1. Please see the illustration above.

Exhale, palms facing the tree and moving in the direction of the tree to push the Qi to the tree. The front leg moves backward one step on 2.

Inhale, palms face down and fingertips are pointed towards the tree as the hands move back to pull the Qi from the tree and the front leg moves backward one step to 3.

Exhale, palms moving forward while facing the tree to push the tree's Qi and as the front leg moves backward to step on 4.

Inhale, palms facing down and finger tips facing the tree as hands move back to pull the tree's Qi and the front leg moves backward to step on 5.

Exhale, palms facing the tree and moving towards the tree to push the tree's Qi and as the front leg moves backward to step on 6.

B. Three steps forward:

Inhale, palms facing down and fingertips facing the tree and hands move back to pull the tree's Qi and as the body weight moves to the front leg and steps on 5.

Exhale, palms facing to the tree and move towards the tree to push the tree's Qi, and the back leg moves forward to step on 4.

Inhale, palms facing down and fingertips facing the tree as the hands move back to pull the tree's Qi and the back leg moves forward to step on 3.

Exhale, palms facing the tree and moving towards to the tree to push the tree's Qi and as the back leg moves forward to step on 2.

Inhale, palms facing down and fingertips facing the tree and hands moving back to pull the tree's Qi and as the back leg moves forward to step on 1.

Exhale, palms facing moving forward while facing the tree to push the tree's Qi and as the back leg moves forward to step on 0.

Repeat three steps backward and forward again. If you started with the right leg, please see the illustration of the pattern of steps on the right.

After the practitioner has finished hand and body movements in front of the tree, turn around and stand with your back facing the tree; the body's distance from the tree will depends on the practitioner feeling the Qi from the tree. Keep the eyes and lips closed and teeth touching each other and the tip of the tongue on the soft palate and behind the front teeth and the spine is straight. Relaxing the body and mind, feel yourself and the tree as one field and start moving the five elements by hand and pores breathing twenty four times or more.

8. Double push channels (Shuang Tui Mai)

Face the tree, both legs apart at shoulder width and knees slightly bent, both hands resting naturally next to the thighs. Close the eyes and lips. The teeth are touching each other and the tip of the tongue is on the soft palate and behind the front teeth and the spine is straight. Stand quietly for awhile.

Illustration of double push channels movements:

A. Three steps backward:

Inhale, palms facing the tree, lift up both arms, palms distance from the tree depends on the practitioner's feeling the Qi between the tree and himself. Lift hands up above the head and close to the head; turn the palms to face the sides of the head. Turn the palms to face the body as they move down, and push the Qi down to the Lower Dantian, the left or right leg takes one step backward on step 1. Please see the illustration of pattern of steps.

Exhale; the hands separate and move from the Lower Dantian, pushing the Qi from the Lower Dantian to the front leg, palms at each side of the front leg's thigh, pushing the Qi from the Lower Dantian to the thighs and foot and back to the tree.

Inhale; the palms facing the tree, palms again moving up from the bottom of tree to just above the head, moving close to the head, then facing the body and moving down to the Lower Dantian as the front leg steps backward to step 2. Exhale; the hands are now moving down to the front leg, palms facing the side of the thighs, pushing the Qi from the Lower Dantian to the front leg and foot and back to the tree.

Inhale; palms facing the tree, keep moving the hands up from the bottom of tree to above the head, moving close to the head, and then moving the hands down with palms turned to face the body, push the Qi down to the Lower Dantian as the front leg steps backward to step 3. Exhale as you separate the hands from the Lower Dantian, moving them down to the front of thighs, palms facing thighs, pushing the Qi from the Lower Dantian to the front leg and foot and back to the tree.

Inhale; palms facing the tree, keep hands moving up from the bottom of tree to the above the head, moving close to the head, then moving down and palms facing the body and pushing Qi down to the Lower Dantian as the front leg steps backward to step 4. Exhale; hands move from the Lower Dantian to the sides of the thigh, facing the thigh, pushing the Qi from the Lower Dantian to the leg and foot and back to the tree.

Inhale; palms facing the tree, keep moving the hands up from the bottom of tree to above the head, moving close to the head, and moving down with palms facing the body, pushing the Qi down to the Lower Dantian as the front leg steps backward to step 5. Exhale; hands move away from the Lower Dantian, down to the front leg, both palms against the side of thigh of the front leg, pushing the Qi from the Lower Dantian to the leg and foot and back to the tree.

Inhale; palms facing the tree, keep them moving up from the bottom of the tree to above the head, moving close to the head, and moving down with palms facing the body and pushing Qi down to the Lower Dantian as front leg steps backward to step 6.

Exhale; the hands move away from the Lower Dantian, down to the front leg, both palms against the side of the thigh of the front leg, pushing the Qi from the Lower Dantian to the leg and foot and back to the tree.

B. Three steps forward.

Inhale, the palms facing the tree, moving up from the bottom of tree to above the head, then close to the head, and moving down with palms turned towards to the body, pushing Qi down to the Lower Dantian as the back leg steps forward to step 5. Exhale; separate the hands as they move from the Lower Dantian to the front of the thighs, palms facing the thigh, pushing the Qi from the Lower Dantian to the leg and foot and back to the tree.

Inhale with palms facing the tree and move the hands up from their level at the base of the tree to above the head and in a position close to the head. Then move the hands down with the palms facing the body and pushing Qi down to the Lower Dantian as the back leg steps forward to step 4. Exhale; hands move from the Lower Dantian to the side of the thigh, facing the thigh, pushing the Qi from the Lower Dantian to the leg and foot and back to the tree.

Inhale and the palms facing the tree, keep them moving up from the bottom of tree to above the head, moving close to the head, and then moving the hands down with palms turned to face the body and pushing Qi down to the Lower Dantian as the back leg steps forward with the step 3. Exhale; remove the hands from the Lower Dantian, moving them down to the front leg with the palms on each side of the thigh of the front leg, pushing the Qi from the Lower Dantian to the leg and foot and back to the tree.

Inhale; palms facing the tree, keep moving them up from the bottom of tree to above the head, moving close to the head, and moving down with palms facing to the body, push Qi down to the Lower Dantian as the back leg steps forward to step 2. Exhale; hands move from the Lower Dantian to the sides of the thigh, facing the thigh, pushing the Qi from the Lower Dantian to the leg and foot and back to the tree.

Inhale; the palms facing the tree, keep them moving up from the bottom of tree to above the head, moving close to the head, and moving down with palms turned and facing the body and pushing Qi down to the Lower Dantian as the back leg steps forward on step 1. Exhale; hands move from the Lower Dantian to the sides of the thigh, facing the thigh, pushing the Qi from the Lower Dantian to the leg and foot and back to the tree.

Inhale; palms facing the tree, keep them moving up from the bottom of the tree to above the head, moving close to the head, and moving down with palms facing the body and pushing Qi down to the Lower Dantian as the back leg steps forward on step 0.

Repeat three steps backward and forward again. If you started with the right leg.

After the practitioner has finished these hand and body movements in front of the tree, he turns around so his back is facing the tree. The body's distance from the tree depends on how close to the tree the practitioner needs to be to feel the Qi. Keep the eyes and lips closed and teeth touching each other and the tip of tongue on the soft palate and behind the front teeth, and straighten the spine. Relax the body and mind, feel yourself and the tree as one field and start moving the five elements by hand and pores breathing twenty four times or more.

Chapter Thirteen: Standing Training

Standing training quiets the mind and body with internal movements. Internal movements lead external body movements; flowing in a circle the external movement turns back into internal movement, and each circle will lead to a higher level.

This standing practice can follow the Ping Heng Gong of balance practice or be practiced by itself.

There are three levels of standing practice:

1. Response.
2. Controlling and balancing Qi.
3. Back to the source.

There are nine standing forms:

1. No limitations.
2. Sun.
3. Moon.
4. Spring.
5. Summer.
6. Autumn.
7. Winter.
8. Seven stars.
9. Nine palaces.

Introduction the no limitation standing form

Stand with both legs apart at shoulder width and knees slightly bent, both hands resting naturally next to the thighs. Open your eyes and look forward as far as you can, let the Shen Guang (mind and light) slowly return to the edge of the human universe, which is at arm's length from the body; close the eyes and lips, teeth are touching each other and the tip of tongue is on the soft palate and behind the front teeth and the spine is straight. Remain quiet for awhile.

Inhale; the concentrated Yi and Nian guide the natural universal Qi from every direction to press into the body's pores, the edge of the body universe; exhale, the human body's internal Qi expands through its pores into the natural universe.

After performing the breathing cycle twenty four times, return to normal undirected breaths, relax the body and mind and stand as long as you comfortably.

1. First level practice:

With the Yi and Nian guide the natural Qi presses in through the skin as the practitioner inhales; he exhales, and expels the Qi back to Nature.

Illustration of pores breathing:

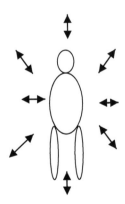

2. Second level practice:

Inhale; the concentrated Yi and Nian presses the natural Qi

through the body's pores to the Lower Dantian as the Middle Dantian Qi through the Duan line moves down to the Lower Dantian; exhale, the Lower Dantian Qi flows through the pores back into nature and the Lower Dantian Qi moves up to the Middle Dantian.

Illustration of pores and the Middle and Lower Dantain breathing:

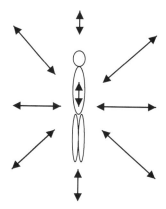

3. Third level practice:

Let the concentrated Yi and Nian guide the universal Qi through the pores from the ball at the edge of the natural universe, to the Lower Dantian and exchanges with the body's Qi and becomes internal Qi. Feeling the strength Li and as the Middle Dantian Qi through the Duan line moves down to the Lower Dantian, exhale, and the internal Qi from the Lower Dantian, is expelled through the pores back to the ball at the edge of the universe and while the Lower Dantian Qi through the Duan line move up to the Middle Dantian. Repeat the process breathing twenty four times.

Illustration of pores, the Middle and Lower Dantian and edge of natural universe breathing:

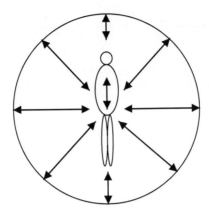

At all the levels practice begins with twenty four cycles of breathing. The body may experience warmth, movement, five elements circulation and movement into acupuncture channels; this is strengthening of Li and Qi pushing and opening the channels and organs as the Qi passes through them.

Chapter Fourteen: Capturing the Sun's Jing of essence and the Moon's light

Capturing the sun's essence and the moon's light is practicing to capture, dissolve, exchange and match the natural forces of the sun and moon to understand the relationship between the human Xin of information and Ling of soul, body and time, space and the universe.

There are three levels:

(1). The first level is standing practice for harmonizing Yin and Yang and nourishing Yuan (original) Qi.

(2). The second level is moving the combined human nature and Yin and Yang.

(3). The third level is the sitting practice for the practitioner to protect the self and take control of the forces of Jing and the light from the Moon.

1. Capturing moonlight.

The moon's light is Yin reflected from the sun's Yang light and is Yin embracing Yang, the Lungs are at the upper position where is Yang embracing Yin; the Yin function nourishes the blood and Qi. This practicing is balancing and harmonizing the Yin moon embracing Yang and Lungs' Yang embracing the Yin.

Perform this practice the night before the full, the night of the full moon and the night after the full moon only.

A. Standing to capture the moonlight.

Face the moon, both legs relaxed at shoulder width and knees slightly bent, both palms are turned towards the moon. Open the eyes to watch the full moon, lips closed and teeth touching each other; tongue on the upper palate and behind the front teeth and a straight spine. Memorize the brightness of the full moon, close your eyes and bring the full moon in front of the eyes at the edge of the human universe, watching the full circle of the moon's brightness.

Illustration of the moon and the edge of human universe:

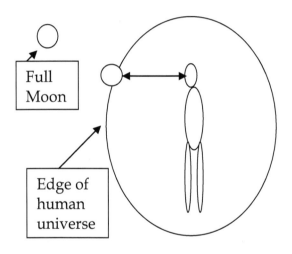

B. Capturing the moon with intense fire and strong, rapid breathing and concentration.

Exhale; there is a bright full moon being sent out from the body to match nature's moon in front of your eyes at the edge of the human universe. The tongue is relaxed in the mouth.

Inhale; bring the full moon from in front of your eyes at the edge of the human universe to between the eyebrows and down into the Lungs and with tongue on the soft palate and behind the front teeth. Exhale; relax and the tongue is relaxed in the mouth. Repeat twenty four times. The first step involves breathing in and out through the nose. The second step is breathing in through the nose and out from the mouth. The concentrated Yi and Nian capture the full moon's bright light, filling the Lungs and strengthening Li in the Lungs.

C. Using optimum fire to move and dissolve the five elements.

After twenty four intense breaths, capture the moonlight in the Lungs. Inhale; the concentrated Yi and Nian from the Lungs dissolve the bright light of the full moon. Exhale; send the bright light down to the Kidneys. Inhale; the Kidneys dissolve into Qi and bright light.

Exhale; the Kidney Qi and light move down to the Urinary Bladder and dissolve. Inhale and exhale; the Urinary Bladder dissolves into the bright light. Inhale; move the Urinary Bladder Qi and light to the Liver to dissolve. Exhale; the Liver Qi and light are powerfully flowing. Inhale; the Liver Qi and light move up to the Heart and dissolve. Exhale and inhale; the Heart dissolves into the bright light. Exhale; the Heart Qi and light move down to the Spleen and Stomach and dissolve. Inhale and exhale; the Spleen and Stomach dissolve into bright light. Inhale; The Spleen and Stomach Qi and light move to the Lungs and dissolve. Repeat six times.

Or guide the movement of the five elements by hand.

Lungs:
Inhale; the palms angle up to above the Lungs, relax and while inhaling and exhaling, the hands are moving, squeezing, and pulling out the inhalation and pushing back the light the exhalation. Repeat several times.

Kidneys:

Exhale; the palms angle down to above the Kidneys, relax and while inhaling and exhaling, the hands are moving, squeezing, and pulling out the inhalation and pushing back the exhalation. Repeat several times.

Urinary Bladder:
Exhale; the palms angle down to above the Urinary Bladder, relax and while inhaling and exhaling, the hands are moving, squeezing, and pulling out the inhalation and pushing back the light the exhalation. Repeat several times.

Liver:
Inhale and place the palms above the Liver, relax and while inhaling and exhaling, the hands are moving, squeezing, and pulling out the inhalation and pushing back the exhalation. Repeat several times.

Heart:
Inhale; the palms move above the Heart, relax and while inhaling and exhaling, the hands are moving, squeezing, and pulling out the inhalation and pushing back the light the exhalation. Repeat several times.

Spleen and Stomach:
Exhale; the palms angle down to above the Spleen and Stomach, relax and while inhaling and exhaling, the hands are moving, squeezing, and pulling out the inhalation and pushing back the light the exhalation. Repeat several times.

Lungs:
Inhale; the palms angle up to above the Lungs, relax, and while inhaling and exhaling, the hands are moving, squeezing, and pulling out the inhalation and pushing back the light the exhalation. Repeat several times.

Repeat the moving the five elements six times.

D. Intense fire guides the mild fire returns the light to its source and its original position.

After moving the Qi from the organs of the five elements back to the golden metal Lungs, use intense fire to guide the mild fire of strong and easy breathing and through back to the source of Lungs, until the bright moonlight of the full moon shines in the Lungs and the body.

Keep the eyes and lips closed and teeth touching each other; the tip of the tongue is on the soft palate and behind the front teeth and the spine is straight.

Exhale; push the moonlight Lung Qi through the pores of the whole body to the edge of the human universe. Inhale; bring back the moonlight Qi from the edge of human universe to fill the Lungs. After repeating the exercise six times, the breathing is relaxed with deep inhales and long slow exhales.

E. Bathe your entire body in the invisible moonlight with intense and mild optimum fire.

Stand naturally with eyes and lips closed, teeth touching each other, the tip of the tongue is on the soft palate and behind the front teeth, breathe naturally, watching where the internal Qi and light move in the body. Observe the channel and the connection between the human body and the natural universe.

F. Back to the source.

Return the full moon from the body out through the space between the eyebrows back to the natural moon in the sky.

2. Capturing the Sun's Jing

The sun is a Yang force embracing Yin, the heat and bright light are Yang; Yang force burns up the substance of Yin. The human Liver is Yin embracing Yang; it stores blood and is in the middle and lower part of body that belongs to Yin, and it is a strong Yang character organ; it smoothes Qi energy and is a decision making organ. This section is practicing harmony between the Yang Sun embracing Yin and the human Liver's Yin embracing Yang.

A. Preparing for the Sunrise.

Practitioner stands where he can see the sun rising from the horizon and closes his eyes naturally. Both palms are turned towards the sun; the body and mind are relaxed. Stand quietly until the sun begins to rise. Open the eyes to watch and to wait for the sun to climb above the horizon.

Illustration of sun rising:

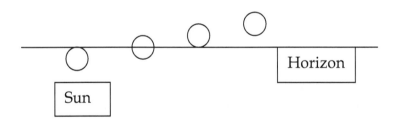

B. Capturing and refining the sun's intense fire.

The eyes are open to just glimpse the sun as it rises over the horizon.

Exhale; the tongue is relaxed in the mouth, the Liver and Gall Bladder Qi expands through the whole body as a red fire ball. Inhale through the nose, with the tip of the tongue lightly pressed behind the front teeth and the palms facing the sun, the concentrated Yi and Nian seeing a fire dragon from the east and the sun captured by the eyes move down to the Liver and Gall Bladder, and they become extremely red and dissolve into Qi. Exhale through the mouth, tongue relaxed down, the Liver and Gall Bladder are red with the sun's Qi expanding through the whole body as a red fireball.

Repeat three to six times before the sun rises above the horizon.

After the sun is almost above the horizon, close the eyes, palms facing the thighs, the tip of the tongue behind the front teeth; hold this position and begin the next section's practice.

C. Mild and intense moving the five elements.

Exhale; the concentrated Yi and Nian guide the Liver is dissolving the bright sun's red light. Inhale; move the Qi and light to the Heart and dissolve the red light. Exhale; move the Heart Qi and light down to the Spleen and Stomach and dissolve the red light. Inhale; move the Spleen and Stomach Qi and light up to the Lungs and dissolve the red light. Exhale; the Lung Qi and light move down to the Kidneys and dissolve the red light. Exhale; the Kidney Qi and light flow down to the Urinary Bladder and dissolve the red light. Inhale; The Urinary Bladder Qi and light move up to the Liver and dissolve the red light. Repeat six times.

One can use the hands on the organs to guide the Qi through the five elements from Liver to Heart, from the Heart to Spleen and Stomach, from the Spleen and Stomach to Lungs, from the Lungs to the Kidneys, from the Kidneys to the

Urinary Bladder and from the Urinary Bladder to the Liver. Repeat the five element movement six times.

D. Intense fire guides the mild fire returns the light to its source and its original position.

Exhale; expand the green wood Qi from the Liver and Gall Bladder to the skin of the whole body and the color should be red sun Qi at the outer and the wood Liver green Qi in the inner.

Inhale; bring back and capture the green and red Qi from the skin and return it to the Liver; this is fire refining the Liver wood.

Repeat six times, each breath series powerful, fast, long, deep, stable and even. The body will be warm and hot and feeling as if it is inhabited by an aggregate of fire.

E. Bathe in the invisible mild and intense fire.

Relax the body and mind and breathe naturally, envisioning the internal universe as an aggregate of fire, feeling enjoy, emptiness and your body in the clouds. In this moment, there is can see a circle of light around you.

F. Back to the natural universe

The sun's light in the body travels up and out between the eyebrows to shoot back to the sun.

Chapter Fifteen: Moving the Five Elements to Open the Eight Extra Channels

This section uses Shen of mind, body movement and hands' Qi to assist in opening eight extra channels.

Perform this practice whenever you want to move the body.

The eight extra channels are used for balance and connection pathways in the human universe.

There are three levels:

1. Healing the self by opening up and harmonizing with the universe.
2. The feeling self surrenders to the whole universe, gaining an understanding of life and death.
3. Protecting you and healing someone else.

Introduction to the first level:

Healing the self by opening up and harmonizing with the universe.

(1) Preparation for the Exercise.

Stand with both legs apart at shoulder width and knees slightly bent, both hands resting naturally next to the thighs. Open the eyes and look forward as far as you can, let the Shen Guang (mind and light) come slowly back to the edge of the human universe, which is at arm's length from the body. Close the eyes and mouth, teeth touching each other and the tip of the tongue behind the front teeth and a straight spine. Remain quiet for awhile.

Inhale; use the Yi and Nian guide the universal Qi to press into the body through the pores and into the Lower Dantian. The practitioner will feel the strength of Li and the Qi flowing along the Duan line from the Middle Dantian to the Lower Dantian.

Exhale; use the Yi and Nian guide the universe's Qi in the Lower Dantian expand through the pores into the natural universe and the Lower Dantian's Qi move through the Duan line back up to the Middle Dantian.

Repeat six, twelve or twenty four times.

(2) Moving the Five Elements with the hands.

Lower Dantian:
One hand is on the top of the other hand, above the Lower Dantian, moving, squeezing with a pulling out the inhalation and pushing back the exhalation motion while inhaling and exhaling. The concentrated Yi and Nian are in the Lower Dantian. Repeat several times.

Urinary Bladder:
Exhale; the palms are angled down moving to above the Urinary Bladder. Relax, and while inhaling and exhaling. The Yi and Nian are in the Urinary Bladder and the hands are moving, squeezing, and pulling out the inhalation and pushing back the exhalation above the Urination Bladder. Repeat several times.

Liver:
Inhale and angle the palms up to above the Liver, relax, and while inhaling and exhaling. The Yi and Nian and the hands are moving, squeezing, and pulling out the inhalation and pushing back the exhalation above the Liver. Repeat several times.

Heart:
Inhale; the palms angle up moving above the Heart, the Yi and Nian and the hands are moving, squeezing, and pulling out the inhalation and pushing back the exhalation motion. Repeat several times.

Spleen and Stomach:
Exhale; use the palms angle down to above the Spleen and Stomach. Relax and while inhaling and exhaling, the Yi and Nian and the hands are moving, squeezing, and pulling out the inhalation and pushing back the exhalation. Repeat several times.

Lungs:
Inhale; use the palms angle up and separate above the Lungs. The Yi and Nian and hands are moving, squeezing, and pulling out the inhalation and pushing back the exhalation. Repeat several times.

Kidneys:
Exhale; use the palms angle down to above the Kidneys, a hand on each Kidney. The Yi and Nian and the hands are moving, squeezing, and pulling out the inhalation and pushing back the exhalation. Repeat several times.

Urinary Bladder:
Exhale; use the palms angle down, one hand on top of the other above the Urinary Bladder. The Yi and Nian in the Urinary Bladder and the hands are moving, squeezing, and pulling out the inhalation and pushing back the exhalation. Repeat several times.

Repeat this entire series six times.

1. Opening the Lower Body Yinyao, Yangyao and Yinwei and Yangwei channels

This drawing illustrates the Yinqaio, Yangyao, Yinwei and Yangwei channels:

Yangqiao

The Yangqiao channel starts from the lateral side of heel; ascending along the side of the body, shoulder face and head, ending below the lateral occipital bone.

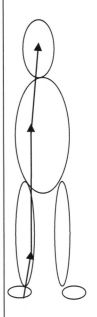

Yinqiao

The Yinqiao channel starts from the posterior aspect of the navicular bone, ascending to the posterior border of the thigh and straight upward along the abdomen, chest, sideways to the Adams apple, ending at the inner canthus.

Yangwei

The Yangwei channel begins at the heel. Ascending to the external ankle, it runs upward, passing through the hip region and further upward along the posterior aspect of the hypochondriac and costal region and the posterior aspect of axilla to the shoulder, from there it further ascends to the forehead and turns backward to the back of the neck, where it becomes the cervical spine.

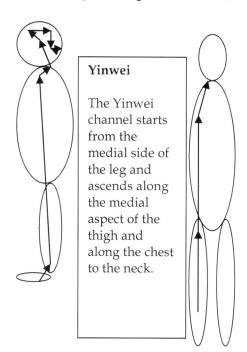

Yinwei

The Yinwei channel starts from the medial side of the leg and ascends along the medial aspect of the thigh and along the chest to the neck.

Open the eyes and change the body weight to the left or right leg.

(1) Exhale; the tongue lies flat and relaxed on the bottom of the mouth, fingers face down, back of hands face each other, and from the Lower Dantian, move both hands up to shoulder level, keeping arms and hands open and facing the sky, the concentrate Yi and Nian from the Lower Dantian travels up to the sky.

(2) Inhale; tip of tongue is behind the front teeth, hands back, arms down and fingers face each other and palms face down to the Lower Dantian. The Yi and Nian guide the natural Qi from the sky to the Lower Dantian.

(3) Hold the breath with hands on top of each other above the Lower Dantian, moving, squeezing, pulling, and pushing back.

(4) Exhale; the tongue is relaxed, change the body weight on one leg, both palms push the Lower Dantian Qi to the weightless leg, both palms face the each thigh, continuing push the Qi from the leg and foot back to the natural universe. Move the hands up to shoulder level, arms and hand open until palms and face up to the sky, as the same time the body turns 90 degrees and the weight on both legs.

(5) Inhale; tip of tongue is behind the front teeth, hands back, arms down and fingers face each other and palms face down to the Lower Dantian. TheYi and Nian guide the natural Qi from the sky to the Lower Dantian.

(6) Hold the breath with hands on top of each other above the Lower Dantian, moving, squeezing, pulling, and pushing back.

(7) Exhale; the tongue is relaxed, changing the body weight on one leg, both palms push the Lower Dantian Qi to the weightless leg, both palms face the each thigh, continuing push the Qi from the leg and foot back to the natural universe. Move the hands up to shoulder level, arms and hand open until palms and face up to the sky, as the same time the body turns 90 degrees and the weight on both legs.

(8) Inhale; tip of tongue is behind the front teeth, hands back, arms down and fingers face each other and palms face down to the Lower Dantian. The Yi and Nian guide the natural Qi from the sky to the Lower Dantian.

(9) Hold the breath with hands on top of each other above the Lower Dantian, moving, squeezing, pulling, and pushing back.

(10) Exhale; the tongue is relaxed, changing the body weight on one leg, both palms push the Lower Dantian Qi to the weightless leg, both palms face the each thigh, continuing push the Qi from the leg and foot back to the natural universe. Move the hands up to shoulder level, arms and hand open until palms and face up to the sky, as the same time the body turns 90 degrees and the weight on both legs.

Repeat the exercise six, twelve or twenty four times.

Illustration of opening the Lower Body Yinyao, Yangyao and Yinwei and Yangwei channels:

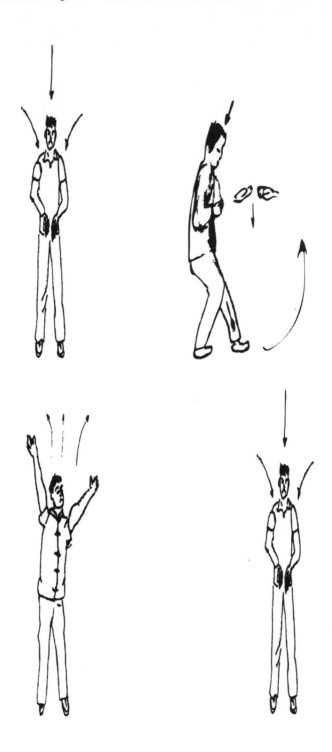

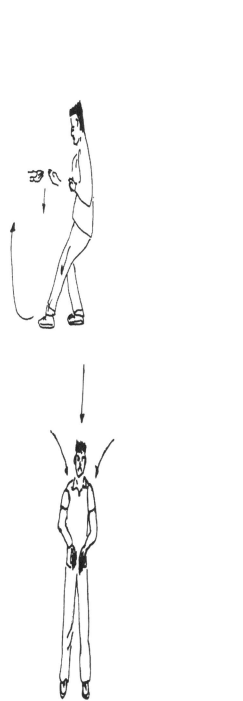

2. Opening the Dai channel

This drawing illustrates the Dai channel:

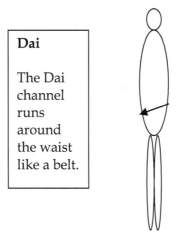

Dai

The Dai channel runs around the waist like a belt.

Mind, body and breathing:

Both hands are placed above the Lower Dantian.

Exhale; the tongue lies flat and relaxed on the bottom of the mouth, move your hands to each side, and then from the Lower Dantian to Mingmen is located between lumbar vertebrae two and three. The concentrated Yi and Nian from the Lower Dantian Qi move the Qi to the Mingmen.

Inhale; the tip of tongue is behind the front teeth, the hands move down to the Lower Dantian, the Yi and Nian push Qi from the Mingmen down to the Lower Dantian.

Repeat six, twelve or twenty four times.

Illustration of opening the Dai channel:

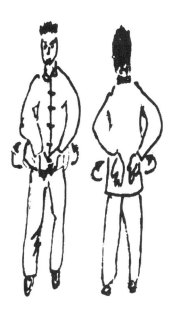

3. Opening the Chong channel

This drawing illustrates the Chong channel:

Chong

The Chong channel originates in the lower abdomen, descends and emerges from the perineum. It ascends and runs insides the vertebral column, while its superficial portion passes through along both sides of the lower abdominal region, and the internal channel ascends up the throat and curves around the lips.

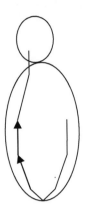

Mind, body and breathing.

Exhale; the tongue lies flat and relaxed on the bottom of the mouth, both hands face up, fingers face each other, the hands move up from the Lower Dantian to the Middle Dantian, located between the sixth and seventh ribs in the center of the sternum. The Yi and Nian push the Qi from the Lower Dantian to the Middle Dantian.

Inhale; the tip of tongue is behind the front teeth; move the downward facing palms from the Middle Dantian to the Lower Dantian. The Yi and Nian push the Qi from the Middle Dantian down to the Lower Dantian.

Repeat six, twelve or twenty four times.

Illustration of opening the Chong channel:

4. Opening the upper body's Chong, Ren, Yangyao, Yinyao, Yangwei, and Yingwei channels

Mind, body and breathing:

1. Exhale; the tongue lies flat and relaxed on the bottom of the mouth, fingers face down, back of hands face each other, and from the Lower Dantian, move both hands up to shoulder level, keeping arms and hands open and facing the sky, the Yi and Nian from the Lower Dantian travels up to the sky.

2. Inhale; tip of tongue is behind the front teeth, hands back, arms down and fingers face each other and palms face down to the lower Dantian. The Yi and Nian guide the natural Qi from the sky to the Lower Dantian.

3. Hold the breath with hands on top of each other above the Lower Dantian, moving, squeezing, pulling, and pushing back.

4. Exhale; the tongue lies flat and relaxed on the bottom of the mouth, fingers face down, back of hands face each other, and from the Lower Dantian, move both hands up to shoulder level, keeping arms and hands open and facing the sky, at the same time turn the body about 90 degree to the left or right. The Yi and Nian from the Lower Dantian Qi travel up to the sky.

5. Inhale; tip of tongue is behind the front teeth, hands back, arms down and fingers face each other and palms face down to the lower Dantian. The Yi and Nian guide the natural Qi from the sky to the Lower Dantian.

6. Hold the breath with hands on top of each other above the Lower Dantian, moving, squeezing, pulling, and pushing back.

7. Exhale; tongue down on mouth, fingers face down, back of hands facing each other, from the Lower Dantian, move hands up to shoulder level, arms and hands open until palms face up to the sky, at the same time the body turns 90 degrees to the left or right. The Yi and Nian from the Lower Dantian move the arms up to open to the sky.

Repeat six, twelve or twenty four times.

Illustration of opening the upper body's Chong, Ren, Yangyao, Yinyao, Yangwei, and Yingwei channels:

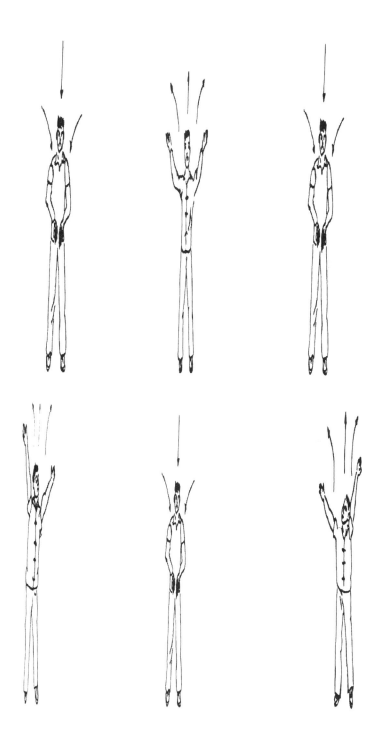

5. Opening the Ren Channels

This drawing illustrates the Ren channel:

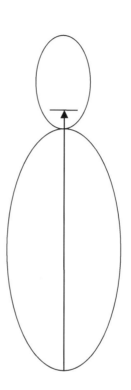

Ren

The Ren channel arises from the lower abdomen and emerges from the perineum, it runs anteriorly to the pubic region and ascends along the interior center of abdomen to the middle of the throat and runs further upward to below the lip, the internal channel, curves around the lips, passes through the cheek and enters the infraorbital region.

Mind, body and breathing:

Exhale; tongue on the mouth, dorsal sides of hands facing each other, from the Lower Dantian, move both hands up to shoulder level, continuing, arms and face up, straight open to the sky. The concentrated Yi and Nian move the Qi from the Lower Dantian through the Ren channel up and open to the sky.

Inhale; tip of tongue is behind the front teeth, hands down, fingers pointing down and back of hands facing each other, until move down to the Lower Dantian. The Yi and Nian guide the natural sky Qi down from the Ren channels to the Lower Dantian.

Hold the breath, hands on top of each other above the Lower Dantian, moving, squeezing, pulling and pushing etc.

Repeat six, twelve or twenty four times.

Illustration of opening the Ren channels:

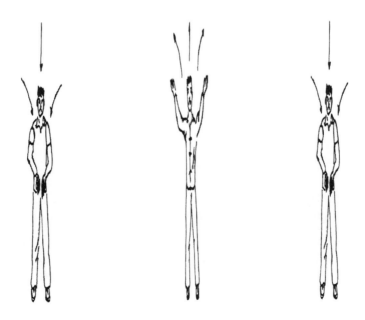

Final exercise of moving the Qi through the five elements by hand:

Lower Dantian:
One hand is on the top of the other hand, above the Lower Dantian, moving, squeezing, and a pulling out the inhalation and pushing back the exhalation motion and the concentrated Yi and Nian is in the Lower Dantian; repeat several times.

Urinary Bladder:
Exhale; the palms are angled down moving to above Urinary Bladder. Relax, and while inhaling and exhaling, the concentrated Yi and Nian are in the Urinary Bladder and the hands are moving, squeezing, and pulling out the inhalation and pushing back the exhalation above the Urinary Bladder. Repeat several times.

Liver:
Inhale and angle the palms up to above the Liver, relax, and while inhaling and exhaling. The concentrated Yi and Nian and the hands are moving, squeezing, and pulling out the inhalation and pushing back the exhalation above the Liver. Repeat several times.

Heart:
Inhale; the palms are angled up and moving to above the Heart. The concentrated Yi and Nian and the hands are moving, squeezing, and pulling out the inhalation and pushing back the exhalation motion. Repeat several times.

Spleen and Stomach:
Exhale and the palms angle down to above the Spleen and Stomach. The concentrated Yi and Nian and the hands are moving, squeezing, and pulling out the inhalation and pushing back the exhalation. Repeat several times.
Lungs:

Inhale; the palms angle up and part above the Lungs. The concentrated Yi and Nian and hands are moving, squeezing, and pulling out the inhalation and pushing back the exhalation. Repeat several times.

Kidneys:
Exhale and the palms angle down to above the Kidneys, a hand on each Kidney. The concentrated Yi and Nian and the hands are moving, squeezing, and pulling out the inhalation and pushing back the exhalation. Repeat several times.

Urinary Bladder:
Exhale and the palms angle down, one hand on top of the other, above the Urinary Bladder. The concentrated Yi and Nian in the Urinary Bladder and the hands are moving, squeezing, and pulling out the inhalation and pushing back the exhalation. Repeat several times.

Repeat the five element movement six times.

Regulating breathing and optimal fire an invisible shower of caring:

Stand with legs apart at shoulder width and knees slightly bent, both hands resting naturally next to the thighs. Lips and teeth are closed; tip of tongue is touching the front teeth. Inhale; use the Yi and Nian guide the natural Qi from the pores into the Lower Dantian. Exhale; use the Yi and Nian, guide the internal Qi from the Lower Dantian, expanding out through the body's pores and into the natural world.

Repeat six, twelve or twenty four times.

Breathe naturally and relax and gently observe the inner body.

Chapter Sixteen: Ba Gua Yi Qiu Gong

The ancient name for Ba Gua Yi Qiu Gong is Lu Zu Ba Gua Yi Qiu Gong. Ba Gua indicates Taoism's eight directions trigram information concerning the relationship between nature and humans and the universe. Yi indicates intention, Qiu means in the shape of a ball. Gong indicates capacity.

Practicing Ba Gua Yi Qiu Gong is training to deliver Xin of information and Ling of soul, for healing, and connecting to nature.

There are standing, sitting and walking techniques. The Ba Gua Yi Qiu ball may be invisible, red, yellow, white, black or green, representing the five elements. The color of the ball will depend on each person.

Perform this practice whenever you need to move the body or the Shen and Ling of soul will be activated your movements.

1. Standing and sitting practice

Stand in the open in a field, lawn, or near trees, squat down naturally, straighten the spine and place your hands on thighs, the lips lightly closed and teeth touching each other and the tip of the tongue behind the front teeth, or sit with legs cross, keep the eyes open, remain quiet and relaxed.

The palms face each other; move the palms apart as though you hold a beach ball opening up a space for your ball between your palms from shoulder to waist. Keep the eyes and Yi and Nian focused into the center of the ball, with the distance between the palms constant, turning the ball, spinning the ball down and up, clockwise or counterclockwise, or left and right in front of your body, between the palms with a fluid motion.

Illustration of Ba Gua Yi Qiu Gang standing and sitting practice:

2. Movement step practice

There are two movements which are geometric shapes that happen at the same time in this practice. The first one is a circle representing the sky and earth square; the second is Tai Ji Yin Yang movement, adding the Ba Gua Yi Qiu invisible ball to the Yin and Yang circle that the legs are performing.

(1) Sky circle and Earth square

In this practice you will exchange Xin of information and Ling of soul with sky and earth. Sky is represented by a Yang circle; Earth is represented by Yin square; practice the Qi Yang circle and Yin square of harmony.

Stand on an open field, a lawn, or near trees and squat keeping the spine straight. And place your hands on your thighs, lips lightly closed and teeth touching each other and your tongue against the soft palate and behind the front teeth, eyes open. Remain quiet and relaxed.

Place the palms face to each other, open up the distant as far as shoulder, the concentrated Yi and Nian there is a ball between the hands and eyes are focus into center of the ball, keeping palms face to each other and distant, turning and circling the ball forward down and backward up, clockwise or counterclockwise, or left and right in front of body. Keeping palms face to each other and same distant and hands fellow the ball move.

The left foot steps to number 1, representing the earth, the right foot steps to number 2 representing the sky, the left foot steps on number 3 and the right foot steps on 4, the left stops on number 5 and right one stops on number 6, the left foot stops on number 7 and right one steps on 8.

Repeat beginning with the right foot.

The sky circle and earth square movement can begin with either a turn to the right or a turn to the left.

Illustration of sky circle and earth square stepping pattern:

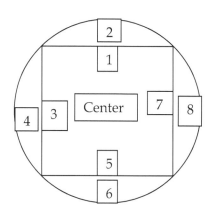

(2) Tai Ji Yin Yang circle.

In this practice you exchange Xin of information and Ling of soul with Yin and Yang.

Stand on an open field, a lawn, or near trees and squat keeping the spine straight. Place your hands on your thighs, lips lightly closed and teeth touching each other and your tongue against the soft palate and behind the front teeth, eyes open. Remain quiet and relaxed.

The palms face each other; hands are at shoulder width apart. Use the concentrated Yi and Nian to feel the ball between your hands. Focus the eyes towards the center of the ball, keeping the palms facing each other. Maintain this distance between the palms, turning and circling the ball forward down and backward up, clockwise or counterclockwise, or left and right in front of body. The palms continue to face each other and hold the same distance, as the hands follow the ball's movements.

Begin with both feet on the center of (5). The left foot steps straight to (1), right foot curls to step into (2), the straight left foot steps into (3), curled right foot steps into the (4), the straight left foot steps back into the center (5), the straight right foot steps into the (6), the curled left foot steps into (7), the straight right foot steps into the (8), the curled left foot steps into the (9), the straight right foot steps into the center (5) and the left foot follows the right into the center square (5), stand with both feet on (5).

Repeat the entire series with the right foot or counterclockwise beginning the pattern.

The diagram below illustrates the Tai Ji Yin Yang circle:

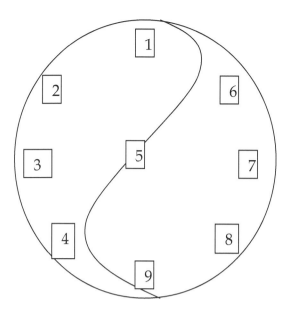

Chapter Seventeen: Tian Gang Bu Gua Bu

In this practice you will exchange Xin of information and Ling of soul with the Ba Gua of Taoism's eight trigrams and gain an understanding of the secrets of the universe.

Perform this practice whenever you need to exchange Xin of information and the Ling of soul between nature and humanity.

Standing outside in an open field, on a lawn or in a garden, with knees bent softly, straighten the spine and place your hands on your thighs, your tongue against the soft palate and behind the front teeth, keep your eyes open, remain quiet and relaxed.

Begin with both feet on the center square Zhong (5) of magic nine squares. The left foot steps straight to Qian (1) square, right foot curls to step into Dui (2) square, the straight left foot steps into Li (3) square, curled right foot steps into the Zhen (4) square, the straight left foot steps back into the center (5), followed by the right (5), both feet stand on the center square, the straight right foot steps into the Xun (6) square, the curled left foot steps into Kan (7) square, the straight right foot steps into the Gen (8) square, the curled left foot steps into the Kun (9) square, the straight right foot steps into the center (5) square and the left foot follows the right into the center square (5), stand with both feet on Zhong (5) .

The diagram below describes the pattern that the feet will follow.

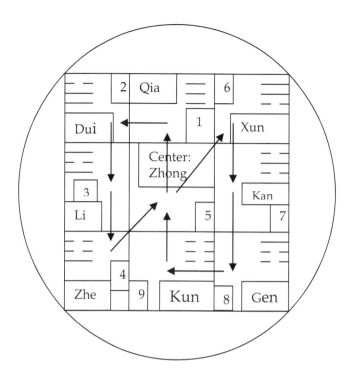

Qian: Heaven and Yang

Dui: Lake and water

Li: Fire

Zhen: Thunder

Xun: Wind

Kan: Water

Gen: Mountain

Kun: Earth and Yin

Hand movements and breathing to accompany the movements of the feet:

In the center (5) square, palms touch each other, fingers up, elbows bent and pointing down, with the first step forward, exhale and let the hands and arms move until they are straight, palms facing the sides, the concentrated Yi and Nian from the Lower Dantian expanding out through the pores to the nature, and from the Middle Dantian the Qi moves from the Duan line down to Lower Dantian. (The Duan line is the line of communication from the scalp through the pituitary gland of Upper Dantian, Middle Dantian and Lower Dantian to the perineum).

Next, leading with the other foot, inhale, returning the hands, arms and elbows and palms facing and touching each other, the Yi and Nian guide the nature Qi through the pores back to the Lower Dantian, and the Lower Dantian Qi from Duan line back to the Middle Dantian. Each step has a chant that goes with it, as shown below.

Repeat the entire series many times.

Illustration of Tian Gang Ba Gua Bu movements:

Chant: This practice is also accompanied by a chant; the words are different for each square.

In (5) square:

Yin Yang Ba Gua Fu Di Zi; Yang Yang Ba Gua Fu Wo Shen.

The meaning of this chant is:
Yin Yang eight trigram supports your disciple; Yin Yang eight trigram supports my body.

In (1) square:

Qian Yuan Heng Li Zhen.

Qian of Yang, source, fortune, wealth and essence.

In (2) square:

Dui Ze Ying Xiong Bing.

Dui of water and hero soldier.

In (3) square:

Li Huo Jia Huo Lun.

Li of fire driving a wheel of fire.

In (4) square:

Zhen Lei Pi Li Sheng.

A clap of Thunder is the sound of Pi Li.

In (5) square:

Yin Yang Ba Gua Fu Di Zi; Yin Yang Ba Gua Fu Wo Shen.

Yin Yang eight trigram support your disciple, Yin Yang eight trigram support my body.

In (6) square:

Xun Feng Jin Tui Li

Xun of wind moves smoothly back and forth.

In (7) square:

Kan Shui Duo Bo Ji.

Kan water wave is moving fast.

In (8) square:

Gen Shan Bu Chu Qi.

Gen of mountain is stable.

In (9) square:

Kun De He Wu Jiang.

Kun of Yin and earth will be steadfast.

In (5) square:

Yin Yang Ba Gua Fu Di Zi; Yang Yang Ba Gua Fu Wo Shen.

Yin Yang eight trigram support your disciple; Yin Yang eight trigram support my body.

The entire practice should be repeated.

Chapter Eighteen: Tian Gang Stars Practice

A practitioner steps into the Star-network to exchange the Xin of information and Ling of soul and for healing the body and understanding the relationship between mankind and the universe.

Perform this practice at night where one can see a panorama of the sky and in an environment that has strong Qi.

North Big Dipper connects to the Kidney.
South six stars connect to the Heart.
Middle five stars connect to the Spleen and Stomach.
West four stars connect to the Lung.
East three stars connect to the Liver.

North Purple Star controls death.
South Heaven's Palace controls life.

Diagram of Star practice:

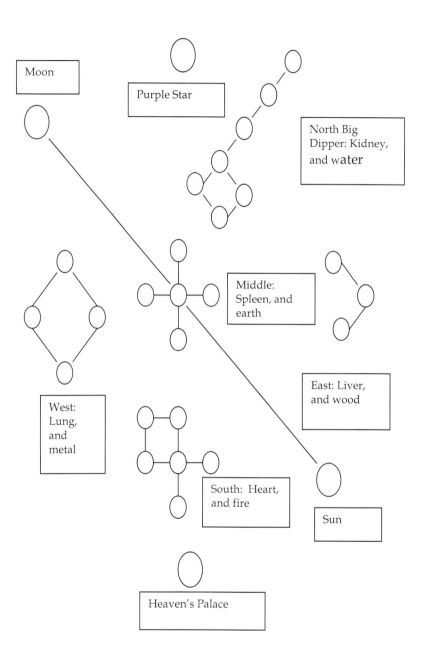

1. Tian Gang Qi Xing of Big Dipper practice

(1) Stepping pattern for the Tian Gang Qi Xing Bu:

Here the practitioner will exchange Xin of information and Ling of soul with the Big Dipper. The Big Dipper is in the north where it affects the water element in the Kidneys. The tail of the Big Dipper makes a complete circle every year; the direction that the tail points indicates the season and where the active Qi is residing.

a. Preparation:
Stand outside where you can see the Big Dipper; relax, straighten the spine, let the hands drop naturally, place the tip of the tongue against the upper soft palate and behind the front teeth. Open the eyes and look forward; bring the Shen Guang (mind and light) to between the eye brows and use the whole body's pores to take long, deep and even breaths.

Inhale; the concentrated Yi and Nian guide the universe's Qi from every direction to press into the body's pores and deposit the Qi into the Lower Dantian with the Li of strength moving with the Qi through the Duan line from the Middle Dantian to the Lower Dantian.

Exhale; let the body's internal Qi expand through the pores to the natural universe and the Lower Dantian's Qi through the Duan line move back to the Middle Dantian.

Repeat six, twelve, or twenty four times.

Moving and dissolving the five elements:

Concentrate more into the Lower Dantian and inhale, the lower abdomen moves in; exhale, the abdomen moves out; repeat several times to prepare for the exercise. During the five elements movement the entire organ system's Shen Guang expands to the boundary of the universe that is within the human body and this universe can simultaneously be as large as all of nature and as small as a dust mote.

Urinary Bladder:
Exhale; the concentrated Yi and Nian push the Qi from the Lower Dantian down to the Urinary Bladder. Exhale; the Qi in the Urinary Bladder is expanding in the human body universe. Inhale; the Urinary Bladder and Qi are contracting. Repeat several times.

Liver:
Inhale; the Qi is moving from the Urinary Bladder to the Liver. Exhale; the Qi in the Liver is expanding in the human body universe. Inhale; the Liver and Qi are contracting. Repeat several times.

Heart:
Inhale; the Qi is moving from the Liver to the Heart. Exhale; the Qi in the Heart is expanding in the human body universe. Inhale; the Heart and the Qi are contracting. Repeat several times.

Spleen and Stomach:
Exhale; the Qi from the Heart is moving down to the Spleen and Stomach. Inhale; the Qi in the Spleen and Stomach are contracting. Exhale; the Qi and Spleen and Stomach are expanding in the human body universe. Repeat several times.

Lungs:
Inhale; the Qi is moving from the Spleen and Stomach to the Lungs. Exhale; the Qi and Lungs are expanding in the human body universe. Inhale; the Qi and Lungs are contracting. Repeat several times.

Kidneys:
Exhale; the Qi is moving from the Lungs down to the Kidneys. Exhale; the Qi and Kidneys are expanding in the human body universe. Inhale; the Qi and Kidneys are contracting. Repeat several times.

Urinary Bladder:
Exhale; the Qi is moving from the Kidneys to the Urinary Bladder. Inhale; the Qi and the Urinary Bladder are contracting. Exhale; the Qi and Urinary Bladder are expanding in the human body universe. Repeat several times.

Lower Dantian:
Inhale; the Qi is moving from the Urinary Bladder to the Lower Dantian. Exhale; the Qi and the Lower Dantian are expanding in the human body universe. Inhale; the Qi and the Lower Dantian are contracting. Repeat several times.

Move the Qi in a circle through the five elements several times as described in earlier practices.

Illustration of Qi Xing Bu movement pattern:

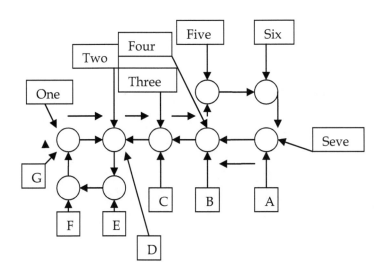

b. Body and leg movement:

Left foot slides to one, right foot slides to two, left foot slides to three, right foot glides to four, left foot moves laterally to five and the right foot follows; right foot glides to six, and turns ninety degrees and left foot glides to seven and turns one hundred eighty degrees, the right foot follows, turning ninety degrees and land to seven parallel with the left foot. The body has now turned one hundred and eighty degrees. From A, right foot slides to B, left foot slides to C, right foot slides to D, left foot move lateral slides to E and right foot fellow, right foot slides to F, and turns ninety degrees, left foot turns one hundred and eighty degrees slides to G, right foot fellows, turning ninety degrees and land to G, parallel with the left foot. The body has now turned one hundred and eighty degrees.

c. Hand movements and breathing:

Palms face each other, and fingers pointing up, elbows relaxed down, when the first foot slides forward, exhale, the hands and arms open until they are extended and palms face out to the side and chant, take a second step forward, inhale, hands and arms return to the beginning position, exhale, forward and chant. Repeat these movements over again for next and next one.

Illustration of Tian Gang Qi Xing Bu movement:

d. Mind and Qi movement:

Inhale; the concentrated Yi and Nian guide the Big Dipper and natural universe's Qi from every directions pressing into the pores of the whole body of the edge human universe, depositing into the Low Dantian and feeling of the Li of strength and the Qi through Duan line from the Middle Dantian to Lower Dantian.

Exhale; the Yi and Nian guide the internal Qi from the Lower Dantian expands through the pores to the natural universe and connecting the Big Dipper and the Lower Dantian's Qi through the Duan line to the Middle Dantian.

Repeat the circle for several times or about 45 minutes.

Chants for each step:

A. Yi Qi Kun Dun Guan Wo Xing

Original Qi nourishes my body.

B. Yu Bu Xiang Tui Deng Yang Ming

Yu steps take me into Yang Ming. (Yang Ming-Sunshine is a brighter level)

C. Tian Hui Di Zhuan Fu Liu Jia

Sky back and earth turn cover Liu Jia. (Liu-six. Jia-the first sky stems in Chinese calendar)

D. Nie Gang Fu Dou Qi Jiu Ling

Step and cover into the Big Dipper has nine souls.

E. Ya Zi Fu Yao Zhong Xie Jing

Pointed and captured evils afraid and scare.

F. Tian Shen Zhu Wo Qian Sheng Qu

Heaven's spirit assists me to become invisible.

G. Yi Qie Huo Yang Zong Bu Qin

There are no accidents.

(2) Alternate Big Dipper Step Practice:

A. Preparation:

Stand in an open area where you can see the Big Dipper. Relax, straighten the spine, let your hands drop naturally, and place your tongue against the upper soft palate and behind the front teeth, open the eyes look forward, bring the Shen Guang from the universe to between the eye brows. Open the body's pores, and regulate your breaths until they are long, deep and even.

Inhale; the concentrated Yi and Nian guide the Big Dipper and natural universe's Qi from every direction, pressing into the body's pores from the edge of the human universe, depositing the Qi into the Lower Dantian and feeling the Li of strength and the Qi through the Duan line from the Middle Dantian to the Lower Dantian.

Exhale; let the human body's internal Qi expand through the pores into the natural universe and connecting the Big Dipper and the Lower Dantian's Qi through the Duan line back to Middle Dantian.

Repeat six, twelve and twenty four times.

Moving the five elements:

Please follow the instructions for Tian Gang Qi Xing Bu.

Body, leg, hand and mind movements:

Place the hands and fingers straight and up, palms facing each other in front of the Middle Dantian; each thumb touching the tip of the little finger, while the other fingers are straight. Hold this position during the Big Dipper practice.

Illustration of Big Dipper's hand form:

All the steps are as same as described in Tian Gang Qi Xing Bu.

a. Step one:

Exhale; left foot steps to number one, both hands face and both hands and arms open until they are extended and palms face out to the side open, the tongue relaxed, the concentrated Yi and Nian guiding the Lower Dantian internal Qi expands through pores into natural universe, connecting the Big Dipper and the Lower Dantian's Qi through the Duan line to the Middle Dantian.

Inhale; the right foot steps on number one, hands close up and palms facing each other, the tip of the tongue on the palate behind the front teeth, the Yi and Nian guide the Big Dipper and natural universal Qi from every direction being pressed into the pores of the whole body edge of the human universe, depositing the Qi into the Lower Dantian and feeling the strength of Li and the Middle Datian Qi through the Duan line back to Lower Datian.

Holding the breath, lift the right foot straight up and step it down hard on the ground while then mind chanting: Shui Jing Zi Yi Tong Ren Gui Shui, Er Bu Wen Er Jing Gui Shen. (The water spirit is controlling Ren Gui of Kidney water); the ears do not listen while the Jing (essence) returns to the Kidneys).

b. Step two:

Exhale; the left foot steps to number two, both hands face and both hands and arms open until they are extended and palms face out to the side open, the tongue down on the mouth, the Lower Dantian internal Qi expands through pores into natural universe, connecting the Big Dipper and the Lower Dantian Qi from through the Duan line to the Middle Dantian.

Inhale; the right foot fellow steps into number two, hands close up and palm face each other, the tip of tongue place on the upper palate behind the front teeth, the Yi and Nian guide the Big Dipper and natural universal Qi from every direction pressing into whole body pores of the edge human universe, depositing into the Low Dantian and feeling the strength of Li and the Middle Dantian Qi through the Duan line back to the Lower Dantian.

Holding the breath, lift the left foot up and stomp on the ground while silently chanting: Shui Jing Zi Yi Tong Ren Gui Shui, Er Bu Wen Er Jing Gui Shen.

Step into three, repeat the same motion, and continue this pattern until reaching number seven and going from A to G.

Repeat the circle again.

(3) Seated practice:

A. Preparation:

Seven practitioners sit in the same pattern as the Big Dipper in the sky, to represent the Big Dipper. The leader sits on two or B. Everyone crosses their legs, relaxes, and straightens the spine, place hands palms up resting on the knees, thumbs touching the tips of the little fingers. The tips of the practitioner's tongues are against the upper soft palate, touching the front teeth, eyes open and looking forward, all bring the Shen Guang to between their eyebrows and use the pores to regulate their breathing until it becomes long, deep and even.

Inhale; the concentrated Yi and Nian guide the Big Dipper and natural universal Qi from every direction pressing into the pores of the whole body of the edge human universe, depositing into the Lower Dantian and feeling the strength of Li and the Qi from the Middle Dantian through the Duan line to the Lower Dantian.

Inhale and silently chant: Er Bu Wen Er Jing Gui Shen. (The ears do not listen while the Dig Dipper's Jing (essence) returns to the Kidneys).

Exhale; the Yi and Nian guide the internal Qi from the Lower Dantian to expand through the pores to the natural universe and connecting the Big Dipper and the Qi from the Lower Dantian through the Duan line to the Middle Dantian.

Exhale and silently chant: Shui Jing Zi Yi Tong Ren Gui Shui. (The Dig Dipper's water spirit is controlling Ren Gui of Kidney water).

Repeat the exercise.

Moving and dissolving the five elements:

And during the five elements movement the entire organ's Qi expands to boundary of the human body universe simultaneously can be as big as nature and as small as a dust mote.

From the Kidneys to the Urinary Bladder, Urinary Bladder to Liver, Liver to the Heart, Heart to Stomach and Spleen, Stomach and Spleen to the Lungs, Lungs to the Kidneys, and Kidneys to the Urinary Bladder. Repeat this circle several times, returning the Qi back to the Lower Dantian upon completion of the exercise.

2. Tian Gang Six Stars practice

Diagram of the Six Stars stepping practice:

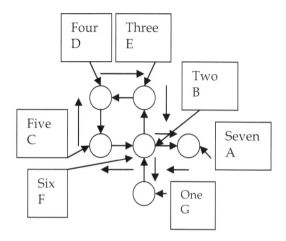

(1) Body, hand, leg and mind movement:

Stand in an open field, relax, straighten the spine, and let the hands drop naturally, tip of tongue on the upper soft palate, gently touching behind the front teeth, eyes open and looking forward. Bring the Shen Guang to between the eyebrows and open the body's pores, and regulate your breaths until they are long, deep and even.

Inhale; the concentrated Yi and Nian guide the Six Stars and natural universal Qi from every direction pressing into the pores from the edge of the human body's universe, depositing Qi into the Lower Dantian and feeling the Li of strength and the Qi through the Duan line from the Middle Dantian to the Lower Dantian.

Exhale; let the human body's internal Qi expand through the pores into the natural universe and connecting the Six Stars and the Qi from the Lower Dantian Qi return along the Duan line back to the Middle Dantian.

Repeat six, twelve, or twenty four times.

The thumb and middle finger touch lightly together at the tips; hold this position during the entire Six Stars practice. Hands are held lightly up; palms are facing each other in front of the Middle Dantian.

Illustration of Six Stars's hand form:

To begin, both feet are together on number one.

Exhale; the left or right foot steps into number two; both arms sweeping out to the sides and remaining parallel to the ground to form a "T" shape; the tongue lying flat in the mouth; the human body's internal Qi expands through the pores into the natural universe, connecting the Six Stars and the Lower Dantian's Qi from the Duan line to the Middle Dantian.

Inhale; the right or left foot steps to number three, hands move back in front of the body, close to each other, palms facing, the tongue placed on the upper palate behind the front teeth, the Yi and Nian guiding the Six Stars and universal Qi from every direction, and passing through the edge of the human universe into the pores of the whole body, depositing Qi into the Lower Dantian as the practitioner is feeling the strength of Li along the Duan line from the Middle Dantian to the Lower Dantian.

Hold the breath, lift the right or left foot up and bring it down hard on the ground with mind chanting: Chi Jing Zi Yi Tong Bing Ding Huo, She Bu Dong Er Shen Gui Xin. (The red fire spirit is mastering Bing Ding of sky stem fire, tongue does not move when the Shen of spirit returns to the Heart).

Continuing the same pattern as you progress to four, five, six and seven, and on number seven and on A the body turns 180 degrees, and steps in the other direction to B, C, D, E, F and G.

Repeat the circle exercise.

Moving and dissolving the five elements:

From the Heart to Stomach and Spleen, Stomach and Spleen to Lungs, Lungs to Kidneys, Kidneys to Urinary Bladder, and Urinary Bladder to Liver again to the Heart; repeat this circle several times, returning the Qi back to the Lower Dantian upon completion of the exercise.

Please refer to the Big Dipper seated five elements ritual for details.

(2) Seated practice:

Six practitioners sit in the same relationship to each other as the Six Stars; the leader sits on number two and B, or F position. Everyone cross your legs, relax, straighten the spine, place

Tian Gang Six Stars seated practice. hands face up on knees, thumbs touching the tips of the middle fingers, tongue placed against the soft palate with the tip touching the front teeth, eyes open and looking forward, each practitioner brings the Shen Guang to between the eyebrows and opens the body's pores, and regulates the breaths until they are long, deep and even.

Inhale; the Yi and Nian guide the Six Starts and universal Qi from every direction pressing into the pores from the edge of the body's universe, depositing into the Lower Dantian the strength of Li and the Qi from the Middle Dantian through the Duan line to the Lower Dantian.

During the inhale silently chant: She Bu Dong Er Shen Gui Xin. (Tongue does not move when the Shen of spirit returns to the Heart).

Exhale; the Yi and Nian guide the internal Qi from the Lower Dantian expanding through the pores to the natural universe and connecting the Six Stars and the internal Qi from the Lower Dantian along the Duan line to the Middle Dantian.

During the exhale silently chant: Chi Jing Yi Tong Bing Ding Huo. (The red fire spirit is mastering Bing Ding of sky stem fire).

Repeat the exercise.

Moving and dissolving the five elements:

From the Heart to Stomach and Spleen, Stomach and Spleen to Lungs, Lungs to Kidneys, Kidneys to Urination Bladder, and Urinary Bladder to Liver again to the Heart; repeat this circle several times, returning the Qi back to the Lower Dantian upon completion of the exercise.

Please refer to the Big Dipper seated five elements ritual for details.

3. Tian Gang Five Stars practice

Diagram of the Five Stars stepping practice:

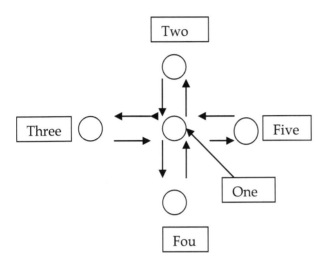

(1) Body, hand, leg and mind movement:

Standing in an open area, relax, straighten the spine, let the hands drop naturally to your sides, tongue placed against the upper soft palate and behind the front teeth, eyes looking forward, bring the Shen Guang to between the eyebrows and open the pores of the whole body, breathing naturally until the breathing becomes long, deep and even.

Place the fingers folded over the thumb, which is lying across the palm of each hand, and hold this position during the Five Stars practice.

Illustration of Five Stars's hand form:

Stand on number one; inhale; begin with hands up, palms with folded fingers facing each other in front of the Middle Dantian, the tongue placed on the upper palate behind the front teeth, the concentrated Yi and Nian guide the universal Qi and the Qi from Five Stars from every direction pressing into the pores of the body, depositing Qi into the Lower Dantian and moving the Qi and the strength of Li along the Duan line from the Middle Dantian to Lower Dantian.

Exhale; the left or right foot steps to number two, both hands, with palms curled, facing the sides of the body with arms spread open to shoulder width, the tongue lying flat in the mouth, let the body's internal Qi expand through the pores into the natural universe, connecting the Five Stars and the Lower Dantian's Qi through the Duan line to the Middle Dantian.

Holding the breath, lift the right or left foot up and bring it down hard on the ground while mentally chanting: Huang Lao Yi Tong Wu Ji Tu, Xi Shi Bu Dong Yi Gui Pi. (The yellow elder is mastering Wu Ji of sky stem earth; arms and legs are still when Yi of intention returns to Spleen)

Inhale; the right or left foot steps back onto number one, hands move back close to each other, palms with fingers folded as above facing each other, the tongue placed on the upper palate behind the front teeth, the Yi and Nian guide the Five Stars and universal Qi from every direction pressing into the pores of the body, depositing Qi into the Lower Dantian and moving the Qi and the strength of Li along the Duan line from the Middle Dantian to Lower Dantian.

Turn the body ninety degrees to the left or right.

Exhale; the left or right foot steps to number three, both hands facing the sides of the body with arms spread open to shoulder width, the tongue lying flat in the mouth, let the body's internal Qi expand through the pores into the natural universe, connecting the Five Stars and the Lower Dantian's Qi through the Duan line to the Middle Dantian.

Holding the breath, lift the right or left foot up and bring it down hard on the ground while mentally chanting: Huang Lao Yi Tong Wu Ji Tu, Xi Shi Bu Dong Yi Gui Pi. (The yellow elder is mastering Wu Ji of sky stem earth, arms and legs are still when Yi of the intention returns to Spleen)

Inhale; the right or left foot steps back onto number one, hands move back close to each other, palms facing each other, the tongue placed on the upper palate behind the front teeth, the Yi and Nian guide the Five Stars and natural universal Qi from every direction, pressing into the pores of the body from the edge of the human universe, depositing Qi into the Lower Dantian and feeling the strength of Li and the Qi along the Duan line from the Middle Dantian to the Lower Dantian.

Holding the breath, lift the right or left foot up and bring it down hard on the ground while mentally chanting: Huang Lao Yi Tong Wu Ji Tu, Xi Shi Bu Dong Yi Gui Pi. (The yellow elder is mastering Wu Ji of sky stem earth, arms and legs are still when Yi of the intention returns to Spleen)

Turn the body ninety degrees to the left or right.

The right or left foot steps onto number four, back to number one and turn the body another ninety degrees and step to number five and back to number one.

Repeat the exercise.

Moving and dissolving the five elements:

From the Stomach and Spleen to Lungs, Lungs to Kidneys, Kidneys to Urinary Bladder, Urinary Bladder to Liver, Liver to Heart, and Heart to Stomach and Spleen; repeat this circle several times, returning the Qi back to the Lower Dantian upon completion of the exercise.

Please refer to the Big Dipper seated five elements ritual for details.

(2) Seated practice:

Five practitioners sit cross legged, representing the Five Stars. The leader sits on the number one spot; hands are face up resting lightly on the knees and fingers are covering the curled thumbs.

Inhale; the Yi and Nian guide the Five Stars and universal Qi from every direction pressing into the pores of the body, depositing Qi into the Lower Dantian and moving the Qi and the strength of Li along the Duan line from the Middle Dantian to the Lower Dantian.

Exhale; let the human body's internal Qi expand through the pores into the natural universe, and connect the Five Stars and the Qi along the Duan line from the Lower Dantian to the Middle Dantian.

Inhale and mentally chant: Xi Shi Bu Dong Yi Gui Pi. (Arms and legs are still when Yi of the intention returns to Spleen).

Exhale and mentally chant: Huang Lao Yi Tong Wu Ji Tu. (The yellow elder is mastering Wu Ji of sky stem earth).

Repeat the exercise.

Moving and dissolving the five elements:

From the Stomach and Spleen to Lungs, Lungs to Kidneys, Kidneys to Urinary Bladder, Urinary Bladder to Liver, Liver to Heart, and Heart to Stomach and Spleen; repeat this circle several times, returning the Qi back to the Lower Dantian upon completion of the exercise.

Please refer to the Big Dipper seated five elements ritual for details.

4. Tian Gang Four Stars practice

Diagram of Four Stars stepping practice:

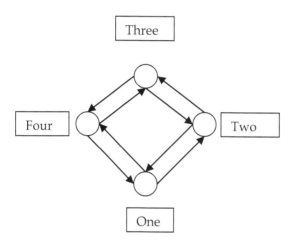

(1) Body, hand, leg and mind movement:

Standing in an open area, relax, straighten the spine, let the hands drop naturally to your sides, the tongue placed against the upper soft palate and behind the front teeth, eyes looking forward, bring the Shen Guang to between the eyebrows and open the pores of the whole body, breathe naturally until the breathing becomes long, deep and even.

Place the tip of the thumb against the tip of the ring finger and hold this position during the Four Stars practice.

Illustration of Four Stars's hand form:

Begin with hands and fingers up and palms facing other in front of the Middle Dantian.

Exhale, the left or right foot steps to number one. The hands are facing the sides of the body with arms spread open to shoulder width, the tongue lying flat in the mouth. Let the body's internal Qi expand through the pores into the universe, connecting the Four Stars and the Lower Dantian Qi through the Duan line to the Middle Dantian.

Holding the breath, lift the right or left foot up and bring it down hard on the ground while mentally chanting: Jin Mu Yi Tong Geng Xin Jin, Bi Bu Xiang Er Po Gui Fei. (Gold mother is mastering Geng Xin of sky stem metal, nose is not making your aware of smells and the Lung spirit's Po returns to the Lungs.)

Inhale; the right or left foot steps to number two, hands move back close to each other, palms facing each other, the tongue placed on the upper palate behind the front teeth, the concentrated Yi and Nian guide the Four Stars and natural universal Qi from every direction, pressing into the pores of the body from the edge of the human universe, depositing Qi into the Lower Dantian and feeling the strength of Li and the Middle Dantian Qi through the Duan line to the

Lower Dantian.

Holding the breath, lift the right or left foot up and bring it down hard on the ground while mentally chanting: Jin Mu Yi Tong Geng Xin Jin, Bi Bu Xiang Er Po Gui Fei. (Gold mother is mastering Geng Xin sky stem of metal; nose is not making you aware of smells, Lung spirit's Po return to the Lungs.)

Exhale; the left or right foot steps to number three, both hands facing the sides of the body with arms spread open to shoulder width, the tongue lying flat in the mouth, let the body's internal Qi expand through the pores into the universe, connecting the Four Stars and the Lower Dantian Qi through the Duan line to the Middle Dantian.

Step onto four and repeat the exercise. You may choose to start from four and go to three, two and one.

Moving and dissolving the five elements:

From the Lungs to Kidneys, Kidneys to Urinary Bladder, Urinary Bladder to Liver, Liver to Heart, Heart to Stomach and Spleen, Stomach and Spleen to Lungs again; repeat this circle several times, returning the Qi back to the Lower Dantian upon completion of the exercise.

Please refer to the Big Dipper seated five elements ritual for details.

(2) Seated practice:

Four practitioners sit cross legged, representing the Four Stars. Hands are face up on the knees and the thumb is touching the ring finger.

Inhale; the Yi and Nian guide the Four Stars and universal Qi from every direction, pressing into the pores of the whole body, depositing Qi into the Lower Dantian and feeling the strength of Li and the Middle Dantian Qi through the Duan line to the Lower Dantian.

Exhale; let the human body's internal Qi expand through the pores into the universe, and connect the Four Stars and the Qi from the Lower Dantian through the Duan line and back to the Middle Dantian.

Inhale and mentally chant: Bi Bu Xiang Er Po Gui Fei. (Nose does not scent; Lung spirit's Po returns to Lungs).

Exhale and mentally chant: Jin Mu Yi Tong Geng Xin Jin. (Gold Mother is mastering Geng Xin sky stem of metal).

Repeat the exercise.

Moving and dissolving the five elements:

From the Lungs to Kidneys, Kidneys to Urinary Bladder, Urinary Bladder to Liver, Liver to Heart, Heart to Stomach and Spleen, Stomach and Spleen to Lungs again; repeat this circle several times, returning the Qi back to the Lower Dantian upon completion of the exercise.

5. Tian Gang Three Stars practice

Diagram of Three Stars stepping practice:

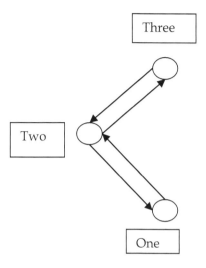

(1) Body, hand, leg and mind movement:

Standing in an open area, relax, straighten the spine, let the hands drop naturally to your sides, tongue placed against the upper soft palate and behind the front teeth, eyes looking forward, bring the Shen Guang to between the eyebrows and open the pores of the whole body, breathe naturally until the breathing becomes long, deep and even.

Place the tip of the thumb against the tip of the index finger and hold this position during the Three Stars practice.

Illustration of Three Stars's hand form:

Begin with hands and fingers up and palms facing other in front of the Middle Dantian.

Exhale, the left or right foot steps to number one. The hands are facing the sides of the body with arms spread open to shoulder width, the tongue lying flat in the mouth. Let the body's internal Qi expand through the pores into the natural universe, connecting the Three Stars and the Lower Dantian Qi through the Duan line to the Middle Dantian.

Holding the breath, lift the right or left foot up and bring it down hard on the ground while mentally chanting: Mu Gong Yi Tong Jia Yi Mu, Yan Bu Lou Er Hun Gui Gan. (The Wood Wizard is mastering Jia Yi of sky stem wood; eyes are not seeing, the Liver spirit's Hun returns to the Liver.)

Inhale; the right or left foot steps to number two, hands move back close to each other, palms facing each other, the tongue placed on the upper palate behind the front teeth, the Yi and Nian guide the Three Starts and natural universal Qi from every direction, pressing into the pores of the body, depositing Qi into the Lower Dantian and feeling the strength of Li and the Middle Dantian Qi through the Duan line to the Lower Dantian.

Exhale, the left or right foot steps to number three. The hands are facing the sides of the body with arms spread open to shoulder width, the tongue lying flat in the mouth. Let the body's internal Qi expand through the pores into the natural universe, connecting the Three Stars and the Lower Dantian Qi through the Duan line to the Middle Dantian.

Holding the breath, lift the right or left foot up and bring it down hard on the ground while mentally chanting: Mu Gong Yi Tong Jia Yi Mu, Yan Bu Lou Er Hun Gui Gan. (The wood wizard is mastering Jia Yi of sky stem wood; eyes are not seeing, the Liver spirit's Hun returns to the Liver.)

Turn the body one hundred and eighty degrees and repeat the exercise.

Moving and dissolving the Five Elements:

From the Liver to Heart, Heart to Stomach and Spleen, Stomach and Spleen to Lungs, Lungs to Kidneys, Kidneys to Urinary Bladder, and Urinary Bladder to Liver again; repeat this circle several times, returning the Qi back to the Lower Dantian upon completion of the exercise.

(2) Seated Practice:

Three practitioners sit cross legged on the three positions representing the Three Stars and the leader sits on the number two spot, hands face up and thumbs touching the tips of the ring fingers; other fingers are straight. The leader sits on the number two position.

Inhale; the Yi and Nian guide the Three Stars and universal Qi from every direction, pressing into the pores of the edge of the human body's universe, depositing Qi into the Lower Dantian and feeling the strength of Li and the Middle Dantian Qi through the Duan line to the Lower Dantian.

Exhale; let the human body's internal Qi expand through the pores into the universe, and the Lower Dantian's Qi moving along the Duan line to the Middle Dantian. Feel the connection to the Three Stars.

Inhale and mentally chant: Yan Bu Lou Er Hun Gui Gan. (Eyes are not seeing; Liver spirit's Hun returns to the Liver).

Exhale and mentally chant: Mu Gong Yi Tong Jia Yi Mu. (The wood wizard is mastering Jia Yi stem of wood).

Repeat the exercise.

Moving and dissolving the five elements:

From the Liver to Heart, Heart to Stomach and Spleen, Stomach and Spleen to Lungs, Lungs to Kidneys, Kidneys to Urinary Bladder, and Urinary Bladder to Liver again; repeat this circle several times, returning the Qi back to the Lower Dantian upon completion of the exercise.

Chapter Nineteen: Appendix

1. Three different kinds of Qi:

a. The first is primordial Qi; every one needs to have this Qi for life.

b. The second is the body's internal Qi, which is combined with primordial Qi to sustain life and enable healing.

c. The third is magical Qi; the capacity of the human body's internal Qi to radiate out and combine with primordial Qi for healing and connection.

2. Jin Dan:

Jin Dan is the golden pill that is created inside the body; an internal medicine and power factory that heals and controls life and death.

3. Yi and Nian:

Yi is intention in the universe with movement and direction.

Nian is thought in the universe without direction or movement.

4. Abdominal breathing technique:

San Xian Gong and all the methods breathing is inhaling with the lower abdomen moving in and the Lower Dantian contracting; when exhaling the lower abdomen moves out and the Lower Dantian expands. During the inhale and the exhale, the emphasis of the abdominal movement is below the navel. The breathing speed is long, slow, even and natural or depends on each section of practice. The inhale is longer than the exhale in the morning. The exhale is longer than the inhale in the afternoon.

5. Sealing three Yins:

Concentrating, breathing, contracting and relaxing the genitals, perineum and anus with a series of movements until the area is sealed and is stable.

6. Set up the furnace and Ding (three legged tripod pot for cooking the Dan of golden pill):

The furnace for the Ding is located below the navel. When there is warm sensation below the navel, exercise the Duan line through the Middle and Lower Dantian to set up the furnace alignment. The Ding is the body and the Ding's cover is the head. Use breathing through the pores to stabilize the skin of the Ding's body

7. Sealing the furnace:

Sealing the furnace is obtained by exercising the Duan line of the Middle and Lower Dantian communication, and breathing through the pores to seal the skin.

8. Human and true breathing:

Basic human breathing is through the nose; true breathing is the Middle and Lower Dantian communication and skin breathing. This section's practice involves nose breathing and Duan line of Middle and Lower Dantian breathing and breathing through the pores at the same time.

9. Three Dantian locations:

Dantian indicates where is the field can make Jin Dan of golden pill. Upper Dantian: The Upper Dantian is from between eyebrows three fingers length into the brain. Middle Dantian: The Middle Dantian is the space between the sixth and seventh ribs from the sternum, three fingers length into the chest. Lower Dantian: The Lower Dantian is about one third below the navel and three fingers into lower abdomen.

10. Kan and Li bonded:

Kan indicates water, Li indicates fire. In this practice through the concentrated Yi and Nian and breathing, the natural sun of Li fire and ocean of Kan water; the human body Heart of Li fire and Kidney of Kan water bond and unite as emptiness within or out.

11. Three types of vision:

There are three types of vision: The first is the normal vision that we all share. The second is a practitioner opens his eyes and looks into the distance, as far as he can, using the vision in his right eye. The third is the practitioner closes his eyes and looks as far as is possible for him, using his Shen Gang (mind and light).

12. The Three Centers:

(1) The three Dantian make up one of the three centers in the body which are used for exchanging Qi, Shen and Jing (essence).

(2) The Kidneys and the Heart and the organs in between them make up another center which is used during the interaction of water and fire.

(3) The Heart and pericardium and the universe of the inner body make up the third center which is used in communication between the Heart, pericardium and body.

Illustrations of the Three Centers:

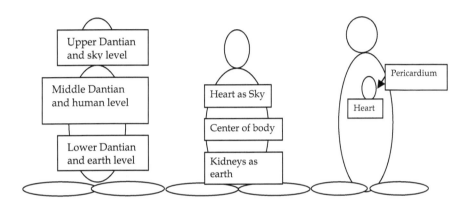

13. Three Cavities:

The Upper Dantian has the cavity of the power of spirit and universe, the Middle Dantian has the capacity for reincarnation and the Lower Dantian carries the power of the self which is used for exchanges between Shen, reincarnation, Qi and the self.

Illustration of three cavities:

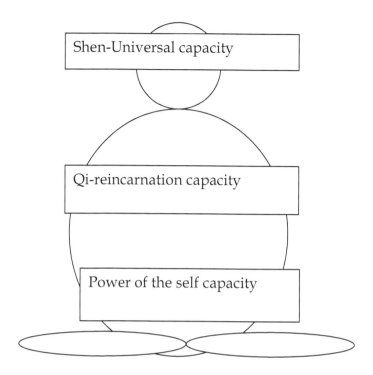

14. Three stages of practice:

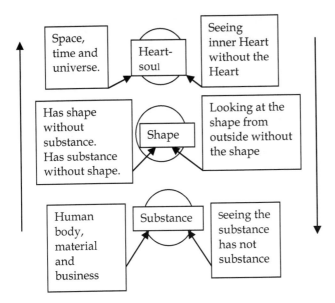

The practitioner moves from the human level to earth level and finally steps into the level of Heaven. The illustration is meant to be seen from the left bottom up from human level to the sky level and at the right from sky to human.

At the first (human) level, one takes care of the body and its basic needs and mortal business. At the second (earth) level, we have dreams which have shape without substance. This is shape without substance. We experience Qi moving in the body; this is substance without shape.

The third Heaven level represents all the Yin (substance) refined to the Yang and Yang of Ling (soul) and Qi matched universe and time and space along which one can travel into different times, space and unite the universe.

15. The pathway travels into the past and beyond:

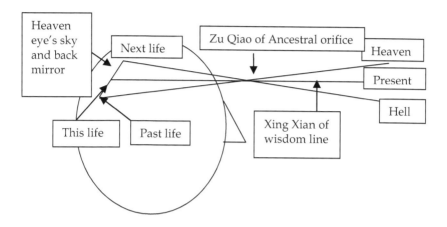

You can control the present and ascend to Heaven, or descend to hell. This processing may be affected by your past life; what you do in the present may affect your next life. The most important process is control of the self. This process is a pathway through to the immortal level.

When a practitioner reaches this level he will need guidance from Master Wang.

There is poem:

No mind, no substance and without shape; one will meet your previous life's owner.

There is one substance left from that life; the dense red sand dust on the platform of the soul.

16. Illustration of the inner lines and pathways of the body:

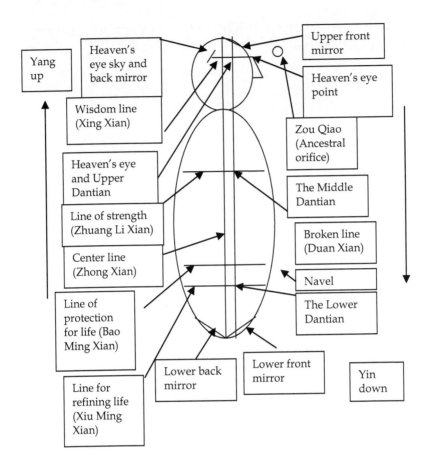

17. Nei Jing Tu illustration of Xiao Chow Tian (microcosmic orbit) inner image explains by Master Wang Liping.

Nei Jing Tu explains the three gates of Xiao Zhou Tian, the route of the microcosmic orbit circulation. The three gates are the Sacrum Gate, the Thoracic Gate, and the Occipital Gate.

The gate of the sacrum is at the end of the spine. There are and seven vertebras and seven points. Practicing refines the seven point's pathway, the internal pathway through the inner

Kidneys, the male to the testis and the female to the ovaries, continuing via the spinal cord pathway called He Che flows in the Cao Xi (narrow creek) to yellow river, up to the Ni Wan (Upper Dantian in the brain).

The thoracic gate or Jia Ji is located around the thoracic spine in the region between 5 and 7.

The occipital gate or Yu Zhen is on the occipital region.

Practicing Zhi Neng Gong (intelligence training,) or San Xian Gong and the Xiu Ming Xian line of refining life, the Zhuang Li Xian line of strength, and the Xing Xian line of the wisdom line will make it easier to make the Xiao Zhou Tian flow.

If the flow of the Qi to the thoracic gate or to the lumbar region is suddenly stopped, the practitioner needs to correct his breathing, making the inhale longer or shorter and the exhale stronger in combination with movements below the navel. This is the blowing wind method, and the wind is called Xun ( ) wind. After the Qi flows to the Ni Wan (Upper Dantian), it flows down in the front of the Ren channel (the center line of the front of the body) transform the Jade fluid to gold fluid to complete the return to the Dan (golden pill).

The three Dantian reside at the front of the body. The Upper Dantian is called Ni Wan, or Hua Chi and the first Hua Chi and upper Hua Chi, it measures one Cun (length measure) long and two Fen (length measure) around, and in it is the emptiness orifice where the Shen stays. From between the eyebrows one Cun away is Ming Tang, and Dong Fang is two Cun away, and Ni Wan is three Cun away.

Please see the diagram below:

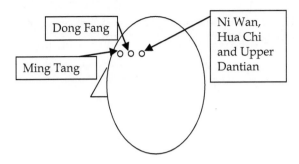

There is an elderly person keeping the gate at the Dong Fang. One needs to pass through him. One is refining into two Cun, there is a crown tightening around his head. This crown is called Luo Tai, and if one can not handle it and gives up, this function of power will be lost, to release the tightness is to find the point of harmony, one needs to keep his eyes closed and maintain a balance between the occipital and the point of Heaven's eye.

There are two hidden points, Jin Qiao and Shang Que Qiao, on the upper mouth and connecting to the nose, where there is a person with both hands supporting the location of Nei JingTu, where the hidden points are located. It may be necessary to seal the Shang Que Qiao by tightly clamping the nostrils shut.

There are two points under the tongue called Jin Jin and Yu Ye which need to be opened, and after they are opened and connected to the throat, which has twelve layers of throat and is called Zhong Lou, the pathway of air and food.

From the trachea to the Lungs, there are many hidden points called Jin; fluid and air come from these places.

The Heart of chest and upper abdomen center region has one orifice that is pictured as one small person. The small person has his own hidden orifice called Jiang Gong where the Metal grandpa and Yellow grandma meet and the dragon and tiger interact. Three Cun long and six Fen straight down is the Tu Fu Huang Ding palace of Middle Dantian that is one Cun long and two Fen around and where Qi is stored, where the Dan is refined in a Ding (the three legged pot that represents the cooking and processing of internal medicine and awakened awareness), and from this palace to the navel is a distance of three Cun and six Fen. The sky has three Cun and six Fen and the earth has three Cun and six Fen. From sky to earth distance is eighty four thousand Li (length measure), and from the Heart to the Kidneys is a distance of eighty four thousand Li.

The Life Gate is located behind the inner navel, where there are seven orifices which connect to the external Kidney of the testis and female of ovaries and the testis has both Jing (essence) and Qi pathways. A female does not have an external Kidney but there is one orifice for a pathway to the ovaries. The male practitioner has to contract the external Kidney and female needs to contract below the navel.

Behind the navel and in front of the Kidneys are the Qi Hai point, measuring one Cun and two Fen around, and there is Hua Chi inside it and the Lower Dantian, described by the ancients. This is a place where there is hidden Jing (essence), and where one can collect internal medicine. There is a furnace and it is upside down. A Ding is above it. This familiar process is for the mortal; reversing the process is necessary to become an immortal. There are two more orifices below, one connects to the inner Kidneys and another one connects to the sacrum, where there is a Xuan Guan (entering the emptiness, one finds substance); this is the region for creating substance from nothing. Xuan Guan has to be refined by fire, without fire it cannot open. Therefore, after abundant Qi and Jing create powerful Qi, Xuan Guan will be automatically opened and it will be the right time to refine the Jin Dan (golden pill) three points.

In this moment, one needs to pay attention to the Qi flow and the transformation of Xia Que Qiao, which is located in the sacrum region. Xia Que Qiao's lower orifice is the whole lower abdomen and is called Kan (☵) Palace and includes the inner Kidneys and the external Kidneys of the testis for a male and for the female, the ovaries which are outer Yin embracing Yang. This Kan (☵) Palace hides Yuan (source) Qi, is life, lead and tiger and is the absorption point and the Kan (☵) furnace is behind the navel and in front of the sacrum. Xia Que Qiao connects to the lower portion of the large intestine and the anus; it passes stool and gas. Between the genital region and anus bridge is Hui Yin. If one can seal the genital region, the perineum, and the anus to prevent leaking, one will attain longevity.

There are six roots which must be sealed to stop any leaking: One is called Sealing the Life and Death root and is done by sealing the genitals, the perineum and the anus, and is also called body root not leaking. Two is clamping the nose to seal the Shang Que Qiao and called nose root not leaking. Three is the ears not listening to external sounds; this is the ear root not leaking. Fourth, teeth lightly touching and lips pressed against each other with the tip of the tongue on the upper part of the mouth; this is the tongue root not leaking. Five, seal the eyes by closing them and returning the light back to the inner body and all will become still, this is eye's root not leaking. Six, the mind does not create any useless thoughts, and is concentrating on lust not occurring, and the dust which is the sex emotion not attaching itself to the practitioner, this is the thought root not leaking and is the most difficult root with which to succeed.

After the six roots have been sealed, one can collect the inner medicine and refine the Jin Dan. Six roots that are not leaking will create the six root vibration naturally. If one has shaking that belongs to the six root vibrations, one may begin to experience the thirty six kinds of vibration, thirty six true (Zhen) persons, three chapters and eight views. As "Ling Bao Jing" said, "Shen controls the Qi's pathway movement, Qi nourishes the Shen, and fullness of Qi will create abundant Shen." Abundance maneuvers the true Qi (Zhen) into the great stillness, and they combine as one to form the Jin Dan great medicine. If one has one vibration below the navel and genital region, and a warm feeling in the lower abdomen, the warm to hot sensation spreads to the whole body, and there will be more vibrations. This is the moment for sealing the lower three orifices and connecting to Xia Que Qiao, after which the body may cool down. As soon as it becomes cool, focus on the two orifices under the tongue, Jin Jin and Yu Ye, at once. The second vibration is when the Kidneys become warm and then hot, with heat concentrated below the navel. The third vibration, both eyes shine and tear. With the fourth, behind the ears, there is wind blowing and at the practitioner must at once pay attention to the ovaries and let the Ci (female) dragon return to the Yin palace. A male will feel the external Kidney, the penis, return inside the abdomen, and this is the time to start to refine the Jin Dan. There is sound and vibration in the brain with the fifth vibration, and the body shakes until one can not handle the shaking anymore. It is necessary to immediately move the five elements of Mao You Zhou Tian and to move the Qi from the Middle Dantian to the Lower Dantian. The sixth vibration follows, and the nose leaks out watery fluid; let it fully drain out and use a clamp to close the nostrils and focus on the Shang Que Qiao, the two points of Jin Qiao in the nose."

Da Zhou Tian is the flow of Qi from the Lung channel to the Large Intestine channel to the Stomach channel to the Spleen channel to the Heart channel to the Small Intestine channel to the Urination Bladder channel to the Kidney channel, then to the Pericardium channel, San Jiao channel, Gall Bladder, to the Liver and back to the Lungs. After this Qi circling stops, the

Ren and Du channel will be opened and Xiao Zhu Tian, the microcosmic orbit circulation, will be opened also and heat will circulate in the body.

Nei Jing Tu illustration: Xiao Chow Tian (microcosmic orbit) inner image.

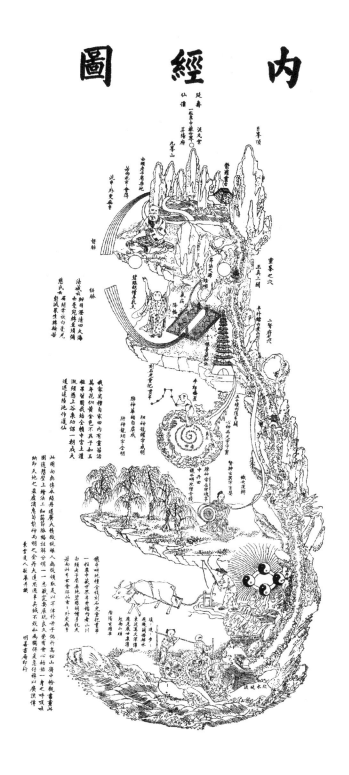

18. Xiu Zhen Tu illustration: Stages of evolving to the innate self.

This classic illustration explains breathing through the body's pores, the relationship of the five organs of elements, functions, characters, and symbolized by the appropriate animals, and location of inner fire and water.

The Chinese calendar is combination of lunar and solar timing. There are twenty four small seasonal sections of fifteen days each in the four season year; which the Qi location of each small season can be seen in the each vertebrae. The illustration also describes the moon circulating in synch with our bodies and shows the location of the Shen Guang (mind and light) and the place from which the immortal body will rise.

Xiu Zhen Tu illustration:

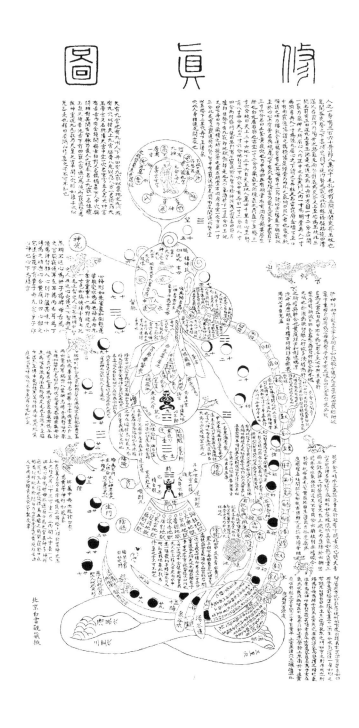

Taoism Texts

There are three Taoist texts; the first one is Zhong Lu Chuan Dao Ji, describing the basic Taoism theory of Mother Nature and human relation for refining the Jin Dan (golden pill). Tai Yi Jin Hua Zhong Zhi is describing the light and true self relation to processing the Jin Dan. Wu Pian Ling Wen is describing the light with inner of stages of processing the Jin Dan.

Zhong Lu Chuan Dao Ji (Zhong and Lu deliver Tao series)

Author: Zheng Yang Zhen Ren of center Yang true person (True person is at the level of Heaven immortal): Zhong, Liquan. Lecture.
Chun Yang Zhen Ren of pure Yang true person: Lu, Dongbin. Gathering.
Hua Yang Zhen Ren of Bright Yang true person: Shi, Jianwu. Delivery.

Chapter One: Discussion of Zhen Xian (True Immortal Level)

1. Lu asks:
After being born, what pathway can we take to be healthy without ever becoming sick, strong without ever becoming old, to live and never die?

Zhong answers:
Human birth results from the combination of father and mother's Qi (energy). The Jing (essence) and blood bond as fetus and placenta. Taichu (vital original stage) form bonds with Taizhi (vital original substance). Yin (substance) nourishes the Yang (energy), the Yang is created. Qi transforms in the fetus three hundred days after the fetus

214

forms a perfect circle. Then Ling light (soul light) enters the fetus and the fetus separates from the mother. After Taisu (Yin and Yang divided stage) has started, ascent and descent motion grows, the yellow sprout grows. After five thousand days growth, the Qi is full.

The body is fully formed in eighty one Jian in length. Here is a fifteen year old virgin boy. The virgin boy contains half Yin and half Yang as light from the east. As he engages in a human life style, he loses his virginity and with it the Yuan (source) Yang, his vital Qi becomes exhausted. Qi deficiency leads to illness, aging, depletion and death. A dull mind damages the Ling light of soul light, the life time force, and shortens longevity. Because of karma, a person's life will be long or short. There is life and there has to be death; there is death and there has to be life. Reincarnation into a degraded form will carry a different level of life expectancy. There is living and disappearing, and the disappeared return to life. If the soul does not awaken it will lose its human form and Ling of soul. Reincarnation into a different lower group of Ling and of another form of soul ensues. If one's true self does not awaken and return to human form it will enter a side pathway from which it cannot liberate itself. Only a true practitioner (the immortal level) can assist you to release the karma from the last life, and guide the change to human form again. After the change back to human form, if one still does not understand, he will cycle through a hundred calamities until he reaches his destiny, but still in hunger and illness or slavery. If the soul still acts as it did previously it will be as a ball bouncing into the wrong path for the next reincarnation.

2. Lu asks:
We are fortunate to be born in China at this time; there is peace and no famine. We are happy to be healthy, free of sickness and wish to live free of worries about death. Master, please tells us again about the most important purpose of life

and death, the theory of living without illness, and eternal life. Would you please teach your poor disciple?

Zhong answers:
Humans need to avoid reincarnation into an unfruitful side pathway. Humans wish to avoid illness, aging, suffering and death. The human level is symbolized by the head touching the sky with feet standing on the earth. It contains Yin and embraces the Yang. If one stays on the human level, it is important not to enter into the ghost level. Practice while on a human level and more forward to the immortal level and into Tian Xian of Heaven immortal level.

3. Lu asks:
A human dies and moves into the ghost level, and must follow the Tao pathway to achieve the Xian (immortal) level. Is not the Xian level the first stage? Why do we need to leave the human Xian level to achieve immortality at the Heavenly Xian level?

Zhong answers:
The Xian (immortal) level is not just one level. The ghost Xian level is pure Yin without Yang. The Tian Xian (heavenly immortal) level is pure Yang without Yin. The human is a mixture of Yin and Yang. A person can enter the ghost Xian level or the Tian Xian level.

If teenagers do not practice the Tao pathway but instead lead a life of sexual excess and greed, burning the candle at both ends, illness and death and descent into the ghost level will follow. However, if they know how to practice, this will be a guide to human sainthood in which the human body is transformed to the Xian immortal level. Immortality, Xian, consists of five levels. The method of practice contains three levels of success. Each practitioner will have different successes.

4. Lu asks:

The method of practice has three levels and Xian (immortal) has five levels. How do the levels differ from one another?

Zhong answers:

The method or technique has three levels: small success, middle success and higher success. The state of immortality, Xian (immortal), has five levels: Gui (ghost) Xian, Ren (human) Xian, Di (earth) Xian, Shen (spirit) Xian and Tian (Heaven) Xian. Gui Xian is the ghost level, Ren Xian is the human level, Di Xian is the earth level, Shen Xian is the spirit level and is close to the Tian Xian and Tian (Heaven) Xian is the Heaven level.

5. Lu asks:

What is the Gui Xian (ghost immortal) level?

Zhong answers:

The Gui Xian is the lowest level of the five immortal levels of Xian. His Shen of mind is not bright and clear. One enters the ghost gate without a last name, and arrives at the three mountains of Taoism without a first name. The Gui Xian can control himself in reincarnation, but cannot enter the Bonlai (one of Taoism's magic islands). Thus homeless, the only possibility is reincarnation as a human fetus again.

6. Lu asks:

Regarding the Gui Xian level, what technique is used and what is the result?

Zhong answers:

In the Gui level, the practitioner does not understand the Tao pathway and wants too fast of a result. Their body is as wood, the mind is as ash, and even though thought focuses within confidently, their mind is not expanding. But In this stable stage, Yin Shen of uncontrollable thought appears. That Yin

Shen is only the clear ghost's Ling of soul; this is not the Yang Shen of controllable Ling of soul and does not lead into the pure Yang Xian (immortal) level. The Gui level practitioner thinks his confident hold of Yin Ling of uncontrollable soul without spreading was perfect enough to result in entry to the higher Xian level, but this is still only the Gui Xian level. It is called Xian, but it is a ghost. The practitioner who is at this level believes he has achieved the goal. But it is only a sham.

7. Lu asks:
What is the human immortality, the Ren Xian (human immortal) level?

Zhong Answers:
The Ren Xian level is the second lowest level of the five Xian levels that do not fully understand the Tao pathway. They possess techniques from the Tao and confidently practice for their lifetime. They combine the five elements (the water element characterized as Kidney, wood characterized as Liver, fire characterized as Heart, earth characterized as Spleen and Stomach, and metal characterized as Lung) Qi but without understanding. The body is stronger, resists external pathogens so they can no longer cause illness, and remains healthy with little sickness. This is Ren Xian level.

8. Lu asks:
What technique and capacity lead to this Ren Xian level?

Zhong answers:
At the beginning when the practitioner hears of the Tao pathway, he has heavy karma and very little fortune. Due to the difficult circumstances of his life he ceases practicing after having attained a low level of capacity and achievement. During his lifetime the practitioner cannot improve further and is unable to regulate the four seasons of the body. The practitioner may stop eating the five tastes (sweet, sour, bitter,

acrid and bland) but does not know there are six Qi (wind, cold, summer heat, damp, dry and fire); he lets go of the seven emotions but does not know that there are ten to guard against. Practicing the washing the mouth technique and concentrating the mind on breathing is wrong.

The practitioner uses sexuality to strengthen himself, laughing at him who practices peace. He loves to take in sky and earth Qi but does not want to practice the diet. He loves to pick the sun and moon's Jing (essence), but does not want to guide and breathe Qi.

He only sits and holds onto the breath, but does not know what is natural. He practices stretching and exercise, but does not know emptiness. He practices collecting female's Yin and Qi, but does not know it is different than reversing the processing between the penis and the testis.

He may nourish the Yang with human breast milk; but does not know it is different than practicing the discipline of the Dan of golden pill. There are many more examples. These are all Taoist techniques, but not the main Tao pathway.

They only practice one method or technique that achieves happiness and longevity. This is the Ren Xian level. There may be another practitioner who only practices for a short time. When confused and practicing the wrong timing and method, the result can be sickness instead of longevity. This happens often.

9. Lu asks:
How about the Di Xian (earth immortal) level?

Zhong answers:
The Di (Earth) Xian level is halfway between the sky and the earth. If the practitioner possesses talent but does not

understand the Tao pathway well, this results in some small success, but not enough achievement. The practitioner may enjoy longevity and no death while remaining at the human level.

10. Lu asks:
How does one practice to achieve the Di Xian level?

Zhong answers:
At the beginning, the practitioner follows the theory of the sky and earth ascending and descending of Yin and Yang communication, the sun and moon cycle predictably of Yin and Yang circulation. The internal body time is matched to the calculation of year, month, and day's timing. He must understand the tiger and dragon of metal and wood communication.

Secondly, he must know Kan (⚏) of water and Li (☲) of fire communication. He must identify clear and turbid water; must understand seasonal, morning and evening interactions. He must harvest the true one Qi (source Qi), inspect the two Yi (Yin and Yang); list the three abilities (sky, human and earth); divide the four appearances (four direction image); know the distinctions of the five elements (water, wood, fire, earth and metal); set up the six Qi (wind, cold, summer heat, damp, dry and fire); gather the seven treasures (water, wood, fire, earth, metal, source Yang and Yin and Yang Qi); order the Ba Gua (relation of natural eight directions, time and space); regulate the nine squares of states where the regulation of sky and the human body take place; reverse the five elements; master the Qi deliveries from son to mother and the relationship and fluid transfer from the husband to the wife; comprehend the three Dantian (upper, middle and lower where the field makes the golden pill) communication for refining the Dan of internal medicine down to the Lower Dantian.

This process of refining the human body to live and never die, keeps the practitioner in the earth's Shen Xian level, this is Di Xian.

11. Lu asks:
What is the Shen Xian (spirit immortal) level?

Zhong answers:
In the Shen Xian state the practitioner is tired of the earthly human life style. The practitioner never stops practicing. Aspects of the practice link together, extracting lead and adding mercury (lead as water essence and mercury as fire essence), refining the Jinjing (golden essence) in the crown of head. Jade fluid returns to the Dan (golden pill).

Refining the body transformed by the five Qi, returns to the Yuan (source). Three Yangs gather into the crown of head. After this processing is fully accomplished, the human body is emptied and the Xian fetus is created. Yin totally disappears and is pure Yang. Beyond the flesh, there is another state that sheds the human body; substance rises into Xian, which is above the human level, into sainthood. There is no more human dust (waste), and one returns to the three mountains of Tao. This is the Shen Xian level.

12. Lu asks:
What is the Tian Xian (heaven immortal) level?

Zhong answers:
The practitioner at the Di (earth) Xian level is weary of the conventional human life style and practices ceaselessly until he sheds his human body substance into the Shen of Tian Xian level. At the Di Xian level the practitioner has attained the level sufficient to permit remaining in the three Taoist islands and to go into the pathway of teaching the Tao to the public to gain more achievement. When the practitioner is fully

accomplished, he follows Heaven's order to return to the magic mountain cave. This is Tian Xian. At the Tian Xian level he may remain in the magic mountain cave, committed to being a Xian level governor. The bottom governor is a water governor, the middle governor is the earth governor and the upper governor is the sky governor. Achieving Heaven and earth is the first reward. If the practitioner continues to benefit society he will be promoted to the next level of governor, passing through thirty six magic caves and back into eighty one Yang Heavens and into three clear and empty natural stages.

13. Lu asks:

Gui Xian (ghost immortal) admittedly does not appear to be an appealing choice. Tian Xian (heaven immortal) seems far away. Please explain the method for Ren Xian (human immortal), Di Xian (earth immortal), and Shen Xian (spirit immortal).

Zhong answers:

Ren Xian is a first level achievement method, Di Xian is a middle achievement method and Shen Xian is a higher level method. They represent three levels of essentially one class of achievement. Using the proper method to learn the Tao, the Tao becomes not difficult. Tao theory is used to progress to the Xian level. Depend on the Tao; the Xian level pathway becomes easier.

14. Lu asks:

Some ancient practitioners did not desire longevity or eternal life nor to rise to the Xian but they still went to Heaven. Why?

Zhong answers:

Some employed a method that does not match the Tao pathway. They listened to different ideas and were stubborn, resisting information and proper technique. They entered a side door; leading to sickness and death. For instance, the disappearing death body technique confuses the public, and the Tao pathway is not heard. Alternatively, some practitioners did not practice for enough time; they had not achieved enough achievement and passed away, but the public thought they had attained the Xian level.

Chapter Two: Discussion of the Tao Pathway.

1. Lu asks:
What is the Tao pathway?

Zhong answers:
The Tao pathway has no shape, and no name, asks no questions, and gives no answers. The exterior of the Tao is infinite and the interior of the Tao is unlimited. One cannot have it through force, but without intention you have and walk through the Tao.

2. Lu asks:
Ancient practitioners started to learn the Tao, began to possess the Tao, finally had the Tao and accomplished Tao. From the dust world (mortal world) into Peng Island (One of magical Taoism island), rising into the sky cave and into Yang Heaven and the three clear levels, finally the successful Taoism practitioner resides. Today, the grand master has said; "We do not need to possess the Tao, but we know and practice it." So, why does the Tao appear hidden?

Zhong answers:
The Tao pathway is not hidden. Lay followers of the Tao just like to hear the name and want to listen, but they do not have the confidence and toughness of mind to go forward; they change their minds from morning to night; memorize how to practice when sitting down and forget about it when standing up; study hard at the beginning and grow lazy at the end and they think the Tao is difficult to understand and practice.

3. Lu asks:
Why is the Tao pathway difficult to understand and practice?

Zhong answers:
If using the sideways technique it is easy to acquire capacity

and to transmit the technique to each other during a lifelong practice. Nonetheless this does not lead to understanding and enlightenment. The practice of the sideways technique is a corruption of the Tao pathway. For instance, some people without understanding the Tao pathway become vegetarian, stop eating, collect Qi, gargle silver, leave their wives, stop tasting food, seek Zen (a Buddhist branch), sit still, cease talking, focus in imagination, collect Yin, are swollen with Qi, keep clean and clear, concentrate on their breathing, stop becoming tired, open the crown of the head, back up the penis, disappear, engage in reading, practice inner burning, still the breath, guide the Qi, inhale and exhale, collect Jing (essence) and strengthen Qi, support and give donations to the public, live in the mountains, identify their true self, stop moving and receiving, etcetera. The components of the spurious sideways technique are so numerous that it is difficult to count them all. These practitioners go about collecting sun and moon essence, sky and earth Qi, image and thought to establish the Jin Dan (golden pill). They bend the body and work hard to try to transform the physical body substance into an immortal level. They inhale more than exhale to try to heal disease and accomplish true fetal breathing (fetus breathing in the uterus), stop thinking and talking to nourish the true self as Taiyi (original vital one) which includes true Qi. And they thought if the practitioner have the control and cause his yellow river to flow in reverse in Xiao Zhou Tian (microcosmic orbit whence the Qi flows from the sacrum through the spine and returns in the circular pattern down through the front of body) to avoid impotence; but this is a lower level of the method of nourishing life; one's body looks like dry wood, his mind is ash; this is just a lower level technique of gathering Shen (mind) etcetera. These are all consequences of the sideways path.

Most of today's intense practitioners, as did the ancient practitioners, pay attention and concentrate the mind, using saliva as medicine. How does it transform? Gathering Qi as Dan (golden pill), how do we retain it? The Liver is characterized as a dragon and the Lungs are characterized as a tiger; how can they interact? The Kan (☵) of water is characterized as lead; the Li (☲) of fire is characterized as mercury; how are they extracted or added? These practitioners water for four seasons to grow the yellow sprout; they concentrate on one thought and want to create great internal medicine, but they are confused and misuse the timing of the month and the year; they do not understand the root of the five elements, nor do they understand the three levels of transformation. They see the branch and the leaf; but they confuse upcoming generations. The Taoist pathway seems further away, unreachable and less understood. The sideways technique has become more and more the common practice. The great grand master's teaching has been lost. The public learns from someone talking on the street. This mouth to ear teaching by persons unaware of Taoist theory is a deeply engrained custom, which is overwhelming. It is not that I do not want to teach the public; it is that the public has karma and less fortune, and does not really understand Heaven's opportunity. The public emphasizes wealth and does not care about health or entrance into the ghost level.

4. Lu asks:
I understand the sideways pathway, can you tell me about the Tao?

Zhong answers:
One cannot ask what the Tao is. There are no answers. The Tao is the present. At the very beginning, the Taibo (vital origin stage) was opened by the Zhenyuan (vital source). The Tao gave birth to the one, one gave birth to the two, and two gave birth to the three.

The first birth is the body, the second birth is function, and the third birth is transformation. Functioning of the body depends upon Yin and Yang. Transformation depends upon copulation.

The Upper, Middle and Lower Dantian are as three abilities; the sky, the earth and human as one Tao pathway. Tao births one, two births Qi. Qi births the three abilities, the three abilities then birth the five elements, and five elements birth everything. In everything, the human is the most valuable and most intelligent and has Ling (soul). Only the human can understand everything and become aware of the true self. By understanding all of the theory, the true human self, and training to achieve perfect, full health and nourishing life to match the Tao, we become solid strong, and long-lived as the sky and earth.

5. Lu asks:
The sky and earth have a long lifetime of thousands of years and without end. The maximum human lifetime is one hundred years. It is difficult to reach even seventy years of age. Why does the Tao allow the sky and earth to last longer than humans?

Zhong answers:
The human life span does not match the Tao. The Tao is not far from the people, it is the people who are far away from the Tao. Those who are far from the Tao wish to take care of their health, but do not know the method to employ; they do not understand the timing and opportunity of sky and earth.

Chapter Three: Discussion of Sky and Earth

1. Lu asks:
Can you tell me about sky and earth's opportunity?

Zhong answers:
The sky and earth's opportunity is in the interrelated function of sky and earth within the Tao pathway. Communication flows from above to below, and back again ceaselessly, mutually reinforcing both realms. This is not widely known.

2. Lu asks:
Sky and earth are the pattern of the Tao pathway. How can practitioners participate in synchrony with this? How do we start? How much effort must this take?

Zhong answers:
Once the Tao gives a form, it has mathematical properties. Sky has the Qian (☰) pathway, one as body, atmospheric and undivided, light, clear and upper and functional as Yang. Earth has the Kun (☷) pathway, two is body, terrestrial, stratified, dense and opaque as Yin. The Tao pathway reverses, Yang embraces the Yin ascending and Yin embraces the Yang descending. They harmonize as the flow of communication between Qian (☰) and Kun (☷). This has been from the beginning of time and is fulfilled each day. Following this Tao cycle will result in daily achievement.

3. Lu asks:
Sky has the Yang ascending Qian (☰) pathway. How does Yang connect to earth? Earth has the Yin descending Kun (☷) pathway. How does Yin connect to sky? If sky and earth have not been coupling, how do the Yin and Yang harmonize? If the Yin and Yang do not harmonize, how do Qian and Kun transform? If the Qian and Kun do not transform, and even if one has begun and processed period time, but one does not

practice in the Tao cycle, how can there be results or accomplishments.

Zhong answers:
The sky pathway is Qian (☰) body, expressing Yang; the Qi flows to upper. The earth pathway is Kun (☷) body, expressing Yin, the water pools downward.

The path from sky Qian (☰) collecting earth Kun (☷) is describe by the trigrams. Qian transformed from Kun one Yao (one of trigram) becomes Zhen (☳), eldest son, followed Qian transformed Kun one Yao is Kan (☵) and the middle son, then Qian changes Kun one Yao to Gen (☶) and the youngest son. This progression is called sky collecting earth, Qian (☰) collecting Kun (☷) through a sequence of three Yangs.

The path from earth Kun (☷) collecting sky Qian (☰) proceeds through the trigrams. Kun transformed from Qian one Yao becomes Xun (☴) and the eldest daughter; Kun transformed one Yao from the Qian as Li (☲) and middle daughter, and Kun transformed one Yao from Qian as Dui (☱) the youngest daughter. This progression is the earth collecting the sky, Kun (☷) collecting the Qian (☰) through a sequence of three Yins.

Three Yangs coupling with three Yins harmonize and a natural substance arises. Three Yins coupling with three Yangs harmonize and create form. Sky and earth combine, Qian (☰) and Kun (☷) collect each other and are the Tao path. This Qian and Kun transformation creates the six Qi (wind, cold, summer heat, damp, dryness and fire). The six Qi harmonize creating the five elements (wood, fire, earth, metal and water). The five elements harmonize to create all. Sky Qian (☰) descends to the earth progresses through three exchanging Yao to earth Kun (☷) where the Yang is hidden within the Yin. The Yang embraces the Yin back up to the sky; earth Kun (☷)'s pathway to the sky progresses through exchanging three Yao to sky Qian (☰) where the Yin embraces Yang and returns to earth.

Yang carries the Yin and this maintains Yin as true (Zhen) Yin. This true Yin ascends upward to the sky due to the Yang. Therefore true Yin descends from the sky, how can it be without Yang? The Yin embraces the Yang; this maintains Yang as true (Zhen) Yang. This true Yang is in the earth due to the true Yin; how can Yang be without Yin?

The Yang embraces the Yin, and the Yin does not decay until returned to earth; Yin embraces the Yang, Yang persists, and then ascends to the sky. Each perpetuates and sustains the other in ceaseless circulation thus manifesting the Tao.

Illustration of the sky and earth communication:

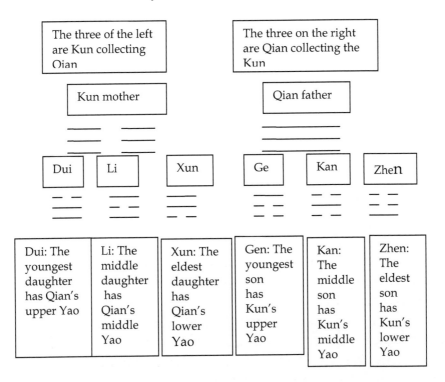

Dui: The youngest daughter has Qian's upper Yao	Li: The middle daughter has Qian's middle Yao	Xun: The eldest daughter has Qian's lower Yao	Gen: The youngest son has Kun's upper Yao	Kan: The middle son has Kun's middle Yao	Zhen: The eldest son has Kun's lower Yao

4. Lu asks:
Sky and earth's opportunity is in the function of the sky and earth within the Tao and that is why sky and earth can be eternal wherein sky and earth are fulfilled. Human beings have intelligence but need a quiet and peaceful mind to follow the Tao pathway. The first level of success is the attainment of joy and longevity. The second level of success is life without death. The last level of success is shedding the flesh and finding liberation to the Xian immortality. How can we harmonize our bodies to the flow of the Tao pathway and match the secret code of Heaven for longevity, and have the immortal body persist and withstand calamities?

Zhong answers:
The Tao pathway has no shape though you have shape. The Tao has no name though you have a name. Sky and earth have the Tao due to the interchange between Qian (☰) and Kun (☷). The sun and the moon have the Tao due to the interchange of Yin and Yang. Mortals have the Tao due to the interchange of an emperor and his assistant's rule; family has the Tao due to the interchange of husband and wife's rule, father and son's rule, the rule of the elders and youth, and even friends' rule.

When father and mother procreate, first the father's Yang enters, then the mother's Yin is moved. This is true Qi coupling with true water as Heart fire and Kidney water communicating to refine Jing (essence). Then if the mother's Yin comes first the water washes away the useless. If the mother's Yang comes first, the Yang embraces the blood receiving the Jing (essence) within the vagina. Jing and blood as embryo includes true Qi in the uterus. Through days and months the true Qi fortifies the human body, as sky and earth communicate and manifesting the Tao pathway as sky Qian (☰) and earth Kun (☷) collect each other, in the process creating three Yin and three Yang. True Qi is Yang, true water is the Yin. Yang is hidden in the water; Yin is hidden in the Qi. The Qi ascends, embracing true water; true water descends embracing the true Qi.

True Yang follows as the water descends, this is Qian (☰) collecting Kun (☷) through the steps Zhen (☳) in upper, Kan (☵) in middle, and Gen (☶) in lower. Using the middle of human body as a criterion, from upper to lower, Zhen is the Liver, Kan is the Kidney and Gen is the Urination Bladder.

The true Yin follows as the true Qi ascends, as Kun (☷) collecting Qian (☰) through the steps the lower aspect Xun (☴), middle aspect Li (☲) middle and Dui (☱) in upper. Using the middle of human body as a criterion, from lower to upper, Xun is the Gall Bladder, the middle aspect Li of the Heart, and the upper aspect Dui of the Lung. When shape and appearance are fully formed, it is time to emerge from the mother.

Postnatally, the Yuan (source) resides in the Kidney. The Yuan (source) creates true Qi. True Qi pilgrimage rises to the Heart where the true Qi creates true fluid, the true fluid descends back to the source. As upper and lower communicate unimpaired the result is longevity.

If the timing is understood and practice of this is never missed, the timing adds and extracts the true fire and water to optimize longevity. The diligent practitioner persists until Yin vaporizes to pure Yang then realizes the extraordinary: transformation from a mortal to immortal.

This is the chance to ascend to a higher, the Heavenly level. This is the secret of antiquity. The practitioner with sufficient confidence and determination to undergo struggle and resist the distraction of fame or fortune or affection may then avoid disease, death and calamity and avoid the soul transfer into being transferred non human being. The only way to go is to foster the transformation of body and soul. It is necessary to clear the mind to the root, retaining the Yuan (source) Yang without exhausting the true Qi.

Excess Qi leads to the burn out Hun (substance) Yin. Abundant Yang results in sufficient Bo (energy) Yang. Ascending and descending must proceed in the proper interchange as with sky and earth's orderly progressions. It must wax and wane as the sun and the moon do in their complimentary perpetual motion.

Chapter Four: Discussion of the Sun and Moon

1. Lu asks:
The Sky and Earth theory are somewhat understood. How does the human body compare to the communication of Sun and Moon? Please let me know.

Zhong answers:
The Tao has no appearance, but births the sky and earth. Tao has no name, but it circulates the sun and moon. Sun and moon are Tai Yang (sun) and Tai Yin (moon)'s essence, encompassing the magnanimity of the sky and earth's movement, assisting in the creation of all. Rising from the east and setting in the west, it divides day and night, south and north communicate, and winter and summer are defined. Day and night are unceasing, winter and summer chase each other. Sun's Po (light) creates moon's spirit Hun (substance); the moon's spirit Hun births the sun's spirit Po and their forward and back in time and matched amount of the Qian (☰) Yang and Kun (☷) Yin calculation, without missing the period of communication between the sky and earth.

2. Lu asks:
East and west divide day and night, why?

Zhong answers:
Chaos was at the beginning, Xuan Huang (emptiness started creating substance) sets the position, and the sky and earth are like an egg. Six combinations (upper, lower, front, back, left and right) are inside; their shape is an oval like an egg. Sun and moon rise and disappear, move up to the sky and under the earth. Up and down, east and west, circulation is as a wheel. The sun rises in the east and sets in the west; the sun is in the sky during the day, disappears at night in the west and rises in the east; that is the sun's rising and setting, which divides day and night.

The moon's movement is different than the sun's; the moon carries the Po (light) to the west, receives Hun (substance) in the east, brightens at night, and hides the spirit Hun (substance) during the day, up and down from the west to east, day after day.

At the beginning of the night the moon's light is shaped like a bow up high, it brightens the west; that is Po (light) birthing the Hun (substance).

After midnight, the moon brightens the south; that is Po (light) hiding a half Hun (substance).

Later before dawn, the moon brightens the east; that is Po with full Hun facing the sun.

Next, the moon is like an imperfect mirror. At the beginning of the day, that is Hun is birthing the Po, and the Hun is hidden in the west.

Next at midday, the moon down low brightens; that is Hun containing a half Po and Hun, hidden in the south.

Later in the evening, the moon is Hun hiding full Po and is opposite the sun; Hun is hidden in the east.

As the circle goes round again, the up and down movement of the moon divides day and night.

Illustration:

Po is light and Hun is substance.

The moon during at night:

North

East: Po has full Hun	West: Po gives birth to the Hun

South: Po has a half Hun

The moon during at day:

North

East: Hun has full Po	West: Hun gives birth to Po

South: Hun has a half Po

3. Lu asks:

Why does the communication of south and north set winter and summer?

Zhong answers:

After winter, at the beginning, the sun rises at the beginning of (Chen) about 7 a.m., the sun sets at the end of (Shen) about 4 p.m. Day and night keep cycling, up and down from south to north until Xia Zhi (the day summer begins). After summer, the sun rises at the end of (Yin) about 5 a.m., and sets at the beginning of (Xu) about 6 p.m. It circulates up and down from north to south until Dong Zhi (the day winter begins). The sun rising up from the south and going down north during winter to summer, changes from winter cold to summer heat. The sun rising up from the north and going down south during summer to winter, changes from summer heat to winter cold.

Summer's day is winter's night; winter's day is summer's night.

After Dong Zhi, the moon rises up from the north and goes down to the south, in synchronization with a summer's day. After Xia Zhi, the moon rises from the south and goes down to the north, in synchronization with a winter's day. This is the circulation of the sun and the moon to set winter and summer.

4. Lu asks:
Sky and earth give the opportunity; Yin and Yang ascend and descend in synchronization just as does the human body's Yin and Yang. How does the communication of the sun and moon compare to the human body?

Zhong answers:
Sky and earth giving opportunity is Yin and Yang ascending and descending. This up and down motion creates the Taiji of Yin and Yang starting communication, Yin and Yang are creating and depending upon each other and circulating over and over again as a lasting Tao pathway.

One who follows the eternal sky and earth pattern follows the sun communication of the sun and moon in timing, interaction, learning the pattern of the moon receiving the sun's Hun, using Yang changing to Yin, Yin transforms to Yang until there is pure Yang. As moonlight pure and bright eliminates unclear Po, bright as sunshine, it irradiates upper and lower. In similar synchronization in the practitioner, Qi transforms into Shen spirit, shedding mortal substance to Xian immortal, and turns into a pure Yang body and eternal.

5. Lu asks:
For the Taoist practitioner following the theory of the sky and earth ascending and descending, the sun's Yang and moon's Jing of essential interaction on time, which comes first?

Zhong answers:
At the beginning, follow Heaven's opportunity; Yin and Yang
go up and down, uniting true (Zhen) water and true (Zhen)
fire as one; refine them into great medicine, let them stay
forever in the Dantian where they can create medicine, which
will survive through calamities, as ageless as sky and earth. If
one is tired of regular life, through diligent practice, one
should learn from sun and moon interaction, using Yang to
transform Yin, eliminating Yin. Qi nourishes the Shen spirit,
concentrating and maintaining Shen spirit, the five Qi make a
pilgrimage to the Yuan of the source, the three flowers gather
in the crown of the head, not distracted by mundane human
affairs, back to the three magical Taoist islands.

6. Lu asks:
If one has this experience and achievement one will be very
happy about having understood this wisdom, but may worry
about not knowing the time interval.

Zhong answers:
The cycle of sky and earth and Yin and Yang ascending and
descending requires one year's interaction and
communication. Sun's Yang and moon's Jing (essential)
interaction takes place during one month's time. The human
body Qi and fluid is the cycle of day and night.

Chapter Five: Discussion of the Four Seasons

1. Lu asks:

What are the relationships between sky and the earth, the sun and the moon, and the year, month, day and hour?

Zhong answers:

There are four levels of time:

The human body has a one-hundred-year lifespan: between ages one to thirty the body is young and vigorous, between thirty to sixty-years-old the body grows to maturity, at sixty to ninety years the body is aging, ninety to one hundred or one hundred twenty are the years of decay. This is the first level of time and how it shows itself in the human body.

There are twelve Chen (unit of time is two hours) in one day; five days as one Hou (unit of time is five days); three Hou is one Qi, (unit of time is fifteen days and is a small section in a season in the Chinese calendar); three Qi equal one Jie (time section is forty five days in the Chinese calendar); two Jie are one Shi (time section of one season); a year has spring, summer, autumn and winter. Spring is the time when the abundant Yin has half Yang, which is why the weather changes from cold to warm. Summer is in the time when the Yang has full Yang, and the weather changes from warm to hot. Autumn is the time when the Yang has half Yin, so the weather changes from hot to cool. Winter is the time when the Yin has full Yin, so the weather moves from cool to cold. This is the second level of time and how it shows itself through the four seasons.

Analogy form the melody has sound Lu; from the Lu has melody, as rhythm one month has thirty days, which equals Three hundred and sixty Chen (unit of time measure), or three thousand Ke (unit of time measure), or one hundred eighteen thousand Fen (unit of time measure).

From the waning to the first quarter of the moon cycle Yin has half Yang, and from the first quarter to the full moon Yang has full Yang. From the full moon to the new final quarter Yang has half Yin, and from the final quarter to the dark moon Yin has full Yin. This is the third level of time and how it shows itself through the sun and moon.

Discuss Gua (the eight trigrams of Taoism) to identify eight directions and the center and four positions.

Relating to the cardinal directions, from north 11a.m. to 1 p.m. (Zi) to east 5 a.m. to 7 a.m. (Mao), corresponding with 11 p.m. to 7 a.m. in the body clock, the Yin has half Yang, which means Tai Yin is giving life to Shao Yang.

From east 5-7 a.m. (Mao) to south 11 a.m. to 1 p.m. (Wu), corresponding with 5 a.m. to 1 p.m. in the body clock, the Yang has full Yang; which means Shao Yang is giving life to Tai Yang.
From south 11 a.m. to 1 p.m. (Wu) to west 5 p.m. to 7 p.m. (You), corresponding with 11 a.m. to 7 p.m. in the body clock; the Yang has half Yin, which means Tai Yang is giving life to Shao Yin.

From west 5 p.m. to 7 p.m. (You) to north 11 p.m. to 1 a.m. (Zi), corresponding with 5 p.m. to 1 a.m. in the body clock, Yin has full Yin, which means Shao Yin is giving life to Tai Yin. This is the fourth level of time and how it shows itself thru the hours of the day.

The time in the body is the most difficult to grasp and the easiest to lose. The months and the years come slowly but pass by rapidly. As sudden as lightening strikes and as rapidly as fire consumes is the turning of the hours into days which become months accumulating into years; we find we have squandered our months and years, with what seems to the speed of light. Many people have lived greedy lives, valuing only accumulation and profit and fame. Others are swayed by their love for their children and grandchildren, so that by the time they finally get a chance to practice Taoism, their bodies are like snow in the spring. It is the autumn-flower's only limitation. And just as the light of the sunset and the full moon cannot shine forever, for practitioners of the Tao, time in the body is the most difficult to keep.

Alluring sunshine and charming scenery, surrounded by beautiful flowers, it is easy to become taken with the surroundings of and cool breezes, blinded to the fact that the water which surrounds the building can also serve to rot the foundation. Basking in the moon light, and drinking the snow, the endless indulgences of amusement, all add up to a waste of precious time. If one did turn his eyes back to study the Tao at this point, they might feel that it is too late, that the sickness in the body is like a boat that is broken. But, who wants to drown because of a sinking boat? If your home has leaks, do you not repair them while you can?

And what of the persons who waste their time of youthful vitality, going outside fun before rooster's crow in the morning. Hearing the drums in the street, they go out thinking only of having a good time, and when the dinner bell is rung, they pretend not to hear so as not to have to return home. And what of the ones who are obsessed with working so that they can fulfill their dreams of accumulating great riches? Can your house of gold and jade protect you from disease? Who will watch your sons and grandchildren when your breath stops? Day follows night endlessly, a clock that waits for no one. This is why the practitioner of the Tao values the time in each day.

2. Lu asks:
Body's timing, Year's timing, month's timing, day's timing, and all are concerned with timing. Master Zhong, why it difficult to understand body timing, and why is it a pity to waste a body's time?

Zhong answers:
A practitioner who has started practicing as a teenager has chosen the best time to have begin, a teenage practitioner's root and source are perfect, solid and strong; they easily obtain results; and they can practice for one thousand days and advance to a higher level. One who begins to practice at middle age has more to correct and encounter before being able to progress and reverse from his present age back to the age of a young child and then to an immortal level.

If the practitioner has not wakened and begun to practice as a teenage, in middle age he will no want to practice, unless he encounters disaster, then he pays attention to quiet and because of sickness, he wants to into Xi Yi (within and out infinite), and when he is a senior in practice, it is to save and care for the Jing and Qi first; therefore strengthening from lower level to the middle level, and deposited there to reverse from old age to infancy, in order fro the practicing body to stay in gather into the crown of the head. Shedding the body's substance and rising to the immortal level is hard now. This is valuable lesson about the body's time.

3. Lu asks:
 The body's timing is difficult to know, how about day's timing?

Zhong answers:
One day for human body has the equivalent of one month's circulation of the sun and moon and one year's time of the sky and earth. The Tao creates and nourishes sky and earth, and

divided the sky and earth realm which has upper and lower, and has eighty four thousand Li (length measure). After Dong Zhi (winter begins), the Yang rises from the earth, one Qi steps forward fifteen days, up to seven thousand Li (length measure), continuing for a for a total of hundred eighty days, when the Yang will have reached the top.

Tai Ji (maximum) creates Yin, and after summer, Yin is descending from the sky. One Yin Qi takes fifteen days and seven thousand Li (length measure), total one hundred eighty days to complete the descent to the earth, Tai Ji begins to create Yang; this pattern is the Tao pathway that never stops.

After the sun and moon circulation and formed, the sun and moon each have eight hundred forty Li (length measure) to travel. After the new moon, in six started the nine, one day counts twelve Shi (time measure of two hours), Po's (Yang and light) hidden Hun (substance) has moved forwards eight hundred forty Li (length measure). After the full moon, in nine started the six, one day is twelve Shi (time measure of two hours), Hun's (substance) Po (Yang and light) steps forward seventy Li (length measure). After fifteen days, total one hundred eighty Shi (unit measure of two hours), Hun's (substance) Po (Yang and light) steps forward eight hundred forty Li (length measure). This describes the solid and strong Tao pathway.

Tao nourishes everything, and is in everything; human is the most valuable form of life and has supreme Ling (soul), Human's Heart and Kidney distant to each other is eight Cun (length measure) and four Fen (length measure), the Yin and Yang ascend and descend with the rhythm of the sky and earth.

Therefore, Qi creates fluid; fluid creates Qi, Qi and fluids create each other and the sky and earth, sun and moon follow the same path. The sky and earth as Qian (sky and Yang) and Kun (earth and Yin) demand each other of Yin and Yang up and down, yearly circulation interaction, continuing year after year as Tao's path. The sun and moon are using Hun (substance) and Po (Yang and light) relationship to create the Jing Hua (essence and light), interaction once each month, and month after month this pattern continues without stopping; this is the Tao path.

The human body knows day and night, but if a practitioner does not know how or when to interact with the universe, when deficiency moment how to strengthen, fullness does not know release, Yin interaction does not know how to create for the Yang, Yang interaction does not know how to refine the Yin. He does not know what part of a monthly cycle is lose or gained, does not practice daily, until a year is lost and then another, one day is passed and one day is lost. He is exposed to excessive winds and lies on damp ground, exposed to extreme hot and cold, never wanting to practice, willingly sick and wasting his time; this is waiting to die.

4. Lu asks:
If the practitioner wastes his time, until illness and death are coming around the corner, because he knows not the method and timing, and misses the Yin and Yang interaction and correct daily and monthly time.

Zhong answers:
The body's time is based on one year timing, a year times uses a month, a month uses a day, and day takes a Shi (time measure of two hours). Using five organs' Qi to synchronize a monthly's abundance and deficiency, a day's forwards and backward, Shi (time measure of two hours) interaction, movement of five Du (unit of degree) to deliver six Hou (unit of weather), the creation of metal, wood, water, fire and earth listed precisely in order, and east, west, south, north and

center have been created with mathematical precision. Refine Jing into true Qi, refine Qi combined with Yang Shen, refine Shen into Tao pathway.

Chapter Six: Discussion of the Five Elements

Illustration of the relationships of the Five Elements to each other:

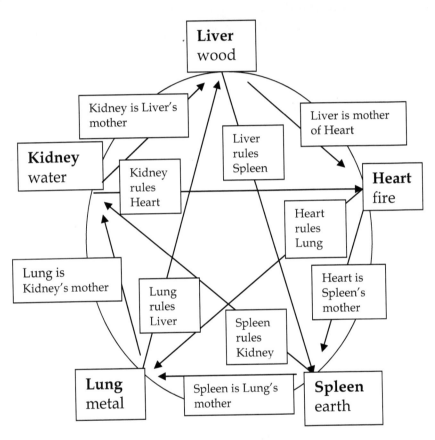

1. Lu asks:

Regarding the five organs' Qi there are metal, wood, water, fire and earth.

The directions these five elements inhabit are west, east, north, south and center. How do they create and rule each and interact with time? Please explain this to me.

Zhong answers:

The path of the Tao enfolds both earth and sky. Earth and Sky are comprised of the realms of the five emperors. From the east, the green emperor commands spring as from the Yin propels Yang; all is begun. From the south, the red emperor commands summer when Yang propels Yang; all is in motion. From the west, the white emperor commands autumn as Yang propels Yin; everything is in form. From the north, the black emperor commands winter, Yin propels Yin, everything culminates and declines.

There are four seasons of ninety days. Once each eighteen days, the yellow emperor commands. In spring, the yellow emperor assists green emperor to emerge. In summer the yellow emperor assists the red emperor to radiate. In autumn the yellow emperor assists the white emperor to consolidate. In winter the yellow emperor assists the black emperor to contract. Five emperors divide responsibility, each one masters seventy two days, total is three hundred sixty days a year, the time it takes for the sky and earth to complete a full cycle of the Tao pathway.

The green emperor's son is mastering time, space and direction of the Jia Yi (sky stem), whose attributions are the wood characteristics of the east. The red emperor's son is mastering time, space and direction of the Bing Ding (sky stem) fire characteristics of the south. The yellow emperor's son is mastering time, space and direction of the Wu Ji (sky stem) which manifests the characteristics of the center of the earth. The white emperor's son is mastering time, space and direction of the Geng Xin (sky stem) with the metal characteristics of the west. The black emperor's son is mastering time, space and direction of the Ren Gui (sky stem) with the attributions of the water characteristics of the north.

These attributes are manifested in turn: wood as green dragon, fire as red bird, earth as yellow Gou Chen (a mythical animal from the earth), metal as white tiger, water as Xuan

Wu, who has the appearance of a black turtle and a snake. Each manifests in turn. The Yi (sky stem) and Geng (sky stem) coalesce in spring to unfurl in elm leaves the green and white of wood and metal. In autumn, the Xin (sky stem) and Bing (sky stem) consolidate to form red date fruit, blending the red and white of fire and metal. The Ji (sky stem) and Jia (sky stem) embody the earth's yellow and wood's green as an autumn melon at the end of summer and early autumn. Water and fire's black and red ripen mulberries in summer as Ding (sky stem) and Ren (sky stem) combine. The Gui (sky stem) and Wu (sky stem) meld as tangerine from water and earth's black and yellow in winter. In this way the five emperors collaborate and create substances beyond number.

2. Lu asks:
How is the sequence of the five elements expressed in the human body?

Zhong answers:
The human head is round and human feet are square, reflecting the appearances of the sky and the earth. Inner self Yin and Yang ascend and descend as sky and earth opportunity.

The Kidney expresses the characteristics of water, the Heart the characteristics of fire, the Liver as wood, the Spleen as earth, the Lung as metal. In the five elements system each element is considered mother to the element that follows it and is called the son. Water is the mother that engenders wood. Wood is the progenitor of fire. Fire is the mother of earth. Earth is the mother lode of metal. Metal is the mother of water.

Similarly, water is the son of metal, metal is the son of earth, earth is the son of fire, and fire is the son of wood, and wood is the son of water.

In the five elements system each element tempers another: water restrains fire, fire renders metal soft, metal dominates wood, wood regulates earth, and earth channels and contains water. The one mastering is a husband and the one receiving is a wife. This is considered the husband-wife relationship within the five elements.

In the mother-son relationship, Kidney-water Qi creates Liver-wood Qi. Liver-wood Qi creates Heart-fire Qi. Heart-fire Qi creates Spleen-earth Qi; Spleen-earth Qi creates Lung-metal Qi, and Lung-metal Qi creates Kidney-water Qi.

In the husband-wife relationship Kidney-water husband's Qi rules Heart-fire wife's Qi. Heart-fire husband's Qi rules Lung-metal wife's Qi. Lung-metal husband's Qi rules Liver-wood wife's Qi. Liver-wood husband's Qi rules Spleen-earth wife's Qi. Spleen-earth husband's Qi rules Kidney-water wife's Qi.

Kidney is Heart's husband, Liver's mother, Spleen's wife and Lung's son. Liver is Spleen's husband, Heart's mother, Lung's wife, Kidney's son. Heart is Lung's husband, Spleen's mother, Kidney's wife, and Liver's son. Lung is Liver's husband, Kidney's mother, Heart's wife, and Spleen's son. Spleen is Kidney's husband, Lung's mother, Liver's wife, and Heart's son.

The Heart manifests internally as blood vessel and manifests externally as color. The tongue is considered the doorway to the Heart. The Heart is subdued by the Kidney, and commands the Lung in the husband-wife relationships. Heart Qi is strengthened by supporting its mother Liver; Heart Qi is calmed by sedating its son Spleen.

The Kidney manifests its essence internally as bone; externally as hair. The ear is the doorway of the Kidney. The Kidney is ruled by the Spleen, and commands the Heart in the husband-wife relationship. The Kidney Qi is strengthened by supporting the Lung, its mother. The Kidney Qi is calmed by sedating the Liver, its son.

The Liver manifests its essence internally as the tendons, externally as nails. The eyes are the doorway of the Liver. The Liver Qi is ruled by Lung, and commands the Spleen in the husband-wife relationship. Strengthen Liver Qi by supporting the Kidney-mother; subdue the Liver Qi by sedating the Heart-son.

The Lung manifests its essence internally as skin; externally as body hair. The nose is the doorway of the Lung. The Lung Qi is ruled by the Heart and commands Liver in the husband-wife relationship. Strengthen the Lung Qi by supporting the Spleen-mother; subdue the Lung Qi by the calming Kidney-son.

The Spleen manifests its essence internally as the Yin organ, nourishing Heart, Kidney, Liver and Lung; the Spleen manifests externally as muscle. The lips and mouth are the doorway of the Spleen. Spleen Qi is ruled by the Liver and commands the Kidney. Strengthen the Spleen Qi by supplementing the Heart-mother; subdue the Spleen Qi by sedating the Lung-son.

This is mankind's five element relationship of creation and rule, command and submission, described as the mother-son and the husband-wife relationship which continually transfigure the Qi through stages of prospering and decline.

3. Lu asks:
So the Heart has characteristics of fire, but how can fire descend? Kidney has characteristics of water; how can water ascend? Spleen Qi is characteristic of earth-center which prospers from the Heart fire Qi, how can Spleen descend to

command Kidney water? The Lung's metal Qi is of the upper body; if it descends, and then the fire of the lower body will weaken it, so how can metal Qi still create water? There are dissimilarities between elements in the creation cycle; there are similarities between elements in the restraining cycle. How are the five elements interactions of creating and controlling, strengthening and subduing perpetuated?

Zhong answers:
Follow the five elements back to their source; all are guided by one Qi. Yuan (source) Yang ascends, raising Zhen (true) water. Zhen (true) water transforms to Zhen (true) Qi. Zhen (true) Qi transforms to Yang Shen (spirit). It starts with the five elements' interrelated locations and the various directions of Qi flowing through the paths of those locations. It starts with one husband and one wife.

The Kidney has the characteristics of water. Water's mother is metal, thus water comes from metal and therefore water has metal within. At the beginning of practice one has to understand water's metal. Water is cautious of earth, after the practitioner has developed internal medicine; earth needs to return to water.

The dragon is Liver's appearance; the tiger is Lung's image. The Yang dragon issues from the Li (fire palace), the Yin tiger is born from Kan (water palace). Each day from Zi (11 p.m.-1 a.m.) to Wu (11 a.m.-1 p.m.), the Yang time to create Yang, the Qi moving through the five elements familiar direction flows to the mother. Five elements transpose, fluid moving from husband to wife from Wu (11 a.m.-1 p.m.) to Zi (11 p.m.-1 a.m.), and in this period Yin refines Yang.

Without the Yang, Yin cannot be generated, without the Yin, Yang cannot be created. When the practitioner refines Yin to vaporize into pure Yang life will be longer.

4. Lu asks:

The five elements come from the Yin and Yang of one Qi. What is that one Qi?

Zhong answers:

The one Qi arises from the union of father and mother. Jing (essence) and blood transform and take shape. The Kidney gives birth to the Spleen, the Spleen gives birth to the Liver, the Liver gives birth to the Lung, the Lung gives birth to the Heart, the Heart gives birth to the Small Intestine, the Small Intestine gives birth to the Large Intestine, the Large Intestine gives birth to the Gall Bladder, the Gall Bladder gives birth to the Stomach, and the Stomach gives birth to the Urinary Bladder. This is Yin expressed as Jing (essence) and blood transformed into shapes. Yang started at the very beginning; one drop of Yuan (source) Yang is within the two Kidneys. The Kidneys are water, water has fire within it that ascends as Qi, and the Qi rises and makes a pilgrimage to the Heart. The Heart is Yang; Yang combined with Yang, at the Tai Ji (maximum) spontaneously creates Yin. The Heart, replete with Qi, creates fluid that flows from the Heart back down to the Kidneys.

The Liver is Heart's mother and Kidney's son. The Liver transmits Kidney Qi to the Heart. The Lung is Heart's wife and Kidney's mother, the Lung transmits Heart fluid from the Heart to the Kidneys. Qi and fluid flow up and down as the Yin and Yang flow between the sky and earth. The Liver and the Lung are the pathways as the energies of the sun and moon flow through the sky and the earth.

The five elements are mathematical. We've discussed their inception, birth and culmination. This is the origin of the Yuan (source) Yang of the one Qi. Qi within creates fluid; fluid within creates Qi. Kidney is Qi's root, Heart is fluid's spring. Ling (soul) roots strongly and firmly in the Huang Hu stage of awakening within quiet when unsolicited Qi spontaneously creates Zhen (true) water. The Heart spring of fluid flows clear and quietly, in the Yao Ming stage of explicit and implicit, unbidden fluid creates Zhen (true) fire. In fire dwells Zhen (true) dragon, in water dwells Zhen (true) tiger. Dragon and Tiger copulate creating the yellow sprout, the yellow sprout achieves the status of great medicine, and this is Jin Dan (golden pill). When Jin Dan is established that is the Shen Xian immortal level.

5. Lu asks:
When the Jin Dan (golden pill) is achieved, refining human substance to the Xian (immortal level), able to travel in ten states, that is understandable. What is the yellow sprout?

Zhong answers:
The yellow sprout is the offspring of the Zhen (true) dragon and the Zhen (true) tiger are.

6. Lu asks:
What is the relevance of the dragon and the tiger?

Zhong answers:
Dragon is not Liver; it is Yang dragon, the Yang dragon came from Li (fire palace) in the Zhen (true) waters realm. Tiger is not Lung; it is the Yin tiger from Kun (water palace) in the Zhen (true) fire's realm.

Chapter Seven: Discussion of the Water and Fire

1. Lu asks:

He who seeks longevity must refine the Jin Dan (golden pill). To refine the golden pill, one must first obtain the yellow sprout. The yellow sprout requires achieving special interaction between the dragon and tiger. The true dragon comes from the Li Gong (fire palace). The true tiger is born in the Kan (water) location. Li and Kan mean water and fire. What are the characteristics of water and fire?

Zhong answers:

Reference is made to water in the human body in the following locations: the four seas, the five lakes, the nine rivers, the three islands, magnificent pond (Hua Chi) , phoenix pond (Feng Chi) , Heavenly pond (Tian Chi) , jade pond (Yao Chi) , Kun pond (Kun Chi), primary pool (Yuan Tan), spacious park (Lang Yuan), spirit water (Shen Shui), golden wave (Jin Bo), beautiful liquid (Qiong Ye), jade spring (Yu Quan), crisp Yang (Yang Su) and white snow (Bai Xue). There are many water places in the body.

Reference is made to fire in the human body only in the following three locations: Emperor's fire (Jun Huo), ministerial fire (Chen Huo), and the citizen's fire (Min Huo).

The source of these three fires is the Yuan Yang (source Yang), which produces true (Zhen) Qi. When true Qi accumulates, the result is good health. When true Qi is deficient, the result is illness. If due to exhaustion of true Qi, the Yuan Yang has become abnormal, is exhausted, and has affected the pure Yang, the Yuan Shen (source spirit) then leaves the body. This is called death.

2. Lu asks:

In the human body, it takes just a drop of Yuan Yang to

support the three fires. Since the three fires arise amidst a gathering of Yin water, they are easily overwhelmed, and it is difficult for them to flare up into a blaze. In this situation, when Yang fire is scarce and Yin water is abundant, this causes a rapid decline, preventing one from achieving longevity. What can we do about this?

Zhong answers:
The Heart is the sea of blood, the Kidney is the sea of Qi, the brain is the sea of marrow, and the Spleen and Stomach are the sea of water and grain. These are the four oceans. Each of the five organs has both fluid and direction: east, west, south, north and center, and these directions are called the five lakes.

The Small Intestine is two Zhang four Chi in length and has nine bends, which are called the nine rivers. The lower part of the Small Intestine is called the Yuan Tan (Source Lake).

The crown of the head is called the Upper Island, the Heart is called the Middle Island, and the Kidney is called the Lower Island. The root source (Gen Yuan) and the spacious park (Lang Yuan) are located among the three islands.

The magnificent pond (Hua Chi) is below the yellow court (Huang Ting) in the abdomen. The jade pond (Yao Chi) is in front of the palace of elixir (Dan Que) in the abdomen. The top of the Kun pond in the brain connects to the jade capital (Yu Jing). The Heavenly pond (Tian Chi) in the brain is directly across from the inner courtyard (Nei Yuan).

The phoenix pond (Feng Chi) is located between the Heart and Lung; the jade pond (Yu Chi) is located between the lips and the teeth. Spirit water (Shen Shui) is produced by Qi. The golden wave (Jin Bo) descends from the sky. The beautiful liquid (Qiong Ye) and jade spring (Yu Quan), which are both nourish and moisten, come from the residence of the red dragon.

When the human body is shed, only then can the white snow (Bai Xue) and Yang crisp (Yang Su) be seen. When one is irrigating to nourish the fire, both the jade liquid (Yu Ye) and the gold liquid (Jin Ye) can be turned into the golden pill. There is a limit for adding these and extract processing and one must invisible bathe. The Middle Dantian and then the Lower Dantian can both be transformed through refining one's shape. The Jade medicine (Yu Yao) and the golden flower (Jin Hua) can be transformed into a yellow and white substance and become refined into the nectar (Gan Lou), which produces a special fragrance. This is called a water effect.

The citizen's fire (Min Huo) ascends to assist the Kidney Qi in creating true water (Zhen Shui). When the Kidney water ascends, it interacts with the fluid of the Heart to produce true Qi (Zhen Qi). This has the minor effect of removing evil spirits and reducing illness and the major effect of refining substances and producing the golden pill (Jin Dan). The microcosmic orbit (Xiao Zhu Tian of microcosmic orbit circulation) can be used to light the fire which ignites in the body; forces the Yang gate to close, and in this way, essence (Jing) can be transformed into the golden pill (Jin Dan).

There are nine other provinces in the body which nourish the Yang spirit; they burn the accumulation of the three corpses and clear up the Yin ghosts. Ascending, they strike the three gates; descending them wear down the seven spirits (Po).

Practice can turn the body into a Qi body which is light and which soars. When Qi is refined into Shen, the body is shed like a cocoon. This is called a fire effect.

3. Lu asks:

As he starts to understand this life process, the patient's fire decreases and the water increases. Yet the body tends to easily decline. The workings of water and fire are many. How can the few overcome the many, the weak vanquish the strong?

Zhong answers:

The numbers two and eight eliminate Yin. Nine and three cause Yang to increase. The bright red golden pill can be made in a matter of days. The numbers seven back and nine circles bring about the return of the immortal fetus.

True (Zhen) Qi is in the Heart and the Heart is the source of all fluids. The Yuan Yang is in the Kidney, also called the sea of Qi.

The Urinary Bladder is the citizen's fire (Min Huo); it is not only as citizen's fire and also the mansion of fluids.

If the practitioner doesn't understand these mysteries, he will have difficulty transforming Qi and will inevitably suffer illness and death

4. Lu asks:

What is transformation? Yang grows and Yin is consumed. How can the golden pill be transformed into the immortal fetus?

Zhong answers:

The distance between the Heart and the Kidney is eight Cun four Fen in length. This corresponds to the distance between the sky and earth. The Qi and fluid are at the Tai Ji (maximum) stage, creating each other, just as Yin and Yang are interacting.

One day has twelve Shi (two hour periods), this is corresponds to one year having twelve months.

The Heart generates fluids, but the Heart doesn't produce the fluid, because the fluid from the Lungs descends to the Heart. Fluid flows like a wife visiting her husband's palace, descending to the Lower Dantian. This can be called the wife visiting her husband's palace.

The Kidney creates Qi, but it does not produce all the Qi by itself. Qi from the Urinary Bladder ascends to the Kidney. The Qi behaves like a son and his mother, moving from lower to upper, facing the Middle source (Zhong Yuan). This can also be called the husband visiting the wife's palace.

Liver Qi guides Kidney Qi upward to the Heart. The Heart and fire communicate and cause vapor in the Lung; Lung fluid bears downward.

Fluid from the Heart is called Heart fluid. Fluid created in the Heart which is not consumed is called true fire (Zhen Huo). Lung fluid conveys Heart fluid downward to the Kidney. Kidney water and Heart fluid communicate, saturating the Urinary Bladder. The Qi of the Urinary Bladder ascends to Kidney; Qi from the Kidney is called Kidney Qi. The Qi created in the Kidney which is not consumed is called true fire (Zhen Huo). True fire comes from water in Huang Hu stage of awakening: within quiet comes substance which cannot be seen by the eyes and cannot be touched with the hands. True water (Zhen Shui) comes from fire in Yao Ming stage of implicit and explicit, followed by essence (Jing). It can be seen, but cannot be held retained. If it can be held retained, it cannot be held retained consistently.

5. Lu asks:
Kidney is water. Qi is created within the water and this is called true fire (Zhen Huo). What substance is within the fire? Heart is fire. Fluids are created within the fire and this is called true water (Zhen Shui). What is the essence of the

water? The substance or essence of water has no shape and it is difficult to obtain. If obtained, what use does it have?

Zhong answers:
The ancient sages who realized the Tao never practiced without using these two substances. They were able to copulate and produce the yellow sprout; finally enough transform a fetus into great medicine. This is called the true dragon and true tiger.

Chapter Eight: A Discussion of the Dragon and the Tiger

1. Lu Asks:

The dragon is Liver's manifestation. The tiger is Lung's manifestation. The Heart fire creates fluid called true water (Zhen fluid). The water is not yet recognized as a true dragon (Zhen dragon), if it is not from the Yao Ming of implicit and explicit stage. The dragon is not found in the Liver, but comes from the Li (☲) of fire palace, why? Kidney water within creates Qi, the Qi is true fire (Zhen Huo). True fire in its in Huang Hu of awakening within quiet stage is hidden true tiger (Zhen Hu). Why is the tiger not found in the Lung, but instead comes from Kan (☵) of water palace?

Zhong answers:

The dragon expresses Yang nature, rising into the sky in flight. The dragon's breath billows out in the form of clouds and all below enjoy the benefits of rain. The dragon is green, its location is the Jia Yi (sky stem), its substance is wood, its timing is spring, the dragon path is benevolence, and it is seen in Zhen (☳) of the Taoism's trigram. It corresponds to the Liver.

The tiger expresses Yin nature, runs along the earth, and its roar creates the wind; it reigns in the mountains and is held in the highest esteem. The tiger is white, it is fond in the Geng Xin (sky branch), its substance is metal, its timing is autumn, its path is honorable, and it with Taoism's trigram Dui (☱). In the body, it corresponds to the Lung.

The Liver expresses Yang its nature while residing in the Yin position. The Kidney Qi feeds Liver Qi in the way of mother and her son, and as water creates wood. The Kidney Qi is the source of Liver Qi. The Liver Qi arises when Kidney is full of Yin, propelling the ascension of pure Yang Qi.

The Lung demonstrates his Yin nature while occupying the Yang position. The Heart fluid supplies the basis for Lung fluid, this is called husband supports his wife, and as fire smelts metal. The Heart's fluid flows to the Lung, precipitation the movement of Lung fluid and the abundant Lung fluid is eliminated the Heart surplus Yang. From the Lung, these pure Yin fluids descend.

The Liver belongs to Yang. This Yang owes its origin to Kidney's surplus Yin, which Qi through the Liver transmutes to pure Yang. Pure Yang includes Zhen Yi (true one) water in the Huang Hu of awakening within quiet stage, transparent and without shape, this is Yang dragon.

The Lung belongs to Yin. This Yin owes its origin to surplus Heart Yang which generates fluid which the Qi through the Lung refines to pure Yin. Pure Yin fluid carries on center Yang (Zhen Yang) Qi, in Yao Ming of explicitly and implicitly stage without being seen, this is Yin tiger.

The Qi is ascending and fluid is descending normally they do not interact, but the Qi's Zhen Yi (true one) water conjoins with fluid, fluid's center Yang (Zheng Yang) Qi conjoins Qi automatically.

If one is mastering this transformation, reserving the Kidney Qi, the Qi collects Zhen Yi (true one) water and the Heart fluid is consolidated, from the Heart fluid collects center Yang (Zheng Yang) Qi. As a son and his mother depend upon and care for each other, days pass, a small orb of the size of grain of millet results, and after a hundred days the medicine is fully complete. Three hundred days later, the immortal fetus has become strong, and after another three hundred days, the fetus is fully established. Round as a marble, colored like a scarlet tangerine; this is the Dan Yao (inner medicine). It keeps its power forever, even surviving catastrophe; this is earth Shen Xian of the realm of immortal spirit.

2. Lu asks:
Kidney water creates Qi; this Qi has Zhen Yi (true one) water which is Yin tiger. This is tiger meeting fluid. Heart fire creates fluid; this fluid has center Yang (Zheng Yang) Qi which is Yang dragon. The dragon and the Yang Qi have bonded together.

Gathering to gather falls in a similar category. Materials are naturally divided by their characteristics, and their patterns of behavior. Qi occurs and the fluid descends, Qi's Zhen Yi (true one) water descends to the five organs. Fluid occurs and the Qi ascends, fluid's center Yang (Zheng Yang) Qi carries water up to the throat (Zhong Lou).

If the true water follows the fluid descending and the tiger does not meet the dragon, then the true Yang follows the ascending Qi, and the dragon does not meet the tiger. How does the yellow sprout appear? Without the yellow sprout how can there be great internal medicine?

Zhong answers:
Kidney Qi occurs in the manner of the sun rising at dawn from the ocean. Fog and clouds cannot obscure this brightness.

Fluid descends drip by drip, how can it win the Qi? When the Qi is strong the Zhen Yi (true one) water will be prosperous. The Heart fluid has been born. As cold weather freezes life, the warmth of breath cannot expel the cold. Qi rises as a jadeite veil, how can it maneuver the fluid? When fluid is strong the center Yang (Zheng Yang) Qi can be strong or weak.

3. Lu asks:

Qi and fluid arise with different timing. With the proper timing of the birth of Qi, Zhen Yi (true one) water is also abundant. With the proper timing of the birth of fluid, center Yang (Zheng Yang) Qi is also prosperous. Why can we not predict abundance and decline?

Zhong answers:
Kidney Qi is easily exhausted, the true (Zhen) tiger is difficulty to have. Heart fluid is difficult to gather, the true (Zhen) dragon is seldom exhausted. Ten thousand books have been written about the Jin Dan (Golden pill); all discuss the relationship of Yin and Yang, the essence of which is the relationship between the dragon and the tiger. Among Taoist practitioners there may be some understanding of the theory of dragon and the tiger, but no knowledge of the timing of their copulation, nor the method of the creation of the elixir. Therefore from ancient times to the present, practitioners are practicing throughout their lives, pausing at their small successes, they achieve longevity but they do not move higher to the immortal level. This is because their bodies do not reach the state of the inner copulation of the green dragon and the white tiger, and therefore they cannot gather the yellow sprout into the Dan Yao (internal medicine).

Chapter Nine: Discussion of the Jin Dan (golden Pill) and the Use of Inner Medicine

1. Lu asks:

Now that the dragon and tiger theory is understood, what is the meaning of the Jin Dan (golden pill)?

Zhong answers:

Medicine can be used to treat disease. There are three causes for disease:

First, there is exposure to wind and dampness, and exposure to the cold after being in the summer heat.

Secondly, there is exhaustion and an excessive, leisurely lifestyle, not eating when hungry, not eating at a routine time, overeating, having an erratic lifestyle, and becoming ill from seasonal changes or the prevalence of certain diseases in certain seasons.

Thirdly, if one does not practice, and burns a candle at both ends, exhausting and depleting the Yuan (source) Qi and Yang, this speeds up the aging process, causing one to become gaunt and silly, the body's Qi depleted, the Hun (controllable Yang Shen of mind) to disappear and the Shen spirit to vaporize. Oh, one sighs, there is no more mastering of the four directions of spirit. Finally, one dies in the wilderness. This is death from sickness.

Seasonal influences are one the causes for disease. Throughout the seasons of spring, summer, autumn and winter, one needs to be able to master and adapt to the changes of temperature of cold, hot, warm and cool. If there is excess Yang, and Yin is deficient, one needs to cool down the Yang. If there is excess Yin, and Yang is deficient, one needs to warm up the Yin.

Elderly people have more illnesses from the cold and young

people have more illnesses from heat. If one is overweight, has excess phlegm and easily gains weight, this tends to lead to stagnation syndromes. Male's illness is due to Qi; female's illness is due to blood. Strengthen the deficiency and calm and eliminate the excess. These conditions may be treated by acupuncture and herbs.

If the patient does not have a healthy lifestyle and has a seasonal sickness, he can be treated and healed by a good doctor with a clear diagnosis and proper medicine.

How does one can treat aging and serious diseases? A wise doctor can cure intestinal tumors and patch up torn muscles, repair the skull and reconnect the extremities. But to reverse wrinkles and grey hair, make the face smooth and beautiful like a child's, keep the body permanently from death, this no one can do.

2. Lu asks:

If one does not have a proper lifestyle, and illness is caused by seasonal influences, a good doctor and high quality herbs can cure the illness. If there is deficiency, decay, diseases of aging, Qi depletion and a painful process towards death, can this be healed? Is there any medicine for these conditions?

Zhong answers:

Disease has three by which it maybe treated. Seasonal disease can be treated by herbs. Diseases of aging can be treated two ways: the first way uses the internal Dan (pill), and the second way uses the external Dan (pill).

3. Lu asks:

What is the external Dan (pill)?

Zhong answers:

Gao Shang Yuan (an ancient master), who taught Taoist

theory explains the Heaven and earth ascending and descending, and the sun and moon circulation theory. From then on, there are many Jin Dan elixir books in existence, and the public has access to the Taoist great pathway.

Guang Chengzi (an ancient master) taught the Yellow Emperor, who in his spare time followed the old teaching and practiced for a long time, but he did not see achievement.

Guan Chengzi used the theory of communication between the Heart and Kidney's true Qi and true water, the Qi and water's true Yin and true Yang, combined into great medicine, and comparable to the connection between metal and stone, with hidden treasure in it. He used this internal medicine theory to refine the great pill in the Kong Dong Mountain.

One of eight stones used is the cinnabar. From cinnabar, mercury is extracted.
One of five metals used is the black lead, and from this lead, silver is extracted.

Mercury is as a Yang dragon, silver is as a Yin tiger. Cinnabar is as red as Heart fire; Kidney water is as black as the blackness of lead. The practicing must follow the Year's fire and Shi (daily timing) of the yearly calendar schedule so that it matches the Qian (☰) and Kun (☷) and Heaven and earth's timing. Monthly, extract and add, refine it, using Wen (mild) and Wu (strong) optimal temperature of fire.

There is a three layers stove inside the body, each layer has nine Cun (length measure), and it is square outside and circular inside. The stove collects the Qi from the eight directions, and matches the changes of the four seasons.

The golden Ding (the three legged pot that represents the cooking and processing of our internal medicine and awakened awareness) includes lead and mercury, as characterized as Lung fluid.

Using sulfur for a medicine mix with Ling (soul) cinnabar is as characterized as an elderly yellow face lady (Huang Po). Take it for three years and one has small success; this Dan will stop hundreds of diseases. Take for six years and one has middle level success; it will produce a longer life. Nine years produces higher level success, so that one can be lifted freely and has a great amount of power, enough to run a thousand and even ten thousand Li (length measure). One cannot go into the Feng Lai (one of the Taoist mountains), but he can stay in the mortal realm through great calamities and never die.

4. Lu asks:
From ancient times until now, there have been many practitioners who have refined the Dan, yet there are very few who achieved full success. Why is this so?

Zhong answers:
There are three reasons practitioners do not succeed. First, they cannot distinguish true from false material for the medicine, they do not know the timing for withdrawing fire and adding the optimal temperature, for mixing up the treasure that vaporized as dust, and they are using the wrong time and day; thus they end with nothing.

Secondly, even if one has good material for the medicine, he may not understand the optimal temperature of fire and timing. Or even if they understand the timing and optimal fire temperature, they may miss the correct material for the medicine, therefore there is no success.

If one has good material for the medicine, and has optimal fire temperature, chooses the correct year, month and day, adds and extracts using the correct time and amount, the Qi will be full and the Jin Dan will be accomplished.

But if anything is missing in the external preparation, one will be unable to achieve the Xuan (emptiness with substance) Crane roars in the sky; missing the bait, with still no success. This is the third reason.

The material for the medicine is the fruit of Heaven and earth's elegant Qi. The optimal temperature of fire is Shen Xian's (Spirit immortal) successful method. In the ancient Three Huang (Three Kingdoms) dynasty, the yellow emperor refines the Jin Dan that needs to circle nine times inner of body for the desired accomplishment

After the five emperors, there is a method of balance with whole Yuan (source) to refine the Dan (pill). It takes three years to refine and establish the Jin Dan.

In the Seven Countries wars, fierce Qi stagnated in the environment and dead bodies were everywhere. The material for the medicine could not receive the Heaven and earth's elegant Qi, and during this time there was no material of the right for the medicine, and successful practitioners escaped to the rock valley where lived peacefully until their deaths. Some of them wrote on bamboo strips and silk the method for distilling the Jin Dan, but their writings were lost and damaged over the years and no longer exist. If just the mortal world's material for medicine is used, the emperor Qin Shi Huang who built the great wall does not need to look for the medicinal material in the island, to extend his life. If the formula for Jin Dan had been in the world of mortals, Wei Bai Yang (one of the Taoist masters) would not have needed to develop the Zhou Yi (Yi Jing of eight trigram sutra). Wrong knowledge has been transmitted to the general population, misleading thousands who exhausted their families and failed in seeking the external medicine because of wrong knowledge.

5. Lu asks:
The external Dan theory came from the Taoist Master Guan Chenzi. Used as internal cultivation, it takes nine years to achieve success. Also, the material for the medicine and the Jin Dan formula are difficult to obtain. At the highest level it can only enable one to fly; it cannot do anything else of a miraculous nature, or make one a saint, nor can it gain the practitioner entrance to the realms of the immortals. Can you tell me the theory of internal medicine?

Zhong answers:
External medicine cannot be used. The practitioner's body root source is not strong enough in old age even with the enlightenment of old age to attain to this achievement. The Kidney is the root of Qi, and if the root does not go deep enough then the leaf is not luxuriant. The Heart is fluid's source, and if the fluid is not clear then it does not flow for a long time. The internal medicine elixir has five metals and eight stones, and it takes days and months to refine them into the three levels. Each level has three levels, which equals nine levels. The dragon and tiger great Dan assists the practitioner to receive the true Qi. It refines the body shape in the mortal world and makes it so light one is able to fly.

If one has practiced internal cultivation, understands coupling at the correct time, and knows the collecting method, then the Xian (immortal) fetus is accomplished, and soon can be liberated into the Xian level in days. If someone is still not awake, and persistently takes the external Dan, adds more fire to cook it, and spends days perfecting the medicine, wanting to enter into the level of Heaven, one can only smile at these useless efforts .

Even if we do not find out the source of the external medicine, we certainly need to explain the details of the internal golden elixir. The substance for the internal medicine comes from the Heart and Kidney, and everyone has this substance. The internal Jin Dan's substance is in Heaven and earth as seen in the external sky and earth. Optimal fire temperature depends on the circulation of the sun and moon calculation that is calculated as husband and wife coupling. The immortal fetus comes and then the true Qi occurs. This true Qi within has Qi like a dragon caring for his bead. Great medicine is accomplished then as Yang Shen comes out; there is an extra body that is sloughed off as a cicada sheds its skin.

This internal medicine depends on the dragon and tiger coupling and producing the yellow sprout. The yellow sprout is divided into lead and mercury.

Chapter Ten: Discussion of Lead and Mercury and their Relationship

1. Lu asks:

Internal medicine comes from dragon and tiger. The tiger springs from Kan of the water palace; it is Qi's water. The dragon came from Li of the fire palace; it is water's Qi. The Yang dragon is formed using mercury refined from cinnabar. The Yin tiger is formed from the silver extracted from lead. The lead and mercury are external medicine; how can they be compared to dragon and tiger coupling, which produces the yellow sprout, and how can the yellow sprout be divided into lead and mercury? What correlates internally to lead and mercury?

Zhong answers:

Embraced as Tian Yi (Heaven's one) substance and the five metals' number one is black lead. Lead creates silver, lead is silver's mother. Cinnabar receives Sun's Qi into the head of all the stones. Cinnabar creates mercury, mercury is cinnabar's son.

It is difficult to extract lead's silver, and cinnabar's mercury. If silver and mercury are combined, they turn into treasure. This is the external lead and mercury combination theory.

Since antiquity theories pertaining to the effects of internal alchemical reactions inside the human body have differed and, in many case been abstruse of father and mother copulation of Jing (sperm) and blood (egg) combine which treasure true Qi guarded in the mother's pure Yin palace of the uterus; Shen (Spirit) is hidden in the environment of Yin and Yang still undivided; in three hundred days the fetus is accomplished, in five thousand days fetus Qi is full. In five elements system, the human body is Jing (essence) and blood in appearance and water came first. The five organs, the first to have been created is the Kidney. In the Kidney's water, hidden in the beginning stage embryo are the father and mother's true Qi; this hidden true Qi is lead. The Kidney creates Qi, the Qi has Zhen Yi (true one) water as the true tiger; this is lead's silver. Kidney Qi delivers to Liver Qi, Liver Qi delivers to Heart Qi, Heart Qi in Tai Ji (maximum) stage creates fluid, the fluid has Zheng Yang (center Yang) Qi within, and cinnabar is the Heart fluid. Mercury is Heart fluid's Zheng Yang Qi, which deposits enough of this Zheng Yang Qi and the Qi and fluid formed a fetus is delivered to the Huang Ting (yellow court) in the middle. Most important at this point is the timing for adding fire at its optimal temperature, which is processing cultivation of the immortal (Xian) fetus. Metaphor it is lead and silver combined into treasure.

Illustration:

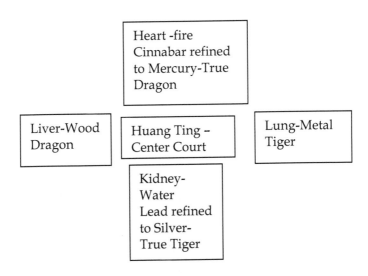

2. Lu asks:

In the realm of the five metals, one extracts silver from lead. Among the eight stones, cinnabar creates mercury. Set up the Ding (the three legged pot that represents the cooking and processing of our internal medicine and awakened awareness); mix the bait of substance to let mercury itself turns from cinnabar and silver turns into treasure. From our body's lead, how to extract silver? From our body's cinnabar, how to extract mercury? How to turn mercury into cinnabar? How does silver turn into treasure?

Zhong answers:

Lead is the father and mother's true Qi combined as one, pure and undivided; after the human body is formed it is hidden in the Kidney, Two Kidneys comparatively of Yin and Yang, lifted up by Qi; this is Yuan (source) Yang's Qi, this Yuan Qi has water within, this is Zhen Yi (true one) water. Water follows Qi rising up; Qi stops then water stops, Qi evaporates and then water disappears. The relationship of Qi and water is as son and mother that are undivided. One usually can see the inner Qi, but the water has not been seen.

If the Zhen Yi water combines with the Heart's Zhen Yang (center Yang) Qi, you have dragon and tiger copulating and creating a yellow sprout; the yellow sprout is a great medicine, and using Zhen Yi water as a placenta, embracing the Zhen Yang Qi, and characterized as at the beginning the father and mother's true Qi, which combines of Jing (sperm) and blood (egg) form the fetus, after transforming for three hundred days, the fetus Qi has fully accomplished, the creation of the body shape and already has Shen (Spirit), separate from the mother. This is form inner and outer matching creates a new form; using this form creates another form.

Within the Taoist practitioner, Kidney Qi communicates with

with Heart Qi; this Qi possesses hidden Zhen Yi water which carries Zheng Yang Qi; Qi transforms water into a fetus with a form like millet, and warms and cares on time without deficiency. In the beginning, Yin carries Yang; next the Yang refines the Yin. Qi transformed into Jing (essence), Jing into mercury, mercury into cinnabar, cinnabar into Jin Dan. The Jin Dan has been produced, true Qi has been self cultivated, refining the Qi into Shen, Shen to liberation. Thus the practitioner is transformed from the earlier dazed stage into a fire dragon, ridding the Xuan (emptiness with substance) crane into the Bon Lai (one of Taoism's magic) Island.

3. Lu asks:
The form coupling the form, form combined to create another form. The Qi coupling the Qi, Qi combined to create Qi, after about three hundred days, the shape divides. How does it differentiate into male and female shapes; how am I myself cinnabar Dan's color?

Zhong answers:
Father and mother copulate; father Jing (sperm) steps in first, and then mother's blood (egg) moving after; the blood covering Jing is female. Female is interior Yang with exterior Yin, as the mother's blood is covering the exterior. If the mother's blood steps in first and the father's Jing comes after, Jing covers blood as male. Male is interior Yin with exterior Yang, as the father's Jing (essence) appears on the exterior.

Therefore, the blood is birthed from the Heart without Zheng Yang Qi. The Jing, which is created in the Kidneys, has Zheng Yang Qi. Zheng Yang Qi is the basis of mercury and is mixed with the Zhen Yi water and harmonizes in the Huang Ting (yellow court) of the middle body. Mercury boils with lead soup; lead cooks by the heat of mercury. Lead without mercury cannot steam up Zhen Yi water. Mercury without lead cannot transform into pure Yang Qi.

4. Lu asks:

Lead in the Kidney creates Yuan (source) Yang Qi; this Qi has Zhen Yi water within, which cannot be seen. If lead has mercury, that mercury can create Zheng Yang Qi. The Zheng Yang Qi refines the lead; activated lead creates abundant Qi, which raises the Zhen Yi water up. The mercury is Zheng Yang Qi and is embraced by Zhen Yi water is a placenta and fetus; they are delivered into the Huang Ting (yellow court), and from here the coupling of dragon and tiger contentedly, but the Yin and Yang stop action, instead using lead soup to cook the Huang Ting, which depletes the Yin and dissipate the true Yang. How can great medicine be created and how can Qi create Qi?

Illustration:

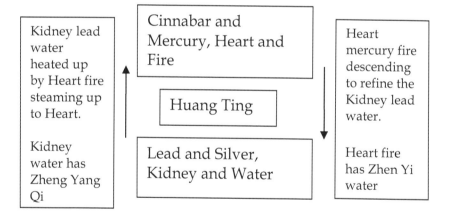

| Kidney lead water heated up by Heart fire steaming up to Heart.

Kidney water has Zheng Yang Qi | Cinnabar and Mercury, Heart and Fire

Huang Ting

Lead and Silver, Kidney and Water | Heart mercury fire descending to refine the Kidney lead water.

Heart fire has Zhen Yi water |

Zhong answers:

Kidney Qi goes into the Heart Qi, the ultimate Qi that creates fluid. The fluid has Zheng Yang Qi (center Yang Qi), coordinated with Zhen Yi water (true one water), this is the dragon and tiger coupling, since one has one millet size as Jin Dan of great medicine everyday, secure into the Huang Ting. The Huang Ting is below the Spleen and Stomach, above the Urinary Bladder and at the Heart's north and Kidney's south, Liver's west and Lung's east; upper is clear and lower is turbid; surrounded by the four colors, it contains two Sheng (volume measure), and the medicine moves through the eight water path day and night. If after the medicine is collected one does not add optimal fire temperature, the medicine will be dissipated and cannot be used. If one just adds fire without collecting, it cannot keep the Yin's Yang; the only effect is to warm and strengthen the Kidney Qi and the lower source.

If one wants to collect medicine which has the correct timing and the optimal fire temperature, first refine the lead, use Qi to increase the fire to strengthen and solidify the great medicine so it will patrol the Lower Dantian forever; this is the collecting and toning method. Refine the mercury to nourish the Dantian, extend life and achieve longevity; this is the earth Xian (immortal).

When one collecting medicine, extract from Yuan (source) lead with the Zhou Hou Fei Jin Jing (behind the elbows fly golden crystal through Xiao Zhu Tian of microcosmic orbit circulation) method. Approaching the extraction of lead one has to add mercury. If one does not add mercury, even returning the Jing (essence) to tone the brain, how can true Qi be created? If true Qi cannot be created, how can one accomplish Yang Shen spirit? One has to add mercury and must extract lead; if one does not extract the lead and wastes refining the mercury to nourish the Dantian, how can one transform cinnabar? If cinnabar is not changed, how can the Jin Dan be attained?

Chapter Eleven: Discussion of Extracting and Adding Theory

1. Lu asks:

Collecting the medicine depend on Qi's water, tempering the fire requires using the Qi's lead. To accomplish great medicine one has to extract lead in all the processing. If mercury is added it can strengthen the Dantian. What is the theory for extracting and adding?

Zhong answers:

In ancient times, the immortal transmitted the Tao to mortals. Since ancient people were innocent, their bodies and minds matched the Tao, but they did not the theoretical background for understanding it.

The sky and earth are as Yang and Yin, ascending and descending, changing between the warm, cool, cold and summer heat's Qi. There are certain seasonal timings in a year, which circulate over and over again as the Tao's pathway; sky and earth have existed since the beginning of time.

Mortals do not know, nor are they concerned with Taoist theory; they are as if blind in a corner. From a distance, the sun and moon's Jinghua (essential) communication theory, goes back and forth as the new moon turns into the full moon; the moon never misses becoming full each month. The circular motion never stops—the Tao is always present. The sun and moon are always present. The cold moves forward and the summer goes backwards; the summer leaves as the cold comes. Ordinary mortals do not realize how the sky and earth (up and down) communicate. The full moon becomes the waning moon, and then the waning moon returns to the full moon. Mortals may not understand the sun and moon circulation theories, and they burn their candle at both ends and waste their limited time. They enjoy wealth and extravagance to satisfy their life's dreams. They love and worry excessively and create karma for the next life. Before the song has stopped, their frustration comes. They may have fame and wealth, but their lover has gone. Greed for money and material wealth will lead one to have ten thousand calamities for a long time. They love their son and grandson and wish to be with them forever. The greedy mind never stops, in vain hoping for life to last forever, but the Yuan Qi (source Qi) and the true Qi (Zhen Qi) have been exhausted. It is only at the moment one has a severe disease that the mind quiets down. Death is here now, and one can finally let go of it all.

The true Xian (immortal) and higher saint, having sorrow for this reincarnation, hopes the mortal will not go into depravation, and passionately wants the public to have knowledge of the sky, earth, sun and moon theory, and understand that they last forever. First there is the sky and earth, Yang and Yin, up and down; next there is the sun and moon's Jinghua (essence and light) communication. If you have not yet reached the secret code of Heaven and understood the communication between the sky and earth, moon and sun and Yin Yang balancing theory, you are still just guessing about the magical Xuan (emptiness has substance) path.

Using internal medicine as compared to using external medicine is like comparing having emotion to having no emotion. No emotion is metal and stone. Metal and stone are external medicine. Having emotion is Qi and fluid. Qi and fluid are internal medicine.

Huge as the sky and earth, bright as the sun and moon, external medicine has metal and stone; internal medicine has Qi and fluid. After collecting one needs to add; after adding one needs to extract. Extracting and adding are the basis of transforming.

After Dongzhi mid winter, Yang rises from the earth, and the earth extracts the Yang's Yin. Tai Yin (the first level Yin) extracts the Yin's Yang into Jue Yin (the deepest level Yin), Shao Yang (second level Yang) adds Yin's Yang into Yang Ming (the highest level Yang). Jue Yin extracts Yin's Yin into Shao Yin (the middle level Yin). Yang Ming (the highest level Yang) adds Yang's Yin into Tai Yang (the first level Yang). This is Yin adding and extracting to transform to Yang from winter to summer. Otherwise, cold could not be transformed to warm, and warm could not change to hot.

After Xiazhi mid summer, Yin descends from sky and the sky extracts the Yin's Yang. Tai Yang (middle level Yang) extracts the Yang's Yin into Yang Ming (the highest level Yang), Shao Yin (first level Yin) adds the Yang's Yin into Jue Yin (the deepest level Yin). Yang Ming (the highest level Yang) extracts the Yang's Yang into Shao Yang (middle level Yang), and Jue Yin (the deepest level Yin) adds the Yin's Yang into Tai Yin (first level Yin). This is Yang adding and extracting Yang to enable the transforming from summer to winter. Otherwise, heat could not transform to cool, and cool could not change to cold. This is the effect of the sky and earth, Yang and Yin, up and down which change into the six Qi of Shao Yang, Tai Yang, Yang Ming, Shao Yin Tai Yin, and Jue Yin.

Illustration of Six Qi:

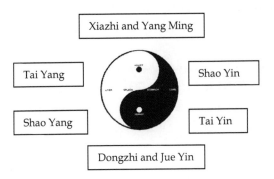

Xiazhi and Yang Ming

Tai Yang

Shao Yin

Shao Yang

Tai Yin

Dongzhi and Jue Yin

Xiaozhi mid summer: Yin descends from the sky and the sky extracts the Yin's Yang.

Tai Yin, the middle level Yin of cool extracts the Yin's Yang into Jue Yin of the deepest level Yin of cold.

Shao Yang, first level Yang of warm adds Yin's Yang into Yang Ming of the highest level Yang of heat.

Tai Yang, middle level Yang of warm extracts the Yang's Yin into Yang Ming of the highest level Yang of heat.

Shao Yin, first level Yin of between cold and hot adds the Yang's Yin into Jue Yin of the deepest level Yin of cold.

Jue Yin, the deepest level Yin of cold extracts Yin's Yin into Shao Yin of the first level Yin of cool.

Yang Ming, the highest level Yang of hot adds the Yang's Yin into Tai Yang of the middle level Yang of between warm and hot.

Yang Ming, the highest level Yang of hot extracts the Yang's Yang into Shao Yang, the first level Yang of warm.

Jue Yin, the deepest level Yin adds the Yin's Yang into Tai Yin of middle level Yin of cool.

Dongzhi mid winter: Yang rises from the earth; the earth is extracting Yang's Yin.

From the dark moon to the new moon, the moon receives and adds the sun's Hun (substance) and sun transforms and extracts the moon's Po (light) at the beginning of the cycle. As the new moon becomes full in fifteen days, the moon is extracting the sun's Po (light) and the sun is adding back the moon's Hun (substance), until the moon is full.

This is the full moon stage when the moon extracts sun's Po (light) and the sun adds moon's Hun (substance) and the Jinghua (essence and light) is full and brightens everywhere above and below.

For fifteen days after the full moon, the sun is extracting the moon's Hun (substance) and the moon is adding the sun's Po (light). The brightness is decay and Yin Po (substance) is full. This describes the moon waxing and waning and waning and waxing; this is the resulting transformation in nine and six with the interaction having the effect from adding and extracting.

Illustration:

The moon receives and adds the sun's Hun (substance) and the sun transforms and extracts moon's Po (light)

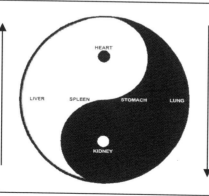

The moon is extracting the sun's Po (light) and the sun is adding moon's Hun (substance)

The sun is extracting the moon's Hun (substance) and the moon is adding the sun's Po (light)

The moon extracts the sun's Po (light) and the sun adds moon's Hun (substance)

People in general do not understand the method of Heavenly communication, and just guess at the Xuan (emptiness has substance) theory.

The true Xian (immortal) uses the human's desires for health and long life and gold and silver, by using lead and mercury and refining them into treasure, and uses gold and stone and refines them into medicine, as a way to follow the Taoist pathway.

If one uses no emotion and metal and stone with optimal fire temperature and adds and extracts in the preferred amount into external medicine, this results in longevity.

If one uses the part of oneself which has emotion's Zheng Yang Qi (center Yang Qi) and Zhen Yi (true one) water, and knows their coupling time, and understands the collecting method, and takes days and months, the Qi within has Qi, the Qi refines into Shen (spirit), and opens into liberation. This success has been rare from ancient time to the present.

From the mortal realm to the Heavenly there are few people who understand the theory of the Tao, that one needs strong aspiration and must renounce all worldly business, and follow the sky and earth, sun and moon pattern, into infinity, must avoid confusion with the path of external medicine, and pay attention into the Tao.

About the external medicine theory, from the ancient time to the present, a few theories may be heard, but the mortal still does not understand them, and has misguided him and the public, and has lost the wisdom of the ancients. They have refined cinnabar to make mercury, and have mixed mercury and lead and transformed mercury into copper. They do not care about health, and are crazy with the desire for money and material goods. They have used this method to share with others, using the Tao as a name only, but actually they are seeking profit and only looking to learn the gold and silver alchemy.

Ancient deities and higher Xian (immortals), following the mortal's preference to teaching, explained the lead and mercury theory as characterized inside the body. Furthermore, lead and mercury come from metal and stone. Even non-feeling metal and stone can be refined into treasure, therefore, inside our bodies, our organs and substances have emotion and spirit and they can transform and process inner lead and mercury with character success than external metal and stone, which have no feeling.

The Taoist practitioner does not have to persist in looking for external elixir and the right Ding (the three legged pot) in which to refine external medicine. The human body's lead, as it was since the beginning of Heaven and earth, is due to Taishi (at the very origin of emptiness with whole) which transforms into Taizhi (first original substance), which is the material's mother. Taizhi transforming into Taisu (divided original substance) is the origin of water's metal and functions as fire's water.

The Tao originated with the five elements. The collected medicine needs mercury added to it; adding mercury is needed to extract lead, therefore the process of extracting and adding does not occur outside of the body. From the Lower Dantian (field where one can make the golden pill) into the Upper Dantian, this is Zhou Hou Fei Jin Jing (Behind the elbows fly golden crystal through Xiao Zhu Tian of microcosmic orbit circulation) and the same as hauling He Che (the purple river vehicle) and the start of running the dragon and tiger. This is called reversing the Jing (essence) to nourish the brain which is attempting to attain immortality. Lead flows to the back, mercury descends from the center and from the Middle Dantian to the Lower Dantian. When the dragon and tiger dragon copulate the lead and mercury are transformed into the yellow sprout and the order of the five elements is reversed; from now on, extracting lead and adding mercury nourishes the Xian (immortal) fetus, and the three Dantian exchange energies back and forth.

If the five elements do not reverse, the dragon and tiger do not copulate, the three Dantians do not communicate, then the Xian (immortal) fetus is Qi deficient.

When one extracts lead and adds mercury, after one hundred days the medicine and Qi are fully accomplished; after two hundred days the immortal fetus is solid, after three hundred days the growth of the Xian fetus has been accomplished and true Qi is created. After the true Qi has been created, the Qi can be refined into Shen (spirit). Fully achieved and dissolving the body, the fetus Xian automatically is transformed. This is the immortal Shen Xian (spirit).

2. Lu asks:
From the metal and stone come external lead and mercury, which are refined as an extract and adding them creates treasure. Coming from our inner body are the hidden parents of Kidney's true Qi of lead, those Zhen Yi (true one) water and Zheng Yang Qi (center Yang Qi) are combined as medicine they are transformed into mercury; extracting and adding them can create Shen (spirit). Can true lead and true mercury be extracted and added?

Zhong answers:
At the beginning, one must first use lead refined into mercury; if one only uses lead it is not enough. Hence, to extract lead into the upper palace, Yuan (source) Qi has to assist it and return Jing (essence) into the brain. After number days one has mercury, and Yin evaporates, leaving pure Yang.

Jing (essential) transforms cinnabar, cinnabar turns into gold as true (Zhen) lead. This true lead comes from being united with the self's true Qi. The true lead is created from true Qi and the true Qi within has Zhen Yi (true one) water. Then the five Qi pilgrims to the source and the three Yangs gathering in the crown of the head will be created.

Golden Jin (golden essence) descends into the Lower Dantian, then rises up to refine the body and bones into a golden color, this is the true lead rising into the organs with white light. From the lower to upper and from the upper to lower, returning into the Jin Dan (golden pill) to refine the body; this is golden Jing back and forth power. From front to the back and from back to the front, this motion burns the body into Qi; this is true Qi's transformative function. If one does not have this extract or adding and collecting medicine and adding the optimal fire temperature, and just stops without the action, how can one reach achievement?

3. Lu asks:
When extracting and adding, how can we know the upper and lower, the correct amount of back and forth and front and back without any mistakes?

Zhong answers:
When it is rising one cannot descend, when it is the time to extract one cannot add, it is necessary to move from upper to lower and back and forth without missing the motion and time least bit. This is what He Che's (river vehicle) enables.

Chapter Twelve: Discussion of the He Che (river vehicles)

1. Lu asks:

What is He Che (river vehicle)?

Zhong answers:

An ancient, watching a cloud covering the sun observed that the cloud was like a lid under the sun casting shade below. He watched a leaf floating on a wave, and thought, oh; this leaf can carry material like a boat. Watch the wind making an awning flutter; the awning flaps back and forth ceaselessly; use this idea to make a vehicle; this vehicle has substance and appearance of the sky and earth, the moving wheels reflect the movement of the sun and moon.

High-level Taoists find a parallel vehicle in the body. The internal body has less Yang and more Yin, water is everywhere in the body, and water has the appearance of Yin, therefore, the internal He Che (river vehicle) is running not on land, but on water, and functions to carry substance from upper to lower, from front to back, driving and carrying substance to the eight ponds and four seas; rising to the sky, up to Kunlun (head) then to Jiji (Fire under the water environment), and running down to Fangji (in the lower abdomen); carrying Yuan (source) Yang, straight into Li (in the Heart) palace; carrying the true Qi into Shoufu ("longevity house", in the brain); communicating in the nine states (regions of the abdomen) without stopping; and patrolling the three mountains without rest. The dragon and tiger have been coupling to in order to drive Huangpo (yellow face lady) into the Huang Ting (yellow court); lead and mercury are divided, the golden boy has moved into Jinque (in mouth); Yuquan (spring of jade fluid) is created. This takes only a few seconds and produces a pot of golden fluid.

Without He Che to haul and assist the five elements, the five elements Qi is difficult to unite and form one. Without this vehicle to move through the body, how can the true Yin and Yang interact? The time of the flowing assists in caring for the Yang and refining the Yin as the He Che carries their energies without missing a little bit.

Refining the Yin and nourishing the Yang, the Kun (☷) Yin and Qian (☰) Yang are not pure yet, Yin and Yang do not communicate, the universe has not begun to move, and neither Qi, Jing (essence), nor blood communicate, He Che's capacity is needed.

All the achievements of circulating the essential Qi of the sky and Qi of the earth from exterior nature to the interior of the body; receiving and guiding the body Yuan (source) Yang from mortal to immortal; moving Yin, Yang and true Qi; nourishing and refining the body's Yuan (source) and Shen (spirit); all these achievements we attribute to the He Che.

2. Lu asks:
The He Che has such an important function. From what is the He Che made in the body? What is its substance? When we possess it, how can we utilize it?

Zhong answers:
The He Che is from north Zheng (center) water; the Kidney has hidden true (Zhen) Qi, the true Qi created Zheng (center) Qi is the river vehicle. It is rare to hear of the function of He Che; true Xian (immortal) keeps this secret.

The Qian (☰) Yang collected Kun (☷) Yin to create Kan (☵); Kan (☵) is water and is water's Yin's Jing (essence). Yang collected Yin, after Yang collects Yin, the Yang carries the Yin back in position, through Gen (☶), Zhen (☳) and Xun (☴); using the Yang collecting Yin, Yang takes Yin, haul into the Li (☲), use the Yang to create; this describes He Che (river vehicle) carrying Yin into Yang palace.

The Kun (☷) Yin collecting Qian (☰) Yang to create Li (☲),
Li (☲) is fire and is Yang's essence. Yin collected Yang, Yin
carries the Yang returning to Yang position, through Kun (☷),
Dui (☱) and Qian (☰); using the Yin collecting the Yang, Yin
takes Yang, it moves into Kan (☵) creating Yin. Therefore, the
He Che (river vehicle) carries the Yang into Yin palace.

The He Che is collecting the medicine in the upper nine
palaces (the upper nine magic squares), where gained to
descend into the Huang Ting (yellow court in the middle).
Extracting the lead under the Curve River, hauling it into the
upper Neiyuan (upper Dantian in the brain). Jade fluid and
gold fluid return to Jin Dan (golden pill), hauling it to refine
the body shape and carry the ascending water. Jun (emperor)
fire and Mein (citizen) fire can refine shape; hauling can assist
in refining the Jin Dan and guide fire down. Five Qi
pilgrimage the Yuan (source), hauling in different sequence.
Three flowers gather in the crown of head, and hauling on
different days. After the Shen (spirit) gathering there will be
suffering with more devils arriving, and the He Che carrying
the true fire burns the body and extinguishes the three
corpses. If the medicine should burn out, the He Che carries
the nectar for bathing without wave water.

3. Lu asks:
The He Che originates in north's Zheng (center) Qi, circulates
without stopping and carries Yin and Yang. There are
different achievements for different functions. Master Zhong,
would you please explain in detail?

Zhong answers:
Five elements circulate; from the beginning to end the path is
a circle. Reversing the direction of this five elements pattern,
the dragon and tiger transform to create the yellow sprout.

This is called the small He Che (river vehicle).

Zhou Hou Fei Jin Jing (behind the elbows the golden crystal flies through the Xia Zhu of microcosmic orbit circulation), return the Jing (essential crystal) into the Neiwan (Upper Dantian in the brain), extracts lead, adds mercury for the transformation into great medicine. This is the great He Che (river vehicle).

Dragon and tiger couple and create the yellow sprout; lead and mercury interact to create great medicine. True (Zhen) Qi creates the five Qi pilgrimage and transforms it into center source, Yang Shen achievements that liberate the three Shen (spirits) from the Neiyuan (upper Dantian). The purple Jin Dan achievement often has Xuan cranes (immortal cranes) flying facing each other, white jade and mercury appear as fire dragons flare up while ten thousand golden light beams brighten mortal bones like a beautiful bright Jade tree.

The Yang Shen travels in or out from the body without stagnation and the Yang Shen can travel in and out among mortals, this is Yu Ke level, which is the Purple He Che of the river vehicle achievement.

These three vehicles comprise upper, middle and lower achievements; the three level achievements experience are higher than the three levels of Buddhism. These three levels are named goat, deer and great ox He Che (river vehicle).

Behind the He Che (river vehicle), there are three more vehicles. Gathering fire to attack disease is the Shizhe (messenger) vehicle. If the upper to lower, Yin and Yang combine perfectly, water and fire harmonize to create the Jiji (water and fire harmonized) environment, where thunder emerges from quiet. This is the thunder (Lei) vehicle.

If the mind is overcome by business or emotional attachment, uncontrolled emotion will weaken the true Yang Qi. This is exterior controlling the interior. If a person lives a long period without enough rest, the Qi will be deficient and aging will be accelerated. If the external eight evils or five transmitted diseases attack, the true Qi cannot move, and if the Yuan (source) Yang is inadequate, sickness, premature aging and early death will occur. This is the broken (Po) vehicle.

4. Lu asks:
When the five elements reverse and the dragon and tiger copulate, the small river vehicle is running. When the three Dantians communicate and Zhou Hou Fei Jin Jing (Behind the elbows fly golden crystal through Xiao Zhu Tian of microcosmic orbit circulation), the great He Che (river vehicle) is running. When does the great purple He Che (river vehicle) run?

Zhong answers:
A practitioner who has an enlightened teacher learns to hear the Tao pathway, understands how the sky and earth communicate and can calculate the pathways of the sun and moon. Start by matching the Yin and Yang. Next gather water and fire. Then collect medicine with the optimal temperature, add mercury and extract lead. Now the small He Che runs. When Zhou Hou Fei Jin Jing (Behind the elbows the golden crystal flies through Xiao Zhu Tian of microcosmic orbit circulation) carries Jing (essence) into the crown of the head, Huang Ting (yellow court in the middle) great medicine is being accomplished, and one strike breaks through three gates to enter the Neiyuan (upper Dantian), it runs from the back and refines the front, nourishes the upper and refines the lower. Then the great He Che is definitely running. After the golden fluid and jade fluid return to the Jin Dan, the next steps are to refine the body, the Qi, and Shen, and at the last step, the refined Shen matches the Tao; this is the final

progress in achievements of the Tao. This is the journey from mortal to Xian (immortal) level, and the Purple He Che level has been attained.

Chapter Thirteen: Discussion of the Return to the Dan (the golden pill)

1. Lu asks:
Refine the body into Qi, refine the Qi into Shen, and refine the Shen into the Tao. Would you please explain what the return to Dan (the golden pill) is?

Zhong answers:
The Dan has no color; red and yellow are part of it. The Dan has no taste, sweet and bland cannot mix with it. Dan is Dantian. There are three Dantians: The Upper Dantian is the Shen (spirit)'s home; the Middle Dantian is the Qi's home; the Lower Dantian is the Jing's (essence) region. Essence creates Qi; Qi stays in the Middle Dantian. Qi creates Shen; Shen stays in the Upper Dantian. True (Zhen) water and true (Zhen) Qi combine to create Jing (essence); Jing stays in the Lower Dantian.

The practitioner has all these three Dan. Therefore, Kidney is mastering Qi, but has not yet made the pilgrimage into the Middle Yuan (source); Shen is hidden in the Heart, but does not reach into the upper court yet. If this Jinghua (essence and Qi) doesn't go back and forth and hasn't combined yet, those three Dan are useless.   .

2. Lu asks:
Xuan within has Xuan (emptiness with substance); every person has his own life. Life's Jing (essence) and Qi originally came from the parents' Yuan (source) Yang. If there is no Jing there will be no Qi and no Qi without your own Shen (spirit), this Shen (spirit) is your parents Yuan (source) Shen. This Jing, Qi and Shen are the three Dantians' treasures; when do they say in the Upper, Middle and Lower palaces?

Zhong answers:

The Kidney creates Qi. This is Qi which has the Zhen Yi (true one) water. This water returns down to the Lower Dantian; this is Jing (essence) nourishing the Ling (soul) root; from here, the Qi will automatically grow. The Heart creates fluid; this fluid has Zheng Yang Qi (center Yang Qi). This Qi returns to the Middle Dantian, this Qi nourishes the origin of Ling (soul); the Shen will be growing by itself. Gathering Ling (soul) into Shen, Shen matches the Tao, returns to the Upper Dantian, then sheds the mortal body and liberates.

3. Lu asks:
The Dantian has Upper, Middle and Lower parts, all return to the Dan, can you please let me know what the details and theory of the return to the Dan is?

Zhong answers:
There is small return to the Dan, great return to the Dan and seven return to the Dan, nine circles return to the Dan, golden fluid return to the Dan, jade fluid return to the Dan; Lower Dan return to the Upper Dan, Upper Dan return to the Middle Dan, Middle Dan return to the Lower Dan, using the Yang to return to the Yin Dan, using the Yin to return to the Yang Dan and more. They are not only different in name; there are also differences in the time and criteria for each return.

4. Lu asks:
What is the small return to the Dan?

Zhong answers:
Small return Dan comes from the Lower Yuan (source). The Lower Yuan (source) is master of the five organs and primary source of the foundation of the three Dantians. The water creates wood, wood creates fire, fire creates earth, earth creates metal, and metal creates water, in a mother and son relationship, this creation follows a set pattern for its creation and is like the deep affection between a mother and son.

Fire rules metal, metal rules wood, wood rules earth, earth rules water, water rules fire; these are the ruling relationships; which regulate each others' content, ruling and nourishing each other like husband and wife. Qi and fluid circulate back and forth, from Zi (11 p.m. to 1 a.m.) to Wu (11 a.m. to 1 p.m.); Yin and Yang start; from Mao (7 a.m. to 9 a.m.) to You (5 p.m. to 7p.m.) Yin and Yang stop. It takes one day and one night to return to the Lower Dantian, this circulation is the small return to the Dan. The practitioner is collecting the medicine and adding fire to the Lower Dantian.

5. Lu asks:
The small return to the Dan is now described; what is the great return to the Dan?

Zhong answers:
The dragon and tiger coupling create the yellow sprout; extracting lead and adding mercury create great medicine. In the Xuan Wu (water Kidney) palace, the Jin Jing (golden crystal) started, and Yu Jing's (jade capital mountain) true Qi started to rise; the river vehicle is running up to the hill. The jade fluid is wet and moving into Zhong Qu (center road), from the Lower Dantian into the Upper Dantian, the Upper Dantian back into the Lower Dantian, starting from the back and running into the front and when this circulation is accomplished, this is the great return to the Dan. The practitioner started from the Middle Dantian, dragon and tiger coupling become flying Jin Jing (golden crystal), nourishing Xian (immortal) fetus and creating true Qi, establishing the great Dan.

6. Lu asks:
The great return to the Dan is now known, how about the seven returns to the Dan and the nine circles return to the Dan?

Zhong answers:

The numerical calculations for the five elements are fifty has five, the sky is one and earth is two, sky is three and earth is four, the sky is five and earth is six, the sky is seven and earth is eight, the sky is nine and earth is ten. One, three, five, seven and nine are Yang, totaling twenty five. Two, four, six, eight, ten are Yin, totaling thirty.

Starting from the Kidney, Kidney water is one, Heart fire is two, Liver wood is three, Lung metal is four and Spleen earth is five; this is the five elements creation due to accomplish amount and totaling three Yang and two Yin.

Starting from the Kidney, Kidney water is six, the Heart fire is seven, the Liver wood is eight, the Lung metal is nine and the Spleen earth is ten, these are the five elements established due to their established order and totaling there Yin and two Yang.

After the five element movement pathway has created Kidney water, Kidney has one and six; fire is the Heart, the Heart has two and seven; wood is the Liver, Liver has three and eight; metal is the Lung, Lung has four and nine; earth is the Spleen, Spleen has five and ten. Every organ has Yin and Yang.

Yin is extreme on eight and two is abundant, therefore, Qi flows into the Liver, the Kidney's extra Yin is extinguished by the Liver's eight. Qi flows into the Heart's two and into the Taiji (extreme) stage to create Yin, the number two is in the Heart and eight is in the Liver.

Yang in nine is the maximum and one is abundant, hence the fluid flows into the Lung's nine, and the Heart's extra Yin is extinguished. Fluid goes into the Kidney's one, into the Taiji (extreme) stage to create Yang, the number one is in the Kidney and nine is in the Lung.

Practice in this environment the dragon and tiger copulating, collecting Heart's Zheng Yang Qi (center Yang Qi). This Zheng Yang Qi is Heart's seven, seven returns to the Middle Yuan (source) and into the Lower Dantian nourishes the Xian (immortal) fetus and returns back to the Heart, This is seven returns Dan.

If two and eight Yin are extinguished, true (Zhen) Qi created, but the Heart is without Yin, the Heart's two is extinguished. Great medicine created and Liver without Yin, the Liver's number eight has been extinguished. Therefore, when the number two and eight Yin have been extinguished then the nine and three Yang grow. The Liver uses extreme Yang to assist the Heart, so the Liver's number three is abundant. Seven has returned to the Heart to exhaust the Lung fluid, the Lung's nine circles assist the Heart, the nine and three assist the Yang to grow, this is the nine circle return to the Dan.

Chart of sky and earth and their numerical:

Sky: One	Sky: Three	Sky: Five	Sky: Seven	Sky: Nine
Earth: Two	Earth: Four	Earth: Six	Earth: Eight	Earth: Ten

The five elements' numbers are one, two, three, four and five; these are characterized by three Yangs and two Yins.

Illustration of the five elements' numbers in the inner body:

Numbers one to five are prenatal numbers. The five elements' numbers are one, two, three, four and five; these are characterized by three Yangs and two Yins.

Numbers six to ten are postnatal numbers.

The innate order of creation of the five elements of the prenatal began with the Kidney water is one, the Heart fire is two, the Liver wood is three, the Lung metal is four and the Spleen earth is five.

The order established postnatally began with the Kidney water is six, the Heart fire is seven, the Liver wood is eight, the Lung metal is nine and the Spleen earth is ten.

Fire Heart:
Two and seven.

Wood Liver: Metal Lung:
Three and eight.   Earth Spleen: Four and nine.
                        Five and ten.

Water Kidney:
One and six.

7. Lu asks:
Seven returning is using the Heart's Yang to return to the Heart in the Middle Dantian. Nine circles are used when the Lung's Yang comes from the Heart and returns to the Heart in the Middle Dantian. The seven returning and nine circles are understood; what is gold fluid, jade fluid, upper, middle and lower Yin and Yang communication to return to the Dan?

Zhong answers:
The most ancient sage pointed out that Lung fluid descending into the Lower Dantian is golden fluid returning to the Dan; the Heart fluid descending to the Lower Dantian is jade fluid returning to the Dan; this is good, but not complete. The Lung gives birth to the Kidneys as metal gives birth to water; metal

into the water, how can it return to the Dan? Kidney controls Heart as water rules fire; water into fire, how can it return to the Dan?

Gold fluid is the Lung fluid, Lung fluid as the placenta, embraces the dragon and tiger, and is protected, into the Huang Ting (yellow court). The great medicine is almost created; Zhou Hou Fei Jin Jing (Behind the elbows fly golden crystal through Xiao Zhu Tian of microcosmic orbit circulation) extract behind the elbow, and fly the Lung fluid into Upper palace and then down, returning to the Middle Dantian, and from the Middle Dantian returning to the Lower Dantian; this is the golden fluid returning to the Dan.

Jade fluid is Kidney fluid, Kidney fluid follows the Yuan (source) Qi ascending in its pilgrimage to the Heart, is deposited as gold water, lifted up and filling a full jade pond, spreading as Qiong Hua (jade flower), refining as white snow. If absorbed, from the Middle Dantian to the Lower Dantian, it is the medicine bathing the Xian (immortal) fetus. If it rises from the Middle Dantian into the four extremities it refines the body, and then regenerates mortal bones. Until inner body rises no higher and ceases to absorb, continuing circulation, this is jade fluid returning Dan.

Extreme Yin creates Yang, Yang within has Zhen Yi (true one) water, the water follows the Yang rising up, this is the Yin returning to the Yang Dan.

Extreme Yang creates Yin, Yin within has Zheng Yang Qi, this true Qi follows the Yin descending down, this is the Yang returning to Yin Dan.

The process of refining the brain and the crown of head is from the lower returning to the upper. Jiji (water and fire harmonized) irrigate, from the upper returns to the middle.

Refine the Dan and add more fire; from the middle it returns to the lower. Refine substance and burn the body, from the lower return to the middle.

Reversing the five elements cycle, the three Dantians exchange places back and forth with each other. Refine the shape to transform into Qi; refine the Qi into the Shen. From the Lower Dantian it moved to the Middle Dantian, from the Middle Dantian it moved to the Upper Dantian, from the Upper Dantian moved out to the Tian Men (Tian Men of Heaven's door: the junction of the frontal and parietal bone). Shed the mortal body, into the level of the Xian (immortal) level. The shift of three levels has been accomplished: from lower to upper into higher, into immortal, no return, but returned.

Chapter Fourteen: Discussion of Refining the Body

1. Lu asks:
Return to the Dan is now known, what is refining the body?

Zhong answers:
After birth, the body and Shen (spirit) are exterior and interior. Shen is mastering the body; the body is Shen's house. The body's Jing (essence) creates Qi, Qi creates Shen. Fluid creates Qi, Qi creates fluid, and this is the body's mother and son relationship.

Water creates wood, wood creates fire, fire creates earth, earth creates metal and metal creates water, this describes the five elements' mother and son relationship.

Qi deliveries from mother and son and fluid deliveries from husband and wife are the Yin and Yang relationship in the body. Water transforms into fluid, fluid transforms into blood, blood transforms into Jin (thinner fluid); this Yin has yet to create.

If Yin and Yang are out of balance and the Yin has no way to create, mucous will leak from the nose, tears from the eyes, thick drool from the mouth, and the body will sweat uncontrollably.

Qi transforms into Jing (essence), Jing transforms into the bead, the bead transforms into mercury, mercury transforms into cinnabar; this Yang has yet Yin to create.

If Yin and Yang are out of balance, the Yang decays and there will be sickness, aging, suffering and death. This is because without Yin the Yang cannot be created; Yang cannot be formed without Yin. The practitioner who only practices the Yang without the Yin or practices without refining the substance creates an imbalance of Yin and Yang.

The Qi which the body receives the beginning is the parents' true Qi; the Jing (essence) and blood form the fetus, which stays in the mother's pure Yin uterus. Yin with the Yin creates Yin, form creates form. The fetus has fully abundant Qi, this six Che (length measure)'s body belongs entirely to Yin, and only has one drop of Yuan (source) Yang. If one wants to lengthen life without death one has to refine the body and undergo many great difficulties. If one wants to go beyond mortality and become an immortal, one has to refine the body to transform it into Qi and then to create a body beyond this one.

2. Lu asks:
Body is Yin, Yin has to have form. Using this form, the practitioner must change this form into emptiness within to transform this body to Qi and liberate a mortal to become an immortal; this is best refining form method.

Due to the body's hold on the Qi, and its use of Qi to nourish the body, the first level will be full of joy and longevity; the higher level will be a Taoist's body which will stay in this world forever. Even an elder will return as a child. Those who aren't aged yet will be stable in the face of ageing and have longevity.

Three hundred and sixty years will be as one year old, twenty six thousand years are one calamity, and three twenty six thousand years are one great calamity. One life as sky and earth forever through the many great calamities until an unknown time in the future, this is proven refine body experience. Do the theories of refining the body and transforming opportunity lead to this experience?

Zhong answers:

It requires three hundred days for the human body to form a fetus; after birth, it takes five thousand days for the Qi to be complete. Five Che (length measure) and five Cun (length measure) of body comply with five elements creation's amount. There are people of many sizes, big and small, but they comply with Che (length measure) and Cun (length measure) measurement, matching each other in the correct proportion.

The body can be divided as follows: above the Heart there are nine skies; below the Heart there are nine states. From the Heart to the Kidney is eight Cun and four Fen in length. From the Heart to top of the throat is eight Cun and four Fen in length; from the top of the throat to the crown of the head is eight Cun and four Fen in length. From the Kidney to the crown of head is two Che, five Cun and two Fen in length.

The Yuan (source) Qi becomes full in one day and night, and in three hundred and twenty degrees. Every degree measures two Che and five Cun and two Fen in length, the total being eighty one Zhang in length. Yuan (source Qi) complying with nine and the nine pure Yang's amount, as the distance between the Heart and the Kidney is proportional to the length of sky and earth. From Kidney to crown of the head is two Che and five Cun in length, complying as five elements' five and five pure Yang's amount.

The Yuan (source) Qi follows the breath out to connect the Ying (nutrition) and the Wei (surface) Qi, and sky and earth's Zheng (righteous) Qi. Following the time and season, or connect or disconnect, Zhang (length measure) and Che (length measure) amount are endless. The breath opens the body's channels. One breathe in and one breathe out, sky, earth and human three Cai (abilities) and Zhen (true) Qi circulating in front of throat. Together the inhale and exhale are one Xi (breath). During the day and night, one takes thirteen thousand and five hundred Xi (breaths). Another way; thirteen thousand and five hundred exhalations to breathe out the body's Yuan (source) Qi; thirteen thousand and five hundred inhalations to breathe in sky and earth Zheng (righteous) Qi. In this breathing the root and source are stable and strong; Yuan Qi does not consumed, and captures sky and earth's Zheng (righteous) Qi.

When one uses the Qi to refine Qi, it spreads in full to the four areas, the clear as Rong (nutritive), the turbid into Wei (surface) Qi and all are flowing, with vertical flow in the Jing (channel) and horizontal flow into the Luo (smaller channel), all pleasant. Cold and summer heat cannot harm one, working hard cannot hurt one, the body is light and the bone is healthy, Qi flows and the Shen (mind) is clear, one attains longevity and eternal life, never dies nor suffers a freezing body and ageing.

If root and source are not stable and strong, Jing (essence) and Qi are deficient, the upper Yuan (source) Qi cannot prevent leakage, the lower palace does not have tone, all the inhaled sky and earth's Qi excessively leaks out, the eighty and one Zhang (length measure) Yuan (source) Qi having nine and

nine are damaged; if all are not mastered by the self, captured by the sky and earth, how can the sky and earth's Zheng (righteous) Qi be captured? There is excessive accumulation of excess Yin and Yang deficiency, the Qi becomes weak and sick, then the Qi is exhausted and one dies, eliding into reincarnation.

3. Lu asks:
How can one prevent Yuan (source) from leaking, refine the body and substance to capture the sky and earth's Zheng (righteous) Qi until one can survive even great calamities?

Zhong answers:

If you want to win, it depends on whether there is a strong soldier. If you want to stabilize the country it depends on whether there is abundance. The soldier is the Yuan (source) Qi, the interior soldier, refining the body and substance's Yin; the exterior soldier captures the sky and earth's Zheng (righteous) Qi outside. The body is akin to the country, which has form which can be seen, abundance always and even has extra Qi.

The body's invisible (Qi and essence) are strong and never lacks. Ten thousand family doors are always open, no one looses a thing, and if even one horse is missed the road still has many opportunities.

The front or back of the body are refining the substance and burning, the upper or lower are nourishing the Yang and dispelling Yin. Burning the Qian (☰) of Yang and Kun (☷) of Yin has own timing, refining the Qi and fluid has own day. One uses jade fluid to refine the body, and uses Jia (unit of sky stamp) dragon to soar, turning white snow into mortal muscle. One uses gold fluid to refine body shape, drive the thunder vehicle to descend, the golden light filling up the whole room.

4. Lu asks:

The theory of refining body shape is understood in outline. What are the gold fluid and jade fluid?

Zhong answers:

Gold fluid refines the mortal body shape, the bone becomes the color of gold and the body radiates golden light; if the golden flowers appear in the space automatically, this is the time of five Qi pilgrimage Yuan (source) and three Yang gathering towards the crown of the head; when the body wants to be liberated from mortality, this great attainment is what the Jin Dan (golden pill) can accomplish.

If jade fluid refines the body shape, the body looks like melted Yang and wakens into the shape of a jade tree, jade flower and jade leaf, the mortal body shines and radiates, the body can follow the wind to fly freely, and the body shape will be as Qi.

Even though the practitioner knows the return to the golden pill method, refining the body shape's capacity of achievement gained is also a great gain. If the jade fluid returns to the Jin Dan, it bathes the Xian (immortal) fetus. The Qi rising up uses He Che (river vehicle) to haul the four greats, starts in the Liver; the Liver receives, the eyes have brilliant light and the pupils are like a drop of fresh paint. Second is the Heart, the Heart receives by the mouth and the mouth is full of active magical fluid; this fluid is like pure white snow. Next is the Spleen, receiving it, the muscles become solid and beautiful and therefore all scars are removed. Next are the Lungs; Lungs receive it can smell Heaven's fragrance; the face has the youthful appearance of a teenager. Last are the Kidneys, Kidneys receive it, and the Jin Dan returns to its own house; the ear is hearing the music of strings and flute and the hair at the temples is no longer grey. This is jade fluid refining the body shape.

The gold fluid refines the body shape incomparably. When the Jin Dan starts to return but has not returned yet, the emperor fire shows up as Jiji of the fire and water in balance restarts returning golden pill, with true Yin and Yang fighting; this is refining the substance.

Earth originates controlling the water, if the metal fluid id in the earth, the yellow emperor returns the light, combined as Tai Yin (beginning of Yin).

Fire originates controlling metal, if the metal fluid in the fire is like a red seed in the same furnace, purple Qi will be created.

Water starts fire, Yang dispels Yin and transforms the golden pill in the Huang Ting (yellow court), and refines Yang Shen into the five Qi. The Liver has green Qi and penetrates, the Lung has white Qi and appears, the Heart has red Qi and shows, the Kidney has black Qi rising, the Spleen has yellow color and Qi begins. The Five Qi make a pilgrimage to the Middle Yuan (source), the emperor fire through the Neiyuan (upper Dantian).

The lower Yuan (source) Yin's Yang is pure Yang without Yin, raising up and gathering in the Shen (spirit) palace. Middle Yang's Yang, does not need to create and raises and gathers in the Shen palace. Huang Ting (yellow court) great medicine, vaporized Yin into pure Yang, gathers and rises in the Shen palace.

The five fluids make a pilgrimage into the Lower Yuan (source); the five Qi make a pilgrimage into the Middle Yuan (source), and the three Yangs make a pilgrimage into the Upper Yuan (source). After they make their pilgrimage, they have accomplished the three thousand achievements, and there will be a crane dancing overhead or a dragon flying in the body. One can hear clear music, see immortal flowers falling, purple palaces, and scent a fragrance true and strong. Accomplishing the three thousand achievements is not the feat of a mortal; in just the time to burn one candlewick, he has become a guest in Bolai (one of Taoism's magic islands), liberated into a deity, and has shed the mortal substance and become the Xian (immortal).

Chapter Fifteen: Discussion of the Pilgrimage to the Yuan of Source

1. Lu asks:
Refining the body theory is understood; what is a pilgrimage?

Zhong answers:
After the great medicine is almost achieved, the jade fluid returns to the Dan (golden pill) to bathe the immortal fetus. After the true (Zhen) Qi occurs that true (Zhen) Qi penetrates the jade fluid, rising up to regenerate mortal bones; this is jade fluid refining the body. Zhou Hou Fei Jin Jing (Behind the elbows fly golden crystal through Xiao Zhu Tian of microcosmic orbit circulation), He Che (river vehicle) runs into the Neiyuan (Upper Dantian), from upper to middle, from middle to lower. Golden fluid returns to refine golden sand, the five Qi pilgrimage to Yuan (source), three Yang gathering crown of the head, refine the Qi into Shen (spirit); this is not just to refine the body for its mortal level.

From ancient times up to present not many persons have known of the pilgrimage, although some of the ancestors may have known and kept silent. The true immortal's great method includes sky and earth, and the Taoist three levels of clarity (San Qing) secret, it is the principle of forgetting the word and appearance of the edict of Xuan (emptiness has substance), the excellent theory of not asking and not responding. But the ancients worried about the practitioner who lacks confidence and concentration, has a restless mind that may not have totally understood the sage's theories and being misguided, spread the theory incorrectly, which did not lead to great benefit for all.

2. Lu asks:
To begin to understand the Tao's path for the true immortal, to distinguish the timing to match the timing of nature, to

know the water's and the fire's true source, to be aware of the dragon and tiger not born from the Liver and Lung, observe, to extract and add great theories, judging that lead and mercury are not Kan (☵) water and Li (☲) fire. The five elements reverse calculation; you have taught us the communication between the three Dantians; we are familiar with reversing the Dan and refining this body of theory in order to understand the path to immortality. How can one be liberated from a mortal body into in immortal body, shed substance into Xian (immortal) pathway and refine Qi for the pilgrimage to the Yuan (source)? Please tell me the method?

Zhong answers:
The Tao has no shape; Taiyuan (at the source beginning) shows Po (simple appearance), in the upper realms, is clear and unlike the turbid lower realms, are united as one. The cataclysm of Taiji (Yin and Yang divided), Chaos as a judge divided the sky and the earth, and in the sky and earth, there are the four directions of east, west, south, north and center. Each direction has one emperor and each emperor has two sons, one is Yang and other one is Yin. The two Qi of the Yin and Yang regulate and depend on each other and create the five elements, five elements create each other and command each other to form six Qi, and the six Qi are divided into three Yins and three Yangs.

Human beings begin in the uterus; Jing (essence) and Qi are one, Jing and Qi divide, the first to develop are the two Kidneys, the Kidney at the left is Xuan (Yang), the Xuan Yang Qi ascends to the Liver, The Kidney on the right is Pin (Yin); Pin Yin fluid descends to the urinary bladder. The Xuan and Pin of Yang and Yin came from emptiness, from emptiness comes substance from the parents' true Qi, received from the pure Yin palace. Gu Shen (responding spirit in the emptiness) never dies, and this is the entrance of the Xuan and Pin, corresponding to the sky and earth root. The Xuan and Pin form two Kidneys and after the creation of the Kidneys the five organs and six Yin organs will, in turn, be formed.

The Liver is Jia Yi (sky stamp) wood, an east green emperor. The Heart is fire and Bing Ding (sky stamp), the south red emperor. The Lung is metal and Geng Xin (sky stamp), the west white emperor. The Spleen is earth and Wu Ji (sky stamp), the middle yellow emperor. The Kidney is water and Ren Gui (sky stamp), the north black emperor.

At the moment of conception when there is Yin and Yang, there is no human body in the shape we know. After the fetus is fully completed, comes the intestine and stomach and divided six Qi and three male (Yang) and three female (Yin).

One Qi moves the five elements, the five elements move six Qi. To understand the Yin and Yang, know that Yang has Yin's Yang, Yin has Yang's Yin. Next know the metal, wood, water, fire and earth; the water has fire, fire has water, water has metal, metal has wood, wood has fire, fire has earth. The five elements harmonize with each other, and there are two Qi divided into six Qi, The Tao spreads the five elements.

After the day Dong Zhi (winter begins), one Yang was born in each of the five directions and places, the Yang all started. One emperor commands, there are four emperors assisting. If in the spring, the black emperor does not stop his command, there will be cold without warmth. If the red emperor is not ready for his command there will be only warmth without heat. After the day Xia Zhi (summer begins), one Yin created from five directions and places in the sky, the Yin descends. One emperor commands, the four emperors assist. If in autumn, the red emperor does not ready his command, it will be hot without cool. If the black emperor does not ready his command, it will be cool without cold. After the day of Dong Zhi, the Yang is created from the earth, and the Yang Qi makes a pilgrimage to the sky. After the day Xia Zhi, the Qi pilgrimage to the earth takes place.

A Taoist practitioner must completely understand these theories. During the day and night, one Yang started the five organs Qi pilgrimage to the Middle Yuan (source), and one Yin started the pilgrimage of the five organs fluid to the Lower Yuan (source). Yin's Yang, Yang's Yin, Yin and Yang's Yang, three Yang pilgrimages to the Neiyuan (upper Dantian), The Heart and Shen (spirit) return to the Heavens palace, those are pilgrimages to Yuan (source).

3. Lu asks:
At the time the birth of the Yang, the five Qi make a pilgrimage to the Middle Yuan (source). At the time of the birth of Yin, the five organs' fluids make a pilgrimage to the Lower Yuan (source). During this pilgrimage there is a transformation and Yang has Yang, Yin has Yang, and Yin and Yang's Yang make the pilgrimage to Upper Yuan (source). Continuing this practice, as regular practitioners all know, how can they be liberated from the human being's impermanent world?

Zhong answers:
If one uses the Yuan (source)'s Yang Qi at the one Yang starting moment, the upper pilgrimage to the Middle Yuan (source), and every one follows the same pattern. If one deposits enough Qi to create fluid, and at the one Yin starting moment, the lower pilgrimage to the Lower Yuan (source), and every one follows the same pattern. This alone will not gain liberation from the mortal body; to become a sage it is necessary to shed the flesh and become liberated by using the great medicine from the dragon and tiger coupling. Great medicine occurred that creates the true (Zhen) Qi, since the true Qi is created, using a year equals a month, using a period of a month to determine which time is rising and which time

is the time of decay, using month equals a day, use a day's time to identify what is the matter, use a day equals a Shi (two hour period); use a Shi to determine amount of your breathing.

Use Yang to nourish the Yang, Yang cannot leave any Yin. Using Yang refines Yin; the Yin cannot eliminate the Yang.

In the spring, the Liver is strong and the Spleen is weak; in summer the Heart is strong and the Lungs are weak; in autumn the Lungs are strong and the Liver is weak; in winter the Kidneys are strong and the Heart is weak. The Kidneys have a fundamental importance in humans. At a certain time in each season, the Spleen is strong and the Kidneys weak. Only the Kidney is used constantly and may be damaged in all the seasons, this is the cause of many sicknesses.

Whatever the Jia Yi (sky stem) Liver is in command; this will prevent weakness of the Spleen Qi. When the Bing Ding (sky stem) Heart is commanding; this will prevent the Lung Qi deficiency. The Wu Ji (sky stem) Spleen is commanding; this will prevent weakness of the Kidney Qi. When the Geng Xin (sky stem) Lung is commanding; this will prevent the Liver Qi deficiency. The Ren Gui (sky stem) Kidney is commanding; this will prevent the Heart Qi deficiency. Whenever one organ is stronger and has abundant Qi; there is one organ with weak Qi. This pattern of one strong organ and one weak organ are another reason to cause many sicknesses.

The Heart Qi sprouted at 9-11 p.m. (Hai) and was born at 3-5 a.m. (Yin) prospered at 9-11 a.m. (Si) and weakened at 3-5 p.m. (Shen).

The Liver Qi budded at 3-5 p.m. (Shen) and was born at 9-11 p.m. (Hai), is abundant at 3-5 a.m. (Yin) and weakened at 9-11 a.m. (Si).

The Lung Qi sprouted at 3-5 a.m. (Yi) and was born at 9-11 a.m. (Si), is abundant at 3-5 p.m. (Shen) and deficient at 9-11 p.m. (Hai).

The Kidney Qi sprouted at 9-11 a.m. (Si) and was born at 3-5 p.m. (Shen), prospered at 9-11 p.m. (Hai) and weakened at 3-5 a.m. (Yi).

The Spleen Qi follows the Liver in spring, follows the Heart in summer, follows the Lung in autumn and follows the Kidney in winter.

Everyone does not know the timing of sprouting, birth, strength and weakness; this is also a reason for many sicknesses.

If day, month and hour three Yangs are gathering, refine the Yang to eliminate the Yin; if day, month and hour three Yins are gathering, nourished and stable, the Yang will not disperse. Using the pure Yang's Qi refines the five organs without stopping until they return to the appearance of their origin which flows into the sky's pond (Tian Chi). Starts from the Kidney without Yin, the nine rivers will be without waves; if the Liver without Yin, the eight gates will be closed forever; next the Lungs without Yin with metal and fire in the same furnace; next the Spleen without Yin the jade door will be closed; last the true Qi rising, four Qi gathering into one. Even if there is golden fluid descending, only one cup of water cannot win the bundled fire, water and fire harmonized and united into one and into the Shen palace, still the breathing and observe inner vision, concentrate into one, Shen and consciousness both feeling magical. In this quiet moment, music is often heard, as in a dream, but not really a dream; it is the stage of nihilism. The scene may not be as beautiful or grand as the mortal stage, but overhanging it, there are many storied buildings and palaces with green jade tiles; clouds are flowing between, pearls, jade and damask hang on the buildings and sweetly fragrant smells are everywhere. This is the moment, where the Yang Shen is gathering and returning in Neiyuan (upper Dantian in the brain), The Shen is refined and the Xian (immortal) accomplished; the great Tao is matched.

One strides through the Tianmen (sky gate in the crown of the head), there is immortal body surrounded by golden light, and your self is sitting among the flowers; you can fly in the sky as easily as walk on the flat land; a distance of ten thousand miles is the same as the length of an arm. Reverse it into body, Shen and body united, this can be life as long as the live of the sky and earth. If you tire of staying in the mortal life, you can leave the mortal body on the earth and transform into an immortal body and return to Heaven's ten states.

Tai Wei Zhen Jun (a high level master) in the purple temple will identify you by name and where you came from and compare you with different Xian (immortals) granted residence in the three islands, from now you will travel above the wind and dust, liberated from the human being's impermanent world.

Illustration of the relationships of the Five Elements to each other:

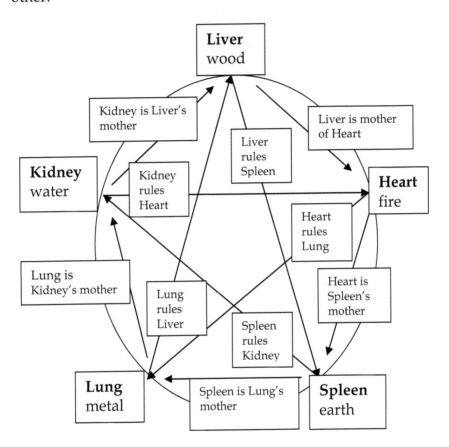

4. Lu asks:
Refining the body, one remains in the world, refining the Qi to rise to the Xian (immortal) stage. Most people do not know the Xuan is (emptiness has substance); without medicine to practicing fetal breathing, the forced to stay in the abdomen, where it may cause stagnation, cold, Qi and Yang deficiency sickness. Practicing out of an obsessive desire for longevity will cause disease. The immortal fetus came from the true Qi; therefore the true Qi will naturally have fetal breathing. Fetal breathing refines the Qi, refines the Qi into Shen. Hence, the practitioner when he refines the Qi needs to determine the

year's month, month's day, day's Shi (two hour period). Sit in a quiet room, forget human affairs and disappear from the community. At this stage, when the mind is still active, you must to try to let it go, or absurdities will come without stopping, wisdom will be lost, and when the goal is to attain the Xian (immortal), but the mind is not able, how can I achieve to the Xian level?

Zhong Answers:
Coupling has individual timing, and it has different laws following the timing route to practice and beseech the Tao; which will be achieved in a day and is easy as turning the hands upside down. Ancient and current practitioners, close the eyes send the Heart (mind) deeply into Xi Yi (emptiness within and out); use inner vision to observe sights within, and the Shen (mind) will be following.

Chapter Sixteen: Discussion of Inner Visualization

1. Lu asks:
What is inner visualization, can you let me know?

Zhong answers:
Inner visualization, sitting for clearing the mind until it is empty and using the visualization figments are used by some of the ancients and some modern Taoists. Not all practitioners agree with this method.

The concern is that the Heart (mind) is like a monkey in motion and Yi (intention) like a horse that never stops. The dread is the material world causing you to lose your will. Using visualization to stable the center from the emptiness, make the eyes not see, ears not hear, Heart not wild and Yi not confused. You need to be able to use the inner visualization method to enter into emptiness and be whole.

Regrettably a youth does not know much, does not know correct timing and or to how to practice. He hopes for achievement only through visualization, uses Yi to achieve Jin Dan (golden pill) and collect medicine. Inhaling and swallowing, looking at the sun and moon, keeping the space of sky and earth in the abdomen, this is a child's game only. The strange one fails to achieve wealth by sitting and visualizing and dreaming of becoming a wealthy man, therefore how can visualization be useful? Like drawing a picture of bread on the floor, how can such bread fill the stomach? There is nothing in the empty Qi; it is as a reflection of flowers in the mirror and moon in the water; nothing can be achieved.

Except for visualization, there is benefit to mastering practitioner's mind. The restless one has a divided Heart and the unquiet one partial thought. Visualization at the right time of the right day can assist in stabilizing the mind. Even when in a quiet and peaceful place, regrettably the mind is tied up with affairs and concentration and moods. Time runs as fast as lightning, even one inch of time wasted is unfortunately as vast as the distance between sky and earth. Practicing yearly and monthly without achievement is due to wild thoughts and a confused mind.

The one good at seeing finds inspiration in the beauty of art but not its vanity. The practitioner good at listening finds inspiration in the sound of the flute, but no the sound of thunder. The use of eyes and ears is a small matter compare of the mind, however if practiced with intention, single-mindedness can master the entire world and permit the practitioner to comprehend everything and do so appropriately and with proper timing, cannot these feats be achieved with the practice of visualization and inner vision?

2. Lu asks:
What are visualization and inner vision, can you tell me?

Zhong answers:
For instance, when you have Yang rising, often thoughts are concerning male, dragon, fire, sky, cloud, crane, sun, house, smoke, afterglow, vehicle, drive, flower, and Qi. This is Yang inner visualization reflecting Yang rising.

When Yin is descending, often thoughts will be about female, tiger, water, earth, rain, turtle, moon, ox, spring, soil, boat, and leaf. This is Yin inner visualization reflecting Yin descending.

Green dragon, white tiger, red bird and Xuan Wu (snake and turtle appearance) have names that have to have their appearance. Five mountains, nine states, four ocean, three islands, golden field, jade girl, river vehicle, double storey building; many metaphors for inner vision are characterized by such names. All use the appearance of emptiness within to establish the mind.

You cannot lose your bait before catching a fish, or catch a rabbit without a trap. A vehicle follows previous vehicle's track. A new machine uses the form of the previous model. The inner visualization method has to have and cannot be stagnating or without such a model, until the Shen is full of emptiness with whole stage; this is true thought and true emptiness. The true thought and emptiness entails a pilgrimage wherein the practitioner must transform himself and breaking through his daze to get close to the process of liberation.

Now there is a grand foundation and achievement will be in a day, the inner visualization can be used. After days spent processing the Tao, into Xi Yi (emptiness within and out) stage, the technique will be shorter, as the practitioner will now have the benefit of having achieved inner visualization.

3. Lu asks:
How do we visualize the dragon and tiger copulating and matching Yin and Yang?

Zhong answers:
At the beginning coupling and matching Yin and Yang to establish Kan (☵) of water and Li (☲) of fire, this visualization can be the nine emperor true person (Jiu Wang Zhen Ren) guiding a boy dressed in red ascending; the nine empress queen true mother (Jiu Wang Zhen Mu) is guiding a girl in a black dress descending, they meet in front of a yellow house where a yellow elderly lady takes over and directs them in a mortal marriage ceremony, and they are happy and joyful. The girl is descending; the boy is ascending, they depart as mortal affair. After they depart the yellow lady holds onto a red tangerine and tosses it into the golden

container in the yellow house.

The boy is Qian (☰) Yang collecting Kun (☷) Yin from the girl, the Yang returns to its source and the Yang embraces the Yin return back into his own village. The girl is Kun (☷) collecting Qian (☰) from the boy, the Yin returns to its source; the Yin embraces the Yang back in her own village. This is the visualization of Kan (☵) water and Li (☲) fire exchanging and matching the Yin and Yang.

There is a black tiger rising from the flame and there is a red dragon descending in the wave; they meet and begin fighting in front of the building and the pavilion, the red door is wide open, and there is a king commanding the smoke and flames. The flames are burning as high as the sky, the wave is more than ten thousand feet high in the sky, the flames leap up and down, smoke and flames are everywhere in the sky and the land. The dragon is curling and the tiger is circling into the golden container and down into the yellow house, settling into the cabinet. We have described copulation between the dragon and tiger creating yellow sprout visualization.

4. Lu asks:
Matching the Yin and Yang, dragon and tiger copulating through inner vision and visualization are understood. How about tempering and refining the Jin Dan visualization?

Zhong answers:
The visualization is of an object shaped like a Ding (three legged pot) and Fu (cooking equipment), colored yellow or black, shaped like a wheel. On the left is a green dragon and on the right there is a white tiger, in front is a red bird and behind is a Xuan Wu (turtle with snake image). There are two assistants standing on the left and right dressed in purple holding a jade tablet and bowing, and many more people holding fire weapons. There is a king dressed in red that is riding a red horse coming from the sky of fiery clouds,

holding the whip to command the flames to burn stronger. Hot flames almost break out the door of the sky to get out. The sky door is not yet totally open, but the smoke and fire are coming down, and all the characters, Ding and Fu, the king, and the assistants in the red flame, are calling to each other to optimize the fire. The container's water condenses without steaming. The bead in the water is glossy. This is tempering and refining the golden pill (Jin Dan)'s visualization.

5. Lu asks:
Inner vision and visualization: is this method limited to collecting medicine and tempering with fire? Do you have anything else?

Zhong answers:
Clouds and thunder are descending, smoke and flames are rising. Or there may be Heavenly rain and exquisite flowers, the wind of fortune and Qi starting from court below. Or there are fairies, colorful phoenixes flying from the green palace into the golden plate, and holding jade magic dew and nectar while making a pilgrimage to the king: this golden fluid returns to Dan (pill) and Jiji (fire below water harmonizing environment) visualization.

If the dragon and tiger are pulling a car through the fire, rising up to break through the three gates, but the three gates have their own armed customs officials, ready with fierce weapons to frighten the populace. The dragon and tiger first hit the gate, it does not open; they use huge flames to break through, fighting until they get to Kunlun (head) and stopping in Tianchi (pond in the brain) region. Or three magic cranes penetrate through the three levels of Heaven, or double butterflies fly into the three palaces, or the five colorful clouds hold a child in red entering through the Heavenly door. Or the golden and jade car with the king flies through the highest Three Realms. This is Hou Fei Jin Jing (Behind the elbows fly golden crystal through Xiao Zhu Tian of microcosmic orbit circulation); this is He Che great river vehicle visualization.

A messenger dressed in red rides through the line, from the city of Jizhou (name of the city) to Yanzhou (name of the city) and then to the city of Qingzhou (name of the city), traveling into Xuzhou (name of the city), into Yangzhou (name of the city), Yangzhou into Jingzhou (name of the city), going from Jingzhou (name of the city) into Langzhou (name of the city), and on into Yongzhou (name of the city) and after Yongzhou, resting in Jizhou (name of the city). East, west, south, north, stopping awhile in Yuzhou (name of city), and then retracing his route, over and over, in a circular pattern. He collected all the gold and jade, if anything gets in his way, he has an official proclamation commanding the nine states to be harmonized, and he rides to the cities over and over again without ceasing. Or he travels over five mountains, beginning with Hengshan (name of mountain). He goes by boat across the five lakes, or travels to the northern marsh. Or he uses Heaven's order to command the five emperors, or uses emperor's power to command the five governors. This is the return to the Jin Dan (golden pill) visualization.

Pearls and jade scattered, thrown on the ground, or in the rain, dew and nectar nourish all the material of world; ocean waves and tides fill hundreds of rivers and creeks. The Yin creates ten thousand abundances, and the fire and flame shooting through the sky and earth, smoke filling the universe. These are refining body visualization.

Visualize the crane flying out from the nest, a dragon bursting out from his cave, or the five emperors' faces up in the sky, five color clouds flowing, or you riding a colorful phoenix penetrating the sky and touching the ground. Travel up to Heaven in dreams; see Heaven's flower petals everywhere, hear immortal music in the palace of golden light filled with abundant flowers. This is visualizing a pilgrimage. After this journey, there is no need to practice further visualization, move on into inner vision.

6. Lu asks:
Inner vision is unlike the former method, Can you tell me why?

Zhong answers:
Ancient and modern practitioners who have not mastered Heaven's secret yet and still do not understand why, are just following the method and trying to speed up seeking liberation. They inhale more than they exhale breathing as a fetus, quieting the mind and closing their eyes for inner vision, but limited in stillness creating Yin Shen (uncontrolled mind); this is only a clear Ling (soul) ghosts, not a pure Yang's Xian (immortal).

The true Xian (immortal) and higher sage, collecting internal medicine, refining with the optimal fire temperature and extracting lead and adding mercury, returns to the golden pill and refines the body to complete the pilgrimage to Yuan (source) and combine the Qi.

Explaining the details over and over again is necessary when the public cannot understand and is not quite paying attention to inner vision. But inner vision comes with the Yin and Yang transforming and this is the time when the mortal attains transformation to an immortal.

The Taoist practitioner, who is not lacking inner vision and pays attention in all the previous methods of interaction's time and day and follows all the rules, the one who has confidence and never misses even a little bit of practice, will see achievement.

To make use of this inner vision, first, do not care about the time or day. Second, there are no rules. In a place where there is a room of deep tranquility, practice day and night, know who is Yang Shen (controlled spirit) and expels Yin ghost (uncontrolled mind). The monk Dharma faced the wall for nine years, becoming liberated from the Neiyuan (Upper Dantian in the brain); the first Buddha Shankyamuni, with great focus to liberate, took himself out of his mortal cage in six years.

Therefore, the inner vision is difficult to obtain. It starts from the upper to lower, purple He Che (river vehicle) hauling Heaven's wealth into the Heavenly palace, who is not pleased? Spending life going back and forth into downtown luxury, usually such people can not see with inner vision, but we all have the capability.

A Taoist practitioner who often keeps quiet and holds on without attachment, has been lonely a long time, but after having gained full achievement, flips into joy and happiness, where he sees pavilions, pagodas and fancy dressing with pearls and jade, fairy musicians playing flutes and metal instruments, with delicious dishes, exquisite flowers and all he sees is beautiful.

If a practitioner does not understand it, keeps his image and thinks himself in Heaven; this is from his inner Neiyuan (Upper Dantian in the brain), he imagined a true view, circulate inner without out, he will be trapped in a daze, and keeping his body living in the mortal world, without the quality of shed flesh into Shen Xian (Shen immortal level) and not yet truly having reached Heaven, remaining in the state of inner vision. Or the Yin ghost and outside evil have created this scene due to his thoughts; this is evil invading.

If the Taoist practitioner has a confused mind, becoming filled with evil, he ends up on the wrong side, and finally cannot become an immortal; instead he will be imprisoned into three the dead and seven Po (uncontrolled Yin Shen) state of wishing someone to die to have his happiness; he has become as nine insects and six thieves, cast aside from human society and being welcome nowhere.

Chapter Seventeen: Discussion of the Nine Difficulties and the Ten Evils

1. Lu asks:

Inner vision gathers Yang Shen, refines Shen to liberate which is out from the Neiyuan (Upper Dantian in the brain), above the Tian Men (Tian Men of Heaven's door: the junction of the frontal and parietal bone crown of the head) into sainthood. The liberated Spirit freely travel back and forth, in and out, with precise. If one wants to life in this world the Shen and the body are together. If one wants to shift to the Shen Xian (immortal spirit) can travel great distances to the Taoist island of Bon.

After having attained three thousand achievements and going from the Neiyuan (Upper Dantian) to state of liberation, but only for those who know how to maneuver around the Yin ghosts and demons, now there is another challenge?

Zhong answers:

The practitioner must have the faith to carry through, without succumbing to temptation from money, business, fame or other human matters. One must be in command of oneself, have a strong mind and work hard without wavering, through loneliness and emptiness. The one, who has the highest goal, may become trapped in the middle level of achievement. The one has middle level goal, may reach a lower achievement level, then that is all one can reach. If one does not understand Tao theory and see that the Tao pathway and Heaven's opportunity, and one followed by learning a little technique here, or hearing of another's' journey there. Even years of effort can be wasted with a stumble; years of study can fail to bring insight into the pathway's function. Old age creeps up and soon one is drawn into another incarnation. Misunderstanding of the Taoist path to longevity and liberation abounds, misrepresentations damage confidence in the Way. Losing oneself in uncontrollable thoughts and selfish materialism means there is no hope of mastering the ten evils and nine difficulties.

2. Lu asks:
What are the nine difficulties?

Zhong answers:
Before the great medicine can be established there are nine difficulties the practitioner must face.

The first difficulty is the body's vulnerability to winter cold and summer heat, to hunger and thirst, to the need for different dress for the changing seasons. The true (Zhen) Qi is weak so the body is in constant need.

The second difficulty is familial responsibility to husband or wife, to children and parents. One has obligations and rarely has free time. The desire to practice the Tao full time is hindered by a reluctance to flee these responsibilities.

The third difficulty is the mental burden of caring for one's family and home. Those we love we worry about constantly, and have great difficulty, because of this habit of perpetual concern. Even if we have peace and quiet the mind leaps to consider all that could go wrong. Thus affection creates difficulty.

The fourth difficulty is that of the successful, obsessed with contemplating their riches and successes. Fame and fortune are difficult to move beyond and the seeker stagnates in self satisfaction.

The fifth difficulty is the teenager who refuses to practice self-cultivation, wasting his Qi until sickness results; he stubbornly refuses to wake to reality. The one Yin root becomes established, suffering and disaster are the outcome.

The sixth difficulty is the urgent need for finding a teacher without knowing how to tell an authentic teacher from an eloquent imposter who has no real understanding.

The seventh difficulty is the distraction of having a shortsighted teacher or confused friends sharing wrong or incomplete information. Many grasp the leaves and branches without understanding the full system; misguided they share their small fragmented knowledge with others. They are as unaware of the true path as the world before the sun and moon: after the sun and moon have risen, it will be bright and everyone can see, in the manner that the thunder is hidden, but if the thunder comes everyone will hear it and be scared. The confused practitioner is like a candle's light attempting to illuminate, the fog in the well in his effort to see the sky. Isn't any way to comparison?

The eighth difficulty is one's own mutability. One may sit with determined discipline in the morning, but by evening may have changed his mind. Being satisfied with brief practice sessions, making a strong start, but soon becoming lazy and slack, keeps one from advancing.

The ninth difficulty is the slipping away of time, the inner body loses the year, year looses a month, a month looses a day, and a day looses a Shi (two hour period). The young cannot turn away from fame and fortune; the elders cannot turn away from children and grandchildren. Personal distractions have no expiration, no boundaries. The squandered months and years speed by.

The Taoist practitioner has to avoid those nine difficulties, there is one or two may in the way, and he cannot attain the highest level of achievement.

3. Lu asks:
Those are the nine difficulties, what are the ten evils?

Zhong answers:
The ten evils are divided into three categories. One category is of the flesh beyond our body. The second category is dreams. The third category of evil is inner vision.

We see beautiful flowers, hear inspiring music, the tongue seeks sweets, the nose wants wonderful aromas, the mind wants thoughts of comfort and fulfillment...we recognize these but don't identify them as six evil demons.

For example, a house made of jade and other treasures, with carved beams, pearl shades and embroidered curtains all of beautiful design...coral, gold and jade everywhere. We perceive these things but fail to identify them as the evil of wealth.

Another example, a strong horse with a golden saddle, a huge household governing ten thousand families, envoys flying the flags of dignitaries, the colors green and purple on the doors. We can see these but do not recognize that this is the evil of wealth and power.

Imagine ocean waves and mist, warm and relaxing sun, rainstorms with thunder and lightning, dramatic music, crying and sadness. We can perceive all of these but do not realize they are the evil of the emotions.

Think of relatives and tragedies, disasters befalling families and children, illness, bereavement, separation, estrangement, divorce. We recognize these but don't identify these as the evils of affection.

When emergencies occur, such as fire, falling from heights,

crop failure, poisoning, being robbed or executed, we can perceive these but fail to identify them as the evil of calamity.

Then there are ten places of Yang energy, Three Clear Jade emperors, four gods and seven Yao (bright), five mountain spirits and eight kings all commanding with dignity and moderation, flying back and forth. We recognize these but don't identify them as the evil saints.

Imagine soldiers and horses, shiny weapons and straight spears, bows and arrows at the ready, poised to fight and kill, we recognize these but don't identify these as armed soldiers of evil.

Imagine an outing of fairies, in beautiful dress with red armbands, offering golden cups of wine; we can perceive these but do not realize they are the evil of happiness.

There is the nightlife of seductive females fluttering around you in wispy clothes; we can perceive these but do not realize they are the evil of sensual females.

Now I have described the ten evils. Recognize these evils, but do not obsess about them, for even that can hold you back from the Tao. To see beyond the flesh; the Heart must be confident and unwavering. Look between dreams but do not linger; see but do not then loose the Shen. Sharpen your inner vision to see what is true and authentic; see what is true and what is false; the Shen does not follow mortal familiar wave and identify false as truth. Stoke the true fire of the three treasures (inner Jing, Qi and Shen fire) to purify the body and the evil demons will dissolve of themselves. The Zi He Che (purple river vehicle) hauls the Yang Shen through the Neiyuan (Upper Dantian into the brain) into Heaven and liberation. He who tends to the Tao with a quiet Heart (mind) is still easily swayed when the environment becomes difficult.

It is not easy to escape the ten evils and nine difficulties. Even those of good reputation may fail to grasp the real and miss the Tao.

Out in the normal dusty human world, even while staying in a quiet place aiming at Xuan Men (entering emptiness, one finds the substance), one may not be clear of the nine difficulties, caught by one or two of the evils, he is still on the Tao, but can only attain small or medium achievements, whether at the level of an immortal, or in Ren Xian (human immortality) or Earth Xian (earth immortality). If we do clean up evil and other difficulties step by step as proscribed using the inner vision of Yang Shen (controlled mind), within days we will belong to the three Taoist magic islands.

Chapter Eighteen: Discussions on Experience

1. Lu asks:

No one wants to be sick; the Taoist practitioner also wants to be healthier and live a longer life. Further cultivation leads to avoiding death, living forever, and to the liberated state of the Xian (Immortality). Mortals stay in this world, and the Taoist practitioner wants to be higher above in the cave of Heaven. He will have be willing to work hard and live simply in a neutral state to be able to stay in the calm stage of mind in the wilderness of a desolate land. Therefore, even while practicing, one but does not know the depth of power, the method of exchange, and changes their mind in an unpredictable manner between morning and night, what will the order and actual result be?

Zhong Answers:

If the dedicated practitioner does not have the necessary accomplishments in the end, this is not the fault of Tao; it is the fault of the practitioner who does not have a knowledgeable teacher and who has received wrong methods and followed an incorrect path. If you follow a knowledgeable teacher, and are taught the proper methods and timing, then how can you be without good experience?

2. Lu asks:

What are the details of the rules and timing of the correct methods?

Zhong answers:

The rules have twelve sections: First, match and introduce Yin and Yang. Second, gather the fire and water. Third, is the copulation of the dragon and tiger. Fourth is refinement of the inner medicine Dan (pill). Fifth is Zhou Hou Fei Jin Jing (Behind the elbows fly golden crystal through Xiao Zhu Tian of microcosmic orbit circulation). Sixth is the jade fluid returning to the Dan. Seventh is the jade fluid refining the body. Eighth is the Jin Ye (golden fluid) returning to the Dan (pill). Ninth is Jin Ye (golden fluid) refining the body. Tenth is pilgrimage source and refining Qi. Eleven is using inner vision and the exchange of appearances. Twelve is liberation and the immortal body may divides into many immortal bodies.

At this moment, the practitioner's body is in synchronization with the yearly timing of the rise and fall of Yin and Yang movements of the sky and earth; the monthly timing of the sun and moon communicating; and the daily timing of the four directions and Taoism's eight trigrams, each day has the timing of the ten Heavenly stems, the twelve earthly branches, the one hundred Ke (time measure), and the six thousand Fen (time measure). Just in a period of one day, time is proportionate to a month, a month is proportionate to a year, and a year's experience is followed by the order of nature, until one sheds the mortal body into the liberation of Xian (immortality) without missing any bit of the steps.

Evil lust has been totally diminished; continuing to practice and the body becomes full of the collected Jin Jing (golden essence), the state of mind masters the Yin ghosts, the Heart Qi through flows up automatically, producing sweet saliva in the mouth. Yin and Yang are interacting and one hears wind which thunders in the belly. Next, the Hun (Yang spirit) and the Po (Yin spirit) are adjusted, and one may feel fear in their dreams. The illnesses of the six organs and extremities are healed as by magic. The Dantian is always warm at night, and the face and body becomes healthy and charming. Then the Shen light appears in the dark room. You will have courage, confidence, and not thing in existence can hurt you, or you have a carrying baby appearance. Next the golden gate and jade lock (sexual organ) are sealed and one will never have a wet dream. Next there is one shock of thunder and the joints of the body connect and sudden body sweats. Afterwards the jade fluid cooks and condenses to be like cake, and the Ling (soul) fluid becomes thick like paste to fill the mouth and abdomen, and will gradually avoid fishy smelling food. Next the mortal bones become lighter and transform into the Yang Shen, your steps become treads and gallops and you move as if you're flying. None of the tension of business bothers you and lust has been diminished. Next, maneuver your true (Zhen) Qi into others; it can cure their diseases. Next, inner vision is bright and clear, without darkness or faintness. The pupils are sharp and remarkable; a wrinkled face and grey hair will be regenerated, as if one had a child's face forever. Next, the true (Zhen) Qi gives one so much courage that one needs less food or drink, or as able to drink immeasurably and without becoming drunk. Next, one sees the Shen Qi's bright luster, clear and charming, and there is a scent like the Saint Dan (golden pill) emanating from the body. The Ling (soul) fluid develops a penetrating aroma, and becomes fragrant in your nose and mouth; someone may notice and smell it. The vision sharpens and can clearly see a hundred steps away. Next old body scars are naturally eliminated, and tears, sweat, and saliva disappear. Next, there will be a fully established immortal fetus and enough Qi so that one never needs to eat. The inner Shen is clear and high matching the Taixu (original emptiness stage), a mortal's love and business will naturally diminish. One will eliminate the lower nice insects and the upper three corpses. Next the Hun (Yang spirit) and the Po (Yin spirit) become stable and dreams will cease. The Shen brightens the day and night. Next the Yang Jing (essence) is the body, the Shen is solid and strong, and the body will not be affected by the changes of the four seasons of winter cold and summer heat. Next life and death cease to be bothersome; while sitting in deep inner vision, one travels into Shen Xian's (spirit immortal) country; there is the fairy musician tower, and a beautiful downtown area, which has no comparison with anything in the mortal's world.

When the practice rises to the level of achievement, Yin achieves retribution, the trial grants Three Clarity true signs. The first, one can predict Yin and Yang changes, the behavior of people, and see visions of the scourge and into mortal's dirty business in order to clean up disgusting dealings. Your self can return to the clean and quiet place and let the immortal fetus become visible; knowing that beyond the flesh there is a sacred body. Next, the true (Zhen) Qi is turned into pure Yang; one breath can dry up external mercury. Next the immortal fetus often wants to take off, and there will be a fortunate aura in your bedroom, when you are quiet, music is heard. Next, although one can meet the wealthy in public, they smell as offensively as bad fish since they have not refined their mortal flesh and bones.

One can shift his Shen luster into a Xian (immortal) appearance, like a jade tree and his bones will reveal golden light. You may often have unsolicited pilgrimages from immortals, it's up to you to command and greet them. Next, in quiet observation, around you there will be purple light everywhere, and in your inner vision your body has a golden mask from the crown of the head on down covering the whole body. The body suddenly transforms into a fire dragon or a crane, and takes off this is the Shen Ling (soul) being liberated from the mortal bones and going above and beyond the vulgar flow; detached, you have been liberated. After the colorful light, clouds and fortune's Qi circles around you, exquisite flowers are like Heaven's rain, and cranes soar in opposite directions. Unusual aromas and jade fairies descend to you and raise you to the Heavenly imperial order, while the Xian (immortal) crowns you, dressing you in the regalia of immortality that you have earned with dignity and discipline. You are welcomed and guided to Penglai (Taoist magical island), while at the purple palace pilgrimage Tai Wei Zhen Jun (one of the high level immortals), depending on your original name, where you come from, and how much achievements you have accomplished, decides to give you the deed of a township in one of the three Taoist islands, as Zhen Ren Xian Zi (true person of immortality).

3. Lu asks:
Today, thank you dear master, you told me the theories of Xi Yi (emptiness within and out stage) and between Heaven and earth. I have not just clear and bright eyes, ears and spirit, but also my Shen and Jing (essence) are clean and charming. The body dies and the corpse looks like feces. However, those who know may not practice it and who those know it may not get it. The life and death are most important matters and time is flying. Although with knowledge of the great theory, but without practice eventually it's unsuccessful and in the end they are no different from those who do not know. If I dare to seek the timing of interactions and the way to practice, how do I start, and how difficulty will this knowledge be to acquire?

Zhong answers:
The servant has the book: Ling Bao Bi Fa which has ten chapters, twelve outlines and six subjects. One describes the golden greatness, the second is the book of jade, third is the true source, the fourth is metaphor, the fifth is true tactic, and sixth is the importance of Tao. Included are all the great milestones of Tao pathway and the Three Clear level allusions. The text refers to the guide lines of the movements of Yin and Yang, of Heaven and earth, and the communication laws of the essence of the sun and the moon. It is the real purpose of the five Xian (immortal), three forms of the regulation, and how to choose an auspicious day for being granted to my disciple.

Tai Yi Jin Hua Zhong Zhi (The Secret of the Golden Flower) (Min version)

Author: Lu, Dongbin

Tai Yi is the origin of infinity. Jin Hua indicates a golden light. Zhong Zhi describes vital tactics.

The Min version is credited to Master Min. His version has a practical emphasis.

Tai Yi Jin Hua Zhong Zhi summarized the meaning of the Tian Xin (Heart and mind) or center of within and out, and mirrors modern quantum physics. The Tian Xin is the place where the Ling of soul is located; from here it is possible to travel from the past and to the future. The Jin Hua (innate light) in relation to the inner self forms a bond and creates the Jin Dan (golden pill). And the text also explains what is important for using this method for processing these experiences of the Yuan Shen (true self) instead of Zhi Shen (postnatal mind) to purify the self and progress to the stage of arriving at the source of Tai Yi Jin Hua.

Chapter One: Tian Xin

The Patriarch says: "Tian Xin consists of three intrinsic abilities of the Heart of spirit or Xuan Qiao (the orifice of entering emptiness, where one finds substance). In the Dan of the book of golden elixir, it is written that everyone has these abilities. If one's Heart is open then intelligence is natural, and if it is closed then one will become dull. When it is open, it will promote longevity; when it is closed, it will shorten lifespan. A person believes in one's prediction of mortality which is just the common man's opinion.

Even though they all seek survival, they all commit suicide; do they have different lungs and intestines? It is six dusts to disturbance; the teenager is distracted, and decadence comes as fast as the blink of an eye. I am not happy about it, so I teach them the Tao. Even though the teacher is earnest, the listener will be in a trance. Why? Because they do not understand the Tao and the process. Instead they will blame each other, right or wrong. They will believe this is the way to go for survival. As a result they travel south, when they should be going north.

Do you know the body of Tao is emptiness and the use of Tao is indistinct? Therefore, there should be neither has or has not, and the Qi will flow automatically. Our self uses Tai Yi of the original one as an origin, Jin Hua of golden shiny light is an end; origin and ends support each other; in this is way one will cultivate long life and immortality.

This pathway came from the ancient Xianzhen of the true immortal transmitted by a soul synchronized with another one. The appearance of the original vital Taishang was transmitted to Donghua the immortal, and to the North and South branches.

The Tao is not hidden, but its delivery from mind to mind is secret, though it is not kept as a secret, it is only accessible transmitted from mind to mind. Oral teaching is wonderful, but it is still difficult to learn even when written.

The original vital Taishang is best delivered by mind. If transmitted to the public, one may suddenly reach enlightenment, the teacher does not need to lecture the student, and the student does not need to ask the teacher. But the true believer is pure, once the chance comes to meld with the Shen, one's mind suddenly awakens and the person may face each other and either smile or cry. Whoever enters the Tao and enlightenment shall see the Tao has the same natural pathway. One may enter enlightenment first, then afterwards enter the Tao, or enter the Tao first and enlightenment afterwards. There is no one entering the Tao without either concentration in one or without belief. If there is not concentration in one, then his Jin Hua (golden light) is scattering, if there is no belief then his light is floating. Scattered the light can not gather; floating, the light can not condense. How can one match Taishang's transmitted Heart (mind)?

Confucianism uses introspection; Taoism uses inner vision. Chapter forty-two of the Buddhist sutra reads: "With a Stable Heart of mind in one, what can we not do?" The infinite path is just the one, and this one is the entire whole. What about the whole? Emptiness and quiet without attachment, this is what it is all about.

The Principle of magical processing is also the Heart concentrated in one. Inner vision is the method for setting the Heart at one that is the principle of the transmission of the secrets of the mind. If the student cannot receive the mind's transmission then it can be verbal; if he still does not understand, then it can be written. If one reaches to maximize the achievement of empty Heart into infinity, the suddenly awakened understanding of Xuan of emptiness has the effect of substance's magical tactic; this cannot be described by verbalization or the written word.

The true Xu of emptiness and quiet, true clarity and nothingness, there is a Xuan bead, as a soul mate, this is really secret. This bead comes after entering enlightenment, and it is extremely significant; simply the Tian Xin cave being opened.

Nowadays, those seeking the Tao see it as a huge flood without any end in sight. Those who make it to the other end have used a raft. This is theory reflecting method. If someone does not know how to proceed, how can you show them the raft? As a teacher, I can definitely show them the raft. But the Tian Xin is not inside the body nor is it outside the body, and it can not be opened by touch, only by continued concentration. If you want to know the theory, it is that lust is empty and emptiness is lust. The golden elixir book called it so, none so, none so, but it is so. This is what it is. If the Tian Xin has opened it will be open forever. The method is maintaining loyalty.

There is a shortcut for maintaining loyalty. After letting go of tens and thousands of affairs, use the "Brahmin" sign: ∴(As the sun and moon Tiangang, the bottom left dot represents the moon and the right eye, the bottom left dot represents the sun and the left eye, the center dot which is the third eye is located between and inner of the eyebrows and represents the three-eyed immortals, such as the mother Big Dipper and the Father of Thunder.)

If one knows how to practice, the third eye, between the eyebrows, will be open. This opened eye is called Heaven's eye. In order to keep the eyes' Shen Guang of spirit light automatically stored in the Heaven's eye, the three lights need

to be gathered at the junction of entry and exit from this gate
between the eyebrows. The elixir book called this the sun and
the moon together. When the practitioner uses those three
eyes as the "Brahmin" sign above uses thought like grinding a
mirror, then the three lights will soon gather between the
eyebrows, shine like the sun and use thought to open the
double gates of Heaven's eye and Heaven's mirror. This is the
Yin door for entering the Xuanpin emptiness. As soon one
uses his thought for entering the door, and the light will
appear. Let us not forget the Xuan of emptiness has substance
has two meanings. The Tian Xin cave will automatically open
itself. How to use the Xuan, the details will be told, so listen to
the warning about the return to the source. The source is the
Qi where transformation occurs, which has to be kept in
balance, otherwise one may fall into illusions and the cave will
degrade to evil. .

Students follow and go step by step, there is no fast way to
progress, and there is only pure thought. The Lengyan Sutra
reads: "Pure thought flies and must be created in the sky."
This sky is not the sky of nature; it is the Qian of the upper
palace in the body. As one practices, the body will be in synch
with the sky. The body is a country; the practitioner is the
emperor; the light is the emperor's intention; intention is the
emperor's sovereign command; as soon the light returns, then
the whole body of the Qi makes its pilgrimage to the capital.
The king establishes the capital and makes the laws, holding
the jade Zhishi to control ten thousand counties. The emperor
and his assistant have the same goal, and all the assistants
naturally follow orders.

Concentrate on returning the light; this is the supreme magical
process. After a long time of returning the light, the light will
be condensed, the body transformed into an immortal body.
In Taoism the emperor and his assistant are now in place, as is
the Buddhist king of magical city. The emperor is supported

by his assistant; the Jing of essence and Qi are growing and the Shen is becoming more abundant. Once the body and mind meld together, don't you think the sky has another sky, and beyond the flesh there is another body?

Therefore, the Jin Hua (golden light) is the Jin Dan (golden pill); the bright Shen of transformation comes from everyone's Heart of mind. This magical tactic has to be live and brilliant and still. Neither a supremely wise man can possess it nor can a supremely silent man keep it.

Chapter Two: Yuan Shen, the Original Soul and Shi Shen, the Consciousness of the Postnatal Mind

The patriarch said: "The sky and earth see humans as ephemeral; but the Tao sees even the sky and earth as but a twinkle." However, your Yuan Shen has definitely existed longer than Yuanhui (many thousands of years). The Jing (essence) and Qi will decay along with the sky and earth, but the Yuan Shen will remain; this is as Wuji (the infinite), where the earth and the sky originated.

The practitioner has to protect and care for his Yuan Shen, so he can maneuver the Yin and Yang, and not fall into the Three Realms. This is only possible by seeing your true self.

With mortal reincarnation, the Yuan Shen stays within a square inch, while the Shi Shen is living under and in the Heart. The Heart is muscle and blood, and is the shape and size of a big peach. The lungs embrace the Heart like two wings while the Liver assists it and the Small and Large intestines support it. If one does not eat for a whole day the Heart will be uncomfortable. Fear will bring on palpitations and anger will cause a sensation of fullness or stagnation. Seeing death will bring sadness, seeing beauty will induce dizziness. Is the head noticing slight vibrations?

Someone asked, "Is it fact that square inch can not move"? The square inch is true thought, how can it move"? If it had moved it would be unsatisfied, nevertheless it would be a most amazing thing. When a mortal dies that square inch has moved; this is not good movement. When the light has been distilled into an immortal body beyond flesh, gradually becoming bonded with the Ling (soul), and begins to move, this is a good movement. This secret knowledge has not been transmitted in many thousand years.

Shi Shen, the conscious postnatal mind is in the Heart, like a violent commander that deceives the emperor from afar; until the tables are turned. Now the light is shining in the Yuan (source) palace, and just as the wise emperor has attendants to assist him, the light returns every day like the imperial ministers giving loyal support. Once the internal affairs have been managed, all of the treacherous elements are naturally tamed.

The three supreme treasures of the Dan pathway are Jing Water, Shen Fire, and Yi of intention earth. What is Jing Water? It is the Zhen (true) innate Qi. Shen Fire is the light. Yi of intention earth is the Middle palace's Tian Xin, the mind of Heaven. Shen Fire is the function, Yi of intention earth is the body, and Jing Water is the base.

The mortal body exists because of the Yi of intention earth. The body is not just the seven Zhang (length measure) physical body; it also has the Po (Yin spirit), which works in coordination with the Shi Shen to support life. The Po belongs to Yin and is the substantial aspect of Shi Shen. If the Shi Shen never stops; the Po will be deformed in our reincarnations. Only the Hun (Yang spirit) is within the Shen. The Hun resides in the eyes during the day and stays in the Liver at night. When it is living in the eyes it can see, when it is stored in the Liver, it can create dreams at night.

Dreams are the Shen traveling through the nine layers of Heaven and nine layers of earth in mere seconds. If you wake up in a daze, you have been held back by the body and the Po. Therefore returning the light will refine the Hun, which preserves the Shen, controls the Po, and in turn stops the Shi Shen. The ancients could distill away the dregs of Yin and seek pure Yang by vaporizing the Po and creating the full Hun.

Returning the light is the tactic of vaporizing the Yin Po. There is no exercise to restore Qian (pure Yang), except the tactic of returning the light. Light is the Qian, and returning it is to restore it. By observing this method, the Jing will naturally be abundant, the Shen Fire will burn, and Yi of intention earth will condense. This way the immortal fetus will be solidified. Even a dung beetle can hatch an egg to produce white shell. The beetle's Shen concentrates on producing magic and a worm leaves the shell from a ball of dung. How then could it not be possible to concentrate on the Shen where the Tian Xin rests and create a body?

The one Ling (soul) of your natural self goes into the Qian palace then divides into the Hun and the Po. The Hun is in the Tian Xin; this is Yang with light and clear Qi that comes from the Taixu (infinite emptiness) and has the same form as the Yuanshi (original beginning). The Po is Yin, with turbid Qi that is attached to the visible mortal body. The Hun wants to live, the Po wants death. All lust affecting the mind is commanded by the Po. This is the Shi Shen, which enjoys feeding on blood after death, and in life it causes great suffering. This is Yin returning to Yin, a combining of a common type. Students must completely refine Yin Po to transform it into pure Yang.

Chapter Three: Returning the Light and Concentrating on the Middle of the Center

The Patriarch says: "Return to the light named by the enlightened historical person Wenshi, also named Guan, Yizi." Return to the light in which the Yang of sky and the Yin Qi of earth are condensed. This is about a refined precious state of mind, pure Qi and pure thought. The first tactic consists of two achievements. The first achievement is the cultivation of a refined precious mind which moves to emptiness, which has it, but within emptiness. After one practices for a long time, the second level will be attained. This level is known as emptiness has substance, there is another one beyond the flesh.

Return to the light with a disciplined mind for one hundred days and this light will naturally condense to form fiery Shen. One drop of true Yang can suddenly create a millet bead, similar to the way a fetus is conceived when parents copulate, while you wait quietly. When the light returns, you will have found the optimum fire temperature environment.

Sunlight is the origin of the dominant transformation force. The shape of the sun is mirrored by the shape of the human eye. Leaking of the Shen is a familiar way of mortality. Therefore, the Jin Hua (shiny golden light) pathway is fully the inverse method.

Reversing the light will not only reverse the depletion of body Jing (essence), it will also reverse the natural transformation of true Qi. You need only stop illusion for one moment to undo the effects of thousands of calamities and reincarnations, whether you are one who breathes as a mortal for a year, or one who breathes as a mortal for one hundred years or walked nine long nights.

The loss of the life force begins with first cry of infancy and continues apace to old age until Yang decays into nine implicit sectors and they have never done reversing method. Therefore in the, "Lengyan Sutra" it is said: "Pure thought can fly, pure emotion can degrade." Most people have no desire to learn this, but instead desire emotions of affectionate love, which is a sinking pathway. However, using an inverse method of watching the breathing and listening to the quiet, can cultivate enlightenment. "Yinfu Jing," said: "Opportunity is in the eyes." "Huang Di Su Wen," said: "Personal essences are up in the empty orifices". By understanding this section one can nurture longevity and rise to the Heavens by and by. This is implementing the three teachings of Taoism, Buddhism and Confucianism.

The light is not in the body, nor outside the body. Mountains, rivers, sun, moon, and earth all share this light. It is not only in the body; intelligent and wise, every animate object has this light; it is not only outside the body. The light from the sky and earth brighten everywhere in the numerous universes. The body shines to sky and earth. Therefore, if the sage reverses the light, the light of the sky, earth, mountains and rivers are all reversed as well.

Our body essences support the eyes. The eyes are the most important point in the body. My students should consider this: If for one day you do not sit and quiet your thoughts, this light flows to somewhere, but where does it end? If one can sit quietly quiet for a moment, ten thousand calamities and a thousand occurrences from the moment are totally gone. All the methods attributed to quietude are really incredible! This is a magical tactic. From the start of your effort, begin practicing with coarse to deep breathing then move to fine breathing. Doing this continuously without stopping is the best. Concentration has always been the way; you will feel a cool and a warm sensation you will know, the self should be the width of the sky and ocean and all the ten thousand methods succeed when practiced this way.

There are many legends of sages who reversed the light and Confucians who knew how to stop the light. Buddhists have a vision about the mind and Laozi also had inner vision, those methods are this. However, the words are written about inverse brightness and many people read these texts and can talk about it, but cannot succeed in manifesting such an effect in their own minds because they do not understand the true meaning of the ancient writing. In order to return to a pure perception of the Heart of true self and the original moment of creation and Shen, in six feet of my body, I must perceive that the sky and the earth were not formed in a single moment. But modern people sit for one or two hours motivated by selfish caring. This is what is mistaken for inverse brightness. How can one achieve the correct result in this manner?

The ancestors of the Buddhists and Taoists taught people to look down at the tip of the nose. They did not teach to focus on the tip of the nose, but to locate the Middle Yellow (central axis) by way of the tip of the nose. This is where vision and thought occupy the same place, and where the mind and the Qi also occupy the same place. How can this energy be moved up and down? And how can they be moved up and down suddenly? Where is the criterion? The tip of the nose is a most wonderful key which is used as a landmark for the eye. If the eyes are open too wide, vision is too far beyond the tip of nose, if the eyelids are too tightly closed, then the nose does not appear. If the eyes are open too wide, then the mind will be lost and scattered. Having them too tightly closed will cause a loss in concentration and you may become lost. However, if the eyes use the tip of the nose as a criterion, then the light will penetrate naturally and you will not need to pull the light in or push it out.

Looking down to the tip of the nose, as you begin upon sitting, set this vision as your criterion, then let go while your are in initial quiet. This is similar to the way in which a carpenter draws a line to follow, after which the line has served its purpose and is of no further concern to him.

Concentration and visualization are methods developed by Buddha, as everyone knows. This method uses the eyes to see the tip of the nose while sitting up straight and comfortably and directing the mind into Yuan Zhong of the Origin Middle. The Taoist method directs the mind into the Middle Yellow (central axis); the Buddha's method is the same.

The beginner does not need to care about the tip of his nose but rather on looking straight ahead with level of eyes and your thoughts are in front of the eyes. Light is lively and will penetrate through naturally without a need to focus on the Middle Yellow. These few words describe the essence of this tactic. Others using the Buddhist sutra called the "Xiao Zhiguan", which describes the in and out of the experience of quietude.

The Yuan Zhong describes the magic stage of a sense of wonder. "Middle" includes everything everywhere of thousands of universes. This is a point which activates transformation for all that enter through this door. "Yuan" is the edge of a clue which has no definite solution, and the meaning of "origin" has life and is very wonderful.

Originally the two words for concentration and visualization were not divided but referred to as Dinghui (stillness and intelligence). Once our mind of thinking is developed one should not remain sitting with it unattended, but rather study this kind of thinking. Come to know where it is, where it starts, and where it disappears. Repeat these observations until you understand where it originates. It is unnecessary to talk about it repeatedly. Once grasped it then can be let go of until the mind is stable and peaceful. This is positive visualization. Otherwise you will be practicing the opposite form of visualization which is negative and should not be indulged. As one continues to practice stillness and then visualization, and visualization and then stillness, you will be training in both stillness and intelligence. This is the Dinghui of stillness and intelligence, and is a method to return the light. Returning is stillness and light is visualization. If you practice stillness without visualization you will have returning but without the light. If you practice visualization without the stillness you will have light but without the ability to return the light.

Chapter Four: Returning the Light and Regulating Breathing

The Patriarch said "The most important tactic is to have a pure mind, which does not seek to have experiences, and to let the proven experience come to oneself." At the early stage one has disease and pain, and being dazed and scattered are two common kinds of disease. In these situations concentrate on breathing since breathing is one's own Heart (mind), and the Heart activates the Qi flow, and Qi is transformed from the Heart.

Our mind is fast; within a second, there are delusional thoughts that impact breathing. Therefore, internal breathing with external respiration is cooperating such as the sound and echo corresponding. In one day, there are tens of thousands of breaths, and those tens of thousands breaths that have delusional thought mean the Shen brightness that has been leaking out totally, as death-rotten wood ash. Do you ever lack thought? One cannot be without thought. Can you have no breath? No, you must breathe. Use respiration as a medicine which bonds with the mind.

So to return the light is to regulate breathing; this method is exclusive to the eye and ear lights. One is the vision light and the other is ear light. Vision light is the external sun and moon combined light. Ear light is the internal sun and moon bonded Jing (essence). Jing is light condensed; there are different names for ear and eye light, but the source is the same intelligent Ling (soul) of all.

After sitting with the eyes and lips closed, set a criterion and let go of thought. Actually try to release tension, but also you may fear not, so put your intention to listen to the breathing, which goes deep and makes no sound. However, listen to the silent breathing; if there is a sound that is rough and that hasn't become fine yet, be patient, taking gentle breaths, then more gentle and slight and quiet, and even more slight and quiet after a long time, until suddenly this breathing stops, and true breathing occurs. Your conscious mind can understand itself. The Heart rate slows and then the breathing is thin, if the Heart of the mind is activated, a trickle of Qi moves. With small breaths the Heart of the mind is scrupulous; Qi is activated and so is the Heart.

A stable Heart of mind must take care of the Qi first, if the Heart does not know where to start, it can care for the Qi as entering, and this is the pure Qi of concentration and stabilization method.

The student does not know the character of an action. An action can be pulled by a thread, or a button may be pulsed to cause a movement. If one can run fast to achieve an action, then why not be pure and maneuver quietly to achieve it? This sage explains that the mind and the Qi conveniently interact in order to benefit future generations. The book of the Jin Dan (golden elixir) states: "The hen's mind often hears and intensely embraces her eggs; this is a magical strategy." The chicken egg can form the chick due to heat. But heat is only able to warm the egg shells, and cannot enter them; therefore the hen has to place her thoughts on the egg to lead Qi inside. The hearing is one thought's penetration and as the Qi follows into the egg, it has the warmth needed to form a chick. When the hen goes out, she usually increases the ear's power, and the intensity of her Shen in the eggs does not lessen. The heating is seamless day and night, and the Shen is alive.

If one has a living Shen, then it is because his postnatal mind has died. If a human can turn off the postnatal mind, his Yuanshen (source spirit) will be alive. If the Heart of mind has died, it is not because the Heart is haggard, it is because the Heart of mind is clear on which is the object of concentration. Buddha said "The mind in one can do everything." With the mind forgotten it's easier to care with pure Qi. Qi easily becomes rough; use the mind to maneuver from rough to fine. One knows this method, how can there not be the desire for stability?

Concerning the dazed and scattered conditions, as long as there is quiet practice day after day without interruption, the self will recover. Without sitting in a quiet state, you may become scattered without the self realizing this has occurred. If one knows that his thoughts are scattered then he can eliminate the scattering. Being dazed, one does not know that he is dazed, and this is quite a different state, like being a thousand miles away. The one that does not know that he is dazed is really dazed. If one knows that he is dazed, then he is not fully dazed, and the clear and the bright are still maintained.

Scattering is the Shen traveling. Being dazed is the Shen not being totally lucid. Being scattered is easier to control, being dazed is difficult to manage. There may be a disease with a symptom of pain or itching, and there may be a medicine to cure this disease. Being scattered can be regulated and being confused and bewildered can be recognized by the self, which still can find where it is. Being dazed and numb and dull indicates the dominance of Po (Yin spirit) of pure Yin. But if one is scattered, the Hun (Yang spirit) is there, resisting pure Yin.

When one is sitting in quietness while sleepy is being dazed. One wants to eliminate such a distraction. The practitioner may do that by regulating his breathing. Breathe in and out through the nose and mouth; this is not true breathing, but it provides access to true breathing. When one needs to sit quietly and purify his Qi, how can one quiet his Heart of mind? Use the breathing, breathing in and out is all that the Heart of mind knows. The breath should not be audible. If it is not heard, it will be thin and clear. The natural consequence of coarse loud breathing is an unfocussed and sleepy state.

What is shining? That is the vision's light shining, and the vision seeing inside rather than outside. One's vision does not look outside and naturally awaken and have intention inside; indeed, that is inner vision, but it is not really watching inside. What is listening? That is used by the ear light to listen inside without any external sound. The listener listens to their silence. The watcher is seeing the invisible. Vision does not look outside and hearing does not intend to listen for exterior, if one closes his eyes, min is scattered. The only method is looking inward and listening inside, looking inward and listening the silent sounds and avoid the effects from outside vision or sound; focus on the harmony of the center without being dazed. This is the sun and moon interacting with Jing and light.

The one who is dazed wants to sleep, so he needs to take a walk until the Shen is clear and bright and then try again to sit. In the early morning, if there is time, one should sit for the duration of one stick of incense. In the afternoon, there is more interference; it is easier to become dazed, which may require a greater length of time than one stick of incense to truly enter silence, who may find an entrance does not fall into being dazed.

Chapter Five: Returning the Light and Understanding the Wrong Path

The Patriarch said: "You are gradually making progress and becoming proficient. However, wrong paths are as many as the dry withered branches scattered beneath the cliff. It is at this point that I must enlighten you with specific instructions. Even though you may already understand, I will nevertheless speak about this.

Our path and the path of the Zen Buddhists are different. This can be verified in a very methodical way. First, I will explain their differences, and then later I will provide the proof.

The Zhong Zhi (main tactic) is in practice. Your aim in meditation is to feel relaxed and still, without thinking too much. You must feel lively and your Qi must be harmonized with your mind. Then, you enter stillness.

When entering stillness, one must grasp the crux of the matter. This is not the time to meditate in a shell of nothingness (the so called "void of no memory"). When you have let go of the ten thousand causes, you will feel awake and calm. There should be no struggling or trying. When you enter this state of awakened calm, do not fall into the Hidden Realm. The Hidden Realm is where the Five Yin Demons rule.

In conventional meditation, thoughts which are like withered branches and cold ashes are numerous. Those which are like the wide landscape and the springtime are sparse. This is called falling into the netherworld where Qi is cold and breathing is deep, a place full of wintry, decaying sights. A place we call "wood-stone", meaning completely lifeless.

But do not follow the ten thousand causes. If after entering stillness, emotions suddenly arise, following them will feel comfortable and familiar. This is called "Master becomes the slave" and if sustained will cause one to fall into the realm of lust and desire.

Those who take the higher path create Heaven. Those taking the lower path take the path of the fox or the slave. This is the path of the "Fairy Fox" which lives in the mountains and enjoys the wind, moon, flowers, fruit, the jade trees and jade grass. In this way, for anywhere from three or five-hundred years to many thousands of years, the "Fairy Fox" lives a life of fun and diversion. This is all considered the wrong path or "getting off track".

Having spoken about the wrong path, it is now time to talk about the methodical proof mentioned above.

Chapter Six: Proofs of Returning the Light

The Patriarch said: "Many people require definite proof of area experiences. One has to be opening minded and cannot act in an ignorant way, as if one is bound to thinking of degrees to assist realized beings. It requires care are and attention to inspect and clearly understand this matter."

The quietness has seamlessness to it, an awakened awareness, and euphoria; as if one was in a warm bath feeling drunkenness. In this moment, the whole body is warm and has harmonized the Yang; the light of golden flower also radiates and at first glance, all ten thousand things are quiet, the full moon is bright in the sky, and the great earth feels as if it was in a bright realm. These are the Heart of the mind and body opening and brightening, the golden flower blooming, and the whole body becoming enriched and strong, defying the cold wind and frost. Who would become bored with it? After I have had this experience, my spirit becomes even more vigorous. The body has built a golden house and a white jade platform. I blow a breath of true Qi, which recovers the life of decayed worldly objects. My body has red blood as milk and my seven Che (length measure) tall body resembles gold and treasures. All of this is consolidated in the Jin Hua (golden flower) stage.

The first section of the "Yinguan Jing" says "Sunset accompanies a great body of water, with images of moving trees." The sunset represents the primal foundation and the Wuji (infinite). The highest good is like water, crystal clear, and it flows into the next level, the Taiji (Yin and Yang started). The Zhen ( ) emperor is ruling, and Zhen represents wood and resembles the image of moving trees. Seven pairs of trees represent the brightening of the seven orifices. Qian ( ) in the northwest position shifts to Kan ( ), the image of Qian and Kan is a high tide at sunset. Kan is the

Zi (earth's stem) position, at the winter solstice, the Dong Zhi (mid winter) thunder rumbles underground, and there is hidden rumbling; the Zhen ( ) shocks, and Yang moves out of the ground, represented by image of moving tree. This pattern means forward movement.

The second paragraph speaks of the foundation and next steps, "Earth is ice; glass is treasured ground, the light is gradually concentrated into a lotus platform, and then Buddha makes an appearance. The true golden light appears; it can only be the Buddha, and is the golden level of great enlightenment. This experience has been verified.

There are three experiences that can be proven: The first one is when one sits and is forgotten; his Shen is as if it is in a valley where one can hear a person speaking from miles away, but the words are very clear, as if the person is next to you, and the sound echoes as if in a valley, and one hears without trying to listen. This is the proof of the Shen in the valley. The second experience, when one is quiet; there is bright white as steams full in front of oneself. As if one is in clouds, if one opens the eyes to look, then there's nothing. This is an emptiness room that creates whiteness, the body inside and out is brightened, and good fortune is present. The third experience, when in a quiet state, the flesh is a state of transpiration and is soft as cotton and as hard as jade; on is trying to sit but cannot; the body is floating and rising like steam. This is the Shen returning to the crown of the head and going through the sky. Sitting long enough, the Shen will be raised, just wait patiently for that moment.

Those three experiences are all proven classic experiences. But there are no endless kinds of these experiences depending on everyone's nature and everyone's desire to excel. As the "Zhiguan" sutra reads "All are coming from and depending on your native kindness to appear." This matter is like feeling as if one is drinking water; one knows how to distinguish cold and warm water. The truth is whenever you trust it.

One's innate Qi appears in front of his eyes. As a result of self inspection, one's Qi has had set up the Dan (golden pill). This is the real Millet. There is one Millet that comes by the next and it forms slightly to remarkably. All the innate nature is a Millet and mastering the innate nature, this one unify the true has innate immeasurable capacity. One has one's own power; at this level the most important thing is that one has to have compassion for all beings. This is the first tactic.

Chapter Seven: The Living Method of Returning the Light

The Patriarch said: "If you return the light gradually and systematically step by step, you do not need to give up your occupation." As a famous ancestor said, "When things come up, let them flow through you, when matters come up, understand them, then let them go". If you use the right thought to manage your affairs, then the thought of light is not affected by the situation. By experiencing the scene and then returning right away, you can return the light without tension.

If in daily life practice one can always remind oneself to return the thought of light no matter what happens, and without any other business stagnating in the mind, then this is using every moment to return the light. This is the finest magical process.

In the early morning, it is easier to clear the mind to return to the original state. Sitting for one to four hours is best. However, if you have to deal with people or business, you should use the return the light method, continuing without a moment of interruption. If you practice this way for two or three months, Heaven's true sages will come to confirm your method is true.

Chapter Eight: Relaxation Tactics

The Patriarch's poem: The Jade Clarity has left us with relaxation tactics using four sets of characters which may be translated in the following way:

With Rapture Condense Shen into the Qi point.
In June, one sees snowflakes falling with flying white snowflakes.

At three in the morning, one sees the blazing sun.
In the water, the Xun (☴) wind blows, upper Heaven travels back to be absorbed by the Kun Earth (☷)."

There is also a sentence: Xuan (emptiness has substance) within a Xuan; there is no town which has a true mansion.

In this verse, all the Xuan's mysteries are contained.

The importance of the Tao cannot be found outside of these four characters: "Wu Wei Er Wei" (action through non-action).

Only the Wu Wei of non-action will be unlimited in shape and appearance. There is only one way from Wu Wei of non-action to progress that will not fall into the stubborn emptiness and death of nothingness. All the function is just in one way and the one center. The cardinal function is all in the eyes. Two eyes have the role of the handle on the Big Dipper: to circulate, transform, and move Yin and Yang. The great medicine is true water's metal.

The introduction reverses the light, which is the point of the beginning tactic. Use the exterior light to control the light inside like an assistant who desires to step into a master's level. This is how the middle and lower level practitioner refines the lower two gates in order to progress to the upper gate. The pathway is becoming clearer and more familiar. Everyone loves the Tao and this is the direction to the supreme tactic. For all students, this is the secret of the secret, please be encouraged.

"Return the light" is a general description. As one progresses to the next level, the light will become more abundant and the reversing method will improve. The previous method started from the exterior and moved to mastering the interior. This time the method requires controlling the imperial center to achieve mastery of the exterior. Previously one assisted the emperor; now the practitioner follows the emperor's order. This is a major reversal.

Method: If you want to enter into the quiet stage, first you must regulate the physical body and calm the mind. In so doing, letting go will be peaceful and harmonized. One can let go of the ten thousand origins and become naked without any attachment. Tian Xin will be in the center position, close your eyelids, and like an imperial edict to call a secretary, who would dare not to respond? Next, two eyes shine into the Kun ( ) earth palace, and with the arrival of this inward illumination the true Yang will dare not to respond.

The trigram Li ( ) has fire: exterior Yang with interior Yin and Qian ( ) body. Li has one Yin line in the center as the principle. If one's mind follows the object to create thought, the familiar flows outward. Now reverse the light to illuminate the interior and it will not follow this phenomenon. The Yin Qi has to stay and be illuminated by the light that is pure Yang. Similar trigrams have a good connection, so the Kan ( ) water's middle Yang responds from the Qian ( ) Yang, which rises up. Those two active Yangs meet, then bond and create inner activities, back and forth, ascending and descending. The Self Yuan (source) palace called Taixu (infinity) has unlimited capacity and the whole body has a feeling of lightness and wants to soar like clouds flowing over a thousand mountains. Next since back and forth is invisible one cannot identify whether he is floating or sinking. When the pulse pauses and Qi stops, this is true copulation, called "moonlight covers up ten thousand rivers". Once it is implicit somewhere, then Tian Xin has one move; this one is Yang returning and carries living Zi Shi (midnight) timing. However this information has to be elaborated upon.

Watching and listening as a mortal, the eyes and ears are concentrated with business affair, so even though the phenomenon has gone, it still leaves an imprint in the mortal method. This is the familiar way for everyone. While the emperor of Heaven serves the attendant, habitual patterns associated with the living level of ghosts stubbornly remain.

Today whether one is active or still, every one is the same. But the Zhen (true) person has the activity of inner Heaven's emperor from which all action follows and the role of this action arises from Heaven's root and mastering quiet into the moon's cave. Quiet is infinite and movement without limitation. The up and down movement never stops or has rest intervals. This leisurely communication is between the root of Heaven and the cave of the moon.

Tian Xin is calm, but one moves it and you will loose this tenderness. Tian Xin has moved and responds after it is too late. As soon as Tian Xin, moves, use the true intention rising up in the Qian (☰) Yang palace. While the Shen light is watching the top, Tian Xin is guiding and this movement occurs at the right time. Tian Xin is raising the Qian (☰) Yang top and enjoyment while suddenly an easing off occurs with the use of the true thought to the Huang Ting of the yellow court. Do this while the eyes focus on the middle yellow spirit room which is the state of peace without thought, achieved by watching without watching. In this moment, the body and mind are at a stage of the infinite and the ten thousand origins disappear. Even my Shen room, my Ding (the three legged pot that represents the cooking and processing of our internal medicine and awakened awareness), and furnace, do not know where they are. Look for the physical body but it is not available. This is the sky coalescing into the earth; it is the magical return to the roots of time, and this is Shen condensed into the Qi point.

Once one returns the light, one will find at the beginning it is scattered. If one wants to merge with it, they will find that even with trying to use the six processes it cannot be done. One must conserve the original and add fuel to expand the life force. If one can merge naturally, then no effort is necessary. This will set Shen into the ancestral orifices, soothing and gathering the innate. All attraction has gone into a stage of peace and great stillness. This is deeply hidden in the Qi point, and all the magic returns back the root.

Here is one chapter that has three sections. One section has nine paragraphs and as soon as the day after tomorrow, I will explain it to you.

Today I will explain the chapter that has three sections. Conservation and caring are the beginning of quietude. Soothing and gathering are conservative, caring and deeply hidden. To this end, nourishing and conservation are deep storage. One is in the middle level which can not easily be divided, but has divided nevertheless. This invisible infinite orifice has the thousand and the ten thousand things everywhere, but just has one orifice. It is not easy to divide, but there has been a division, this is unlimited time, whether a million years or just one.

The mortal Heart of mind has to maximize quietness to move, otherwise its movement will be reckless and not movement from the true self. Therefore, one has a sense of having to move in the same natural way that the sexual act promotes movement. The Heaven and earth have no motivation to move. If the sky moves it is not a response. As with sexual movement, lustful words, which have substance, can cause movement, but this is off the true position and the movement is from an external effect.

If one has no thought instead of a thought created, this is true thought. In the state of great peace and stillness, while the Heavenly opportunity is moving suddenly, is there any thought to encourage this movement? If there is no purpose to advancing, then this is the Wu Wei Er Wei (action through non-action)'s meaning.

The first two poems are all including the role Jin Hua of the golden flower. The next two are about the meaning of the communication between the sun and the moon. In June is Li (☲) fire. White snow flake flies is Li's true Yin and will also return to Kun (☷) Yin. Three o' clock in the morning is Kan (☵) water. Sunshine is Kan's (☵) one Yang and will be transferred to Qian (☰) Yang; exchanging Kan (☵) water to fill in Li (☲) fire herein. The next two sentences are about the role and function of the handle of the Big Dipper which controls the entire up and down Yin and Yang movement. Is the water not Kan (☵)? Eyes are Xun (☴) wind, the light of the eyes shines into the Kan (☵) water palace, recruiting sun's Jing essence. Sky is Qian (☰) Yang of upper palace which travels back to be absorbed by Kun (☷) Yin of lower palace. The Shen moves into the Qi and the Sky moves into the earth, taking care of the optimal fire as well. The end of two sentences is the tactic's tactic. The tactic's tactic is bathing, cleaning the Heart of mind, and washing away all worry.

Learning the immortal sage's theory, one has to know how to start at the beginning and stop at the good end. Starting from

Wuji (infinite) and ending up at Wuji (infinite). Buddha is neither here nor there, but where his mind is. This is the most important Buddhist doctrine, and our Taoist doctrine is extreme about emptiness as well. End of Xin (true self) and Mei (life) accomplishment. In short the three religions use one sentence which is about protecting life and eternal's Shen Dan (golden pill).

What is Shen Dan? All has no purpose and that is what it is all about. Taoism's most important secret is invisible bathing, all the complete to achievement, only empty mind to word of all. This statement is a breakthrough which took many decades to discover.

Student unknown one section that has three paragraphs. The Buddhist concepts of "Emptiness, Illusion and Center" are represented by following three concepts: the first concept is seeing everything as empty; the second, understanding the illusory nature of everything and knowing that the empty nature of form does not destroy everything, emptiness is necessary to establish all things. The third, center visualization, is not destroying everything, but eventually nothing is destroyed. After all, to practice visualizing emptiness requires the understanding that all things cannot be indestructible and are impermanent; this is practicing all three visualization concepts. Therefore, practicing emptiness understands form cannot exist without emptiness or emptiness cannot exist without form; so seeing emptiness as nothing; illusion is empty, and center is also empty. Practicing the concept of illusion creates an understanding that the majority of what is seen is illusory and form is empty, emptiness is an illusion as well as is the idea of a center. Practicing the center also uses the concept of emptiness. No name is empty; this empty name is the center. Within the concept of illusion, no name is illusory; this illusory name is the center. At the center, therefore, one need not talk about it any more.

Although I mention the Li (☲) fire or Kan (☵) water sometimes, I never talk about it. The cardinal role all is in two eyes. Hence the cardinal function is using them. Using them for circulating and transforming, but not just transforming and maneuvering the six roots and seven orifices; it is all light hidden there. Why only the two eyes, but not the others? Use Kan (☵)'s Yang and the Li (☲) light to shine and attract, hence it will brighten. Zhuzi (he is also called Yunyang or Yuanyu a northern sect of Taoism). Zhuzi said: "A blind practitioner has difficulty becoming successful, but a deaf practitioner may have success." How similar is our language, but there is still a difference between a main or auxiliary position and between the chief and the assistant.

The sun and the moon were originally a single object. The sun includes true Yin. That Yin is true moon's Jing essence. As the moon cave is in the sun instead of in the moon, the moon cave is the Jing of the sun. Otherwise, only talk about the moon is sufficient. The moon embraces the true Yang and is really the sun's light. The sun's light reflects into the moon and is the sky root. Otherwise, only talk about sky should be sufficient. One day or one month, separated is a half, combined as a whole. For instance, one man and one woman; if living separately are not a family. A marriage has a husband and wife; a complete family. Even a business cannot completely explain the Tao; however, husband and wife separately, after all are two people. Since the sun and moon have become separated they are not a whole. Hence, the ear and eye example uses the same philosophy. I said the blind without ears, the deaf no longer have eyes; this is the case, saying that is a thing, but it is two things. In this way the six of roots are as one root and the seven of orifices are as one orifice. My language is only to disclose their commonality. In actuality we have not gotten two. May close-minded students force themselves into different compartments, thus changing their vision for all time.

Chapter Nine: Discussion of Building the Foundation in One Hundred Days

The Patriarch said in the "Xinyin" sutra that "the returning of wind and mixing with the Jin Hua (golden flower) will lead to the achievement of the Ling of the soul in one hundred days." Most importantly, building the foundation requires one hundred days to achieve the true light. As we are still students, we still use the light of the eyes, not the Shen fire of spirit fire, nor the natural light and the intelligent subtle illumination light.

Within one hundred days of practice, the Jing and Qi will be self-sufficient, and true Yang will be abundant. Water within has true fire. As it continues, this will lead to a natural copulation and spontaneous condensation to form the immortal fetus. I did not know and understand the sky, but as the process goes on, the immortal baby gains form. If one has a little bit of his own ideas, then he will be thrown into heretical thought.

One hundred days establishes the foundation; but it is not literally one hundred days. One day establishes the foundation; is not literally one day. Breathing establishes the foundation; it is not literally one breath.

Breathing is from the Heart of mind, the Heart is the breathing and the Yuan of source Shen, Yuan Qi, and Yuan Jing; their entire movement of ascending and descending, of opening and closing, begins from the Heart of the mind. Whether there is actual being or no, emptiness or form, all are in thought. Just as holding one breath is a lifetime, far more than one hundred days; one hundred days is just one breath.

One hundred days training is about having strength, if day has strength, then it will be effective at night; if night has strength, then it will be effective at day. The one hundred days establishes the foundation of the Jade edict. The superior true person's listening is affected all of us without exception. A true teacher's speech should consider all the students without exception. Xuan of emptiness has substance within Xuan. It is unsolvable, only seeing nature with knowledge, so scholars must have learned from a true teacher, from nature itself to begin. This is all that has been identified.

Chapter Ten: Xing, the Light of our Original Natural Essence, and Shi, the Light of the Conscious Postnatal Mind

The Patriarch said "Returning the light of our original nature has to be done throughout the day, in walking, stopping, sitting, lying, as long as one has the method to grasp the crux, awaken it. As I have previously discussed, the empty room has white light. Is it only the white light that makes it white?"

But as one said, initially when one doesn't see a light, this is effective. If one is seeing a light, but with an intention in your mind, then this is not the Xing light, the light of our original nature. Regardless, if there is an actual light or not, as long as one has no thoughts to have thought. What is no thought? There are a thousand places of no thought which create thought. What is no thought within thought? One thought can be held for a lifetime. This concept is a criterion of thought; it is different than daily thoughts. This is the Heart of the Mind as thought, thought as it is presented in the Heart, and this Heart is the light and the medicine.

With normal vision everyone's eyes see objects without consideration. This is the Xing light, the light of our original nature. Like a mirror that captures images without intending to, such as water having an appearance without intention. After awhile, that will turn into the Shi, the light of conscious thought, and that is the difference between the two. If a mirror has a shadow, then it is no longer a mirror, like water that has an image that is no longer purely reflected. If the light of Xing is shadowed by the light of Shi, then what light is it?

Students who are at the beginning, see the Xing light, then at that moment, switch to Shi light, they cannot seek the light explicitly. It is not without having the light; it is having the

light that has been influenced by the Shi. The Yellow Emperor said "Sounds do not create melody, it is just noise."
This is the meaning.

"Lengyan seeking entrance" said "It is not in the dust, not at the Shi, it is in the root." What does this mean? Dust is the external material world and is the realm which contains things that we don't need to care about. If the mind follows objects that it considered to be associated with it, then identify the external object as your self. Therefore, the attachment of objects in the mind must eventually be returned, and all things return to where they come from. The brightness returns to the natural moon and sun.

If you restore the light for your self, eventually it is not yours. If you have returned it, who has it? Brightness returns to the sun and moon. If one is seeing the sun and the moon's light, but did not want to return it, the sky will have no sun or moonlight and your self will lose the sun and moon's nature.

If one considers having the light of the sun and the moon, does one still has? I do not know the difference in result of bright and dark; when the bright and dark move into a forgotten stage, where is the respectively? Therefore, if there is a return, this is also internal dust. Only one is seeing Xing of nature without return; seeing, but not really, this has included return.

The returning is the circulating Shi, and has to transfer to the Xing light; this is the teaching from the Buddhist Ananda who circulated his Heart and eyes when he started his practice. At the beginning, he said he had eight returns; the first of seven have come one by one. Later, the Buddhist Ananda is holding on Xing of nature his self as crane support, but his Xing still carried the eight Shi that his true Xing had not really been returned. In the end, there was a breakthrough; his true Xing came and he kept on, but it has not actually returned.

When you return the light you are returning the light that you did not want to return at the beginning. Therefore it does need a bit of Shi (conscious thought). For one to circulate you must use the six roots. Going to the Buddhist Pudi level requires using those six roots. The Dust and Shi are not used; to use the root it is required to use the root's Xing. One dose not use the Shi to return the light; use the root of the Yuan of the original Xing. If one uses the Shi to return the light that is the root's Shi, then this is only a bit different, it has changed to the opposite direction.

Using conscious thought is the Shi light, letting go is the Xing light. This small difference is a thousand miles apart; it can not be not identified. If the Shi is used continuously, then the Shen can not be created. The Heart of the mind is not empty, and then the Dan, the elixir, of the golden pill does not condense. The calm Heart is the Dan, the empty Heart is the medicine. Not being stuck thinking about anything is a quiet Heart. Not having a focus on a thing is an empty Heart. What one sees as empty is not really empty. In emptiness, forget the empty. This is true emptiness.

Chapter Eleven: Kan and Li Copulate

The Patriarch said; "When one leaks their Jing essence and Shen of spirit, and indulges in strenuous exertion when copulating, one becomes Li (☲). When one can cultivate the Shen of spirit and Zhi of postnatal knowledge with quietude and conservation this is Kan (☵)."

When one allows the seven orifices to move outward this is Li (☲). When one reverses the movement of the seven orifices inward this is Kan (☵).

Indulging in Lust through the eyes and sound through the ears is Yin.

Mastering the reversal of seeing and hearing is Yang. Kan (☵) and Li (☲) are Yin and Yang. Yin and Yang are the Xing of the natural self and the Ming of life; the Xing and Ming are the physical body and mind, body and mind are Shen and Qi.

The Jing of essence and Shen of spirit do not converge during normal circulation. True copulation is a convergence of Shen and Jing with one breath while sitting in silence.

Chapter Twelve: The Zhoutian (Cosmic Orbit)

The Patriarch said: "The Zhoutian (cosmic orbit) is not mainly achieved by controlling Qi; one uses Heart of mind as a magical tactic. Someone thought, "How can I circulate Zhoutian?" That is excess encouraged thought. It has to be no intention to concentrate and not intention to make it move of deed. Face up to look at the whole seeing the sky from every direction with changes every moment. The Big Dipper is stable; this stable Big Dipper is like our Heart of mind, the Heart is the stable Big Dipper and Qi is moving stars."

To have the body's Qi flow through the entire body, including the extremities, originally did not require much effort. But now, due to the stagnation of Zhi Shen (postnatal mind), one must refine the Zhi Shen and stop scattered ideas, in order that the internal medicine may spontaneously occur. Internal medicine does not have the form of a physical object; this is the Xing of natural light. This natural light is innate true Qi which one most have had great skill to have found, there is no another way to obtain it, to say you can collect is not true. In practicing one has had seeing it for long, hence his Heart of mind brightens and his stress and tension has been leaked with emptiness, his Heart of mind naturally escaped the dust of mortal life. If one wants to have the dragon and tiger copulation today, and fire and water communication tomorrow, eventually it became a delusion. The true tactic is only taught by the fire dragon true person, as told in the book of the elixir.

Day has a Zhoutian (cosmic orbit) and one moment in a day has a Zhoutian. When Kan (☵) and Li (☲) are copulating, this equals one Zhoutian. The body is internal copulation has the same rhythm of natural sky and earth circulation. Our body's Qi circulation sometimes has been stopped, but the natural sky circulation never stops for a moment. If Yin and Yang are harmonized, there is Yang peace on earth, and I am among the palace of center, tens and thousands of everything give enjoyment to this moment. This is described in the book of elixir as invisible bathing, why only occurs with the great Da Zhoutian (great cosmic orbit)?

Stone Temple's Shi said: "A word within a sentence has to have its own importance; in the present time there has been loss of this understanding."

Regarding the optimum fire temperature, there is a difference in degree, whether nor strong or mild can do. Stone Temple's Shi said: "Our generation can be enlightened, but the next one is filled with regret." One is making progress toward spontaneous achievement naturally, if I do not know what the Kan (☵) and the Li (☲) are, or the sky and earth and the nature of their communication, what is one circle or two circles of Zhoutian, Where to find the great or small of the difference or not?

In short, it is difficult to attain true circulation in the body. If there is not true circulation, we are seeing that is very big or small circulation. The inner body true circulation occurs, the whole sky, earth and all the substance are following, even in this square inch can be understood the minimum or maximum.

The Jin Dan of golden pill's optimum fire temperature has to occur naturally. If it is not natural, parallel the sky and earth remain sky and earth, everything remains everything. If they forced together, eventually they do not match, as it just likes the drought environment that is Yin and Yang discord. Even Qian (☰) sky and Kun (☷) earth serve never miss on day, but still seeing that the number of unnatural harmonizing.

I have the ability to communicate between Yin and Yang,

transform and regulate the nature; which at this moment the clouds are streaming and the rain is felling, vegetation intoxicated fitness and mountains are clear and rivers are flowing, even though some cynical suddenly released, this is great Zhoutian.

Question: Living Zishi is a very wonderful time that must be determined precisely to be the Zishi midnight time, it seems be caught in phase state.

Answers: It is not caught in phase state, if there is no criterion, how to recognize the live Zishi? It is not only to know the live Zhishi; surely there is Zhishi at midnight. There is one and two and it is really Zhishi, but it is no really; this is true Zhishi. The true Zhishi does not have criterion or live.

If one does not know the criterion of either live Zhishi or the Zhishi at midnight that one needs to identify, how can you know which one is live or midnight Zhishi and true Zhishi? The living Zhishi is always perceived and always present. After all, while the midnight Zhishi's Qi is clear, live and bright, the living Zhishi is easier to find. If you do not know the living Zhishi, you should inspect the midnight Zhishi; with the midnight Zhishi is apparent. Use this discovery to find the Zhishi in daily activity; this live Zhishi will be experienced through magical processing.

Chapter Thirteen: A Song to Persuade the World

The Patriarch said:

Due to the World-Dan (golden pill) fever, it is my intention to explain this teaching as often as necessary.

A Lord has used this great origin, which is directed at life and death, so it would be a shame to lose it.

Laojun (author of the Dao De Jing) who also suffers from a human body introduced Gushen (the valley spirit) to the world.

My outline seeks the true path; and the Huang Zhong (Middle Yellow middle theory) describes the great Yi (Taoism eight trigrams).

At the center of body is a Xuanguan (Entering the emptiness, one finds substance), between Zi (midnight) and Wu (noon) the criteria for which is to follow the breath.

Reverse the flow of light to the ancestral orifices, which will bring peace to ten thousand spirits, and reveal the source of all medicine which arises from this one Qi.

A transparent screen changes to a golden light, and there is often a blazing red sun light.

Everyone misidentifies Kan (water) and Li (fire) Jing (essence), which transfer Heart and Kidney into the interval state.

When mortal matched Tian Xin (Heart and center of universe), Nature and Tao naturally bonded.

Let go of the ten thousand origins without a bit of effort, this is the innate true Wuji (infinite).

Taixu (original emptiness) has infinite capacity, the moment of life and death is forgotten by your own thoughts.

Thought has been forgotten when seeing the truth, and seeing that within the clear water, there is a bead and unpredictable Xuan (emptiness has substance).

When all the original worry has gone; Jade Clarity will descend to honor the nine dragon's certificate.

Fearlessly step forward through Heaven's gate, maneuver the wind's power and control thunderbolts.

Stilling the Shen and regulating the breathing are the first steps, followed by retreating hiding in the secret of eternal place.

I used a Zhang, Lushen style poem to write this poem. My intention was to help the reader understand the Tai Yi Jin Hua Zhong Zhi edition. After the hour of Zi (11 pm to 1 am) and before the hour of Wu (11 am to 1 pm) are not chronological times but refer to the Kan of water and Li of fire.

Those who have stable breath are all breathing into the root of the Huang Zhong (Middle Yellow), the central axis. Sitting means that the Heart of the Mind does not move. The Jiaji is not only the spine; it is the straight thoroughfare of the Yuqing (Jade Clear) pathway. The two gates are where there is difficulty in using a verbal description. Forgetting the Shen in concentration is the most important thing in emptiness and quietness, even when concentrating observe this fact. The liquid has been dissolved and blood is formed, this is the postnatal returning to the innate. Qi reverts to the Shen, Shen returns to emptiness, emptiness matches the Tao, and the Tao is the goal which fulfills your wish. There are numerous tactics to describe this path, but here is the true one. The thunder that is below ground and shakes the mountain is the true Qi occurring; the true Qi creates the yellow sprouts, when they are unearthed is the true medicine is born. This small sentence of a few phrases describes the self-cultivation. Understanding that this should not be confused with the public puzzles is essential.

The Confucian pedant and his student Yanzi were at the Tai mountain peak watching Wu Gate's white horse. Yanzi exhausted his Shen, but finally saw that the horse had a white cloth. Yanzi used his vision and Shen light too much and too often, so he passed away early in his life. Returning the light is important, indeed!

Returning the light is the use of the pure Heart of the Mind to lead, by only having true breath and concentrated brightness, into the middle palace. After a long time, it will naturally bond with the Ling of the soul; this transformation occurs spontaneously. Finally, with an ever calm mind and stable Qi as the foundation, the Heart has forgotten and the Qi becomes condensed for efficiency. The breath, Qi, and emptied Heart will achieve the internal medicine which is the Heart and Qi as one. The fire reaches the optimal temperature to care for, clear, and brighten the Heart, and one can see the Xing of nature. This is achieving the Tao.

Each student is encouraged to practice. My seven students remember if you miss the time and age it is unfortunate! One day of not practicing is like one day of being a ghost. One breath is like being a true Xian, an Immortal. The experience, transformations, and creations on which this is based will surely cause my seven students to pay attention!

Wu Pian Ling Wen (Five Ling [soul] Articles)

Written by Wang Chong Yang. Transcribed by Qing Xu Zi

Wu Pian Ling Wen was written by Wang Zhong Yang, who is the Dragon Gate branch founder Qiu Chuji's teacher. He explains how the mind needs to practice and to ignite Tian Xin, light and inner vision to create internal medicine of the Jin Dan (golden pill) in five stages.

In the Taoist view of life and reality, the highest level, Taixu (Infinity) is seen as a Ding, the three legged pot that represents the cooking and processing of our internal medicine and awakened awareness; Taiji (Yin and Yang) started to divide into a magical furnace, clear and quietly the magical processing begins. Wuwei, the non purpose- relaxing in the self and without agenda or particular direction is as the Dan, a golden pill, that provides a foundation and internal medicine that allows the self-perfected nature to come forth through the body. Xingming, the Xing is the inherently pure and natural self, likened mercury, and Ming is life, seen as the nature of lead. Dinghui, Ding is stillness and Hui is intelligence; both are seen as water and fire, both can naturally transform and develop into the true seed. They are used not to assist nor forget the optimal fire, but to wash the Heart of mind and worry as an invisible bath. Concentrate and stabilize the breathing as to strengthen and harmonize yourself. Avoidance of distraction, stability of the stillness of the mind, and the ability to not allow one's intelligence to dull while in stillness, are the three important practices, the innate has Xuan Guan (upon entering the emptiness, one finds substance). Brightening the Heart is developing your inner wisdom as your identity, seeing the Xing (true self) is condensed. The three Yuan, the source of nature-Jing, Qi, and Shen are united as a Xian (Immortal) fetus. All is as one in the Dan, the golden pill of achievement. Beyond the flesh there is an immortal body that is detached, breaking into the emptiness as the final outcome.

At the highest level of study and practice, it is understood that three religions of Taoism, Buddhism and Confucian come from the same source and thought. The higher-level practitioner never stops, he moves straight into sainthood, enlightenment and perfection. The body and Shen (spirit) both are magical; with the Tao matches the truth, living in freedom stage of paradise for eternity, and never decaying. This is the great enlightenment of the Jinxian of the golden immortal position.

The true Tao is difficult to pass on; to search to the end is to let go of the human dust.

The waterfall from the mountain grows the yellow sprout; the ground rises and is covered with white snow.

Hui (intelligent moon) shines like the jade green marsh pond; Xuan (emptiness with substance) is like the wind slightly blowing the curved green smoke.

The interaction of wood and metal is love; this is the emptiness of the Taiji of Yin and Yang divided in the same circle.

Preface

This text is the most valuable treasure of Jin Dan, the alchemical path of the internal golden pill. It cannot be passed on to an unworthy person; but if a highly advanced and moral person finds this book, he will have found the right way to practice towards Xian, the immortal level. The author Chong Yang said: "The Xian (immortal) has five levels: ghost Xian, the ghost immortal which is undesirable, Ren Xian, the human immortal which is not worth talking about, Di Xian, the earthly immortal who lives in the world with a very long life, Shen Xian, the spirit immortal level can change from visible to invisible and also exists beyond the mortal flesh. Tian Xian, the Heavenly immortal level is listed above Shen Xian. The Taoist practitioner does not want to be at the middle or lower level, and should strive to learn the highest true law, the ultimate magical Tao pathway of understanding Yin and Yang, Heaven and earth, as well the five elements (phase) they transform. Yin and Yang: the implications of these words are magnificent. Heaven and earth, sun and moon, the five elements (phase); all transformations come from them.

Taiji is formed when Yin and Yang start to divide. From the interaction of Yin and Yang the clear Qi rises and appears to us as the Heaven. The heavy Qi falls to the ground forming the earth, which includes wood and fire essences which are like Taiyang (the beginning of Yang), and metal's water essence which is like Taiyin (the beginning of Yin). Heaven and earth, sun and moon transform from the interaction of Yin Qi and Yang Qi. These two energies are communicating between Heaven and earth and circulating incessantly, transforming into ten thousand classes (all of the things that exist on universe). Human offspring receive the father's essence and the mother's blood, which are metaphors for Heaven's Yang Qi, earth's Yin Qi, the sun's energy and Yang Hun (Yang spirit), the moon's substance and Yin Po (Yin spirit), fire's Yang Shen (self control spirit) and water's Yin Jing (essence). The human body transforms using the same Qi as Heaven and earth. Heaven and earth are humans' great parents. The enlightened one rises above Heaven and earth and Yin and Yang, while the confused one drowns in a huge bitter ocean. If one is not restrained by the five elements (phase) and Yin and Yang then one can attain the highest level, Tian Xian, the Heavenly immortal level. Those who do not reach enlightenment will perish with the rest of creation, which is sad indeed.

Tian Xin (Heavenly Heart) is like a wise ruler, Yuan Shen (source spirit), is a vehicle for Tian Xin. Chong Yang said "Tian Xin is the True Heart of the primary magical circle". The first Buddha Shakyamuni said this true Heart reality was originally magically bright with no stains or attachments, with a clean and quiet body, even a slight stain would cause illusion. Tian Xin is the root of Taiji, (Yin and Yang starting to divide). Nothingness is its body. It is the ancestor of Yin and Yang, and is the True Heart of Heaven and earth, hence the name Tian Xin.

Your Yuan Shen is the true Ling (soul) which has no life or death, and cannot perish or be damaged. It is the brave and calm mind. Tian Xin utilizes Yuan Shen. Yuan Shen is Tian Xin's magical process. Therefore, one uses the stillness and magic circle of Tian Xin to transform the true Heart back to its original, eternal, unstained form. This is the magical Yuan Shen process.

The three treasures are the basis of the process. The exterior three treasures should not leak and the interior three treasures should be self-closing. Chong Yang's notes say, "The exterior three treasures are the eyes, ears and mouth, whereas the interior three treasures are Jing, Qi and Shen." When the exterior treasures are not closed; the interior treasures can easily seep out through the eyes, ears and mouth. Shen escapes through the eyes, Jing from the ears and Qi through the month.

To talk, hear and see is an outward action eventually exhausting the interior Jing, Qi and Shen. As time goes on we gradually age, the three interior treasures become depleted until we die. The three exterior treasures are important to maintaining the potency of the three interior treasures; hence there is a need to fortify and strengthen the three exterior treasures. With the eyes, see but not to the point of excess. With the ears, listen but not to the point of excess, and the mouth, speak moderately and forgo talking nonsense. This is known as the exterior three treasures not leaking.

Not seeing affects the Shen which resides in the Heart, not listening affects the Jing which resides in the Kidney, not talking affects the Qi which is in the Dantian. This is known as the self-closing of the three treasures.

When the human body is connected to Heaven's innate Qi, the innate Qi returns to the body naturally. Chong Yang's notes read, "The Heaven contains innate Qi; the human body is formed from innate Heaven Qi." An immortal practitioner has to be careful and conscious when entering into the stillness of Tian Xin. Let the living and non-desiring Yuan Shen concentrate into Xuan Guan (entering the emptiness, one finds the substance) in the daily motion of walking, standing, sitting and laying. Then the eyes will avoid excessive seeing, the ears will avoid an overindulgence of listening, and the mouth will avoid too much talking. The body's interior is then transformed into a true stage in which the exterior will respond automatically, communicating with the innate Qi naturally, which will then be attributed to the body.

The body's interior and exterior has a front and back, a left and right, an upper and a lower which are postnatal Yin and Yang. There is only a drop of the extreme innate Yang Qi, mixed in a mysterious environment in Yao Ming (awakening within extreme emptiness both clearly expressed and yet only implied); flexible and active, it cannot be seen and asked. Chong Yang's note reads: "In the body, the exterior has the limbs and hundreds of bones, the interior has the five Zhang which are the Lung, Spleen, Kidney, Liver and Heart and the six Fu which are the Large Intestine, Stomach, Urinary Bladder, Gall Bladder and Small Intestine and San Jiao (three cavities). The tears, saliva Jing, Qi and blood have form; they are the postnatal Yin and cloudy substance."

This one drop of extreme Yang Qi is the innate true one (Zhen Yi) Qi and is also named Taiyi (the great infinite origin) embracing true Qi. It awakened from the Huang Fu (awakening within quiet, one finds substance) and Yao Mi (implicit and explicit in awakening within both clearly expressed and yet only implied) quietude to discover substance of innate environment. To find the innate extreme Yang, one has to be in a quiet state; this is the one and only path. In this quiet state one needs to clear excessive thoughts, watching the body until one has entered into a state of emptiness and stillness; suddenly one will find a little true Yang awakening in Huang Fu (awakening within quiet to find the substance stage) one reach it; it seems like one has not, but one really has, and in Yao Ming (explicit and implicit within both clearly expressed and yet only implied) quietude, between yes and no, interior and exterior, unpredictable and difficult to get a glimpse of, neither interior nor exterior. It cannot be explained why, but it arrives.

Although it comes from the external, the internal pregnancy of the immortal fetus is real. Chong Yang's notes read, "All the objects are carrying Yin and embracing Yang; the substance of the human body though cloudy, maintains a little innate Yuan, the source Yang."

At birth one's self is magical and bright. With time, the enslavement to the seven Qing (seven emotions) and six Yu (six desires) begins, attaching from the interior. In addition, working hard in cold and hot environments will deplete one from the exterior, unconsciously exhausting the Yuan (source) with no regard to natural development, until the body perishes.

This being understood, one should practice to reverse his vision and listen, forgetting the material and embracing the true, seeing and listening to but not leaking from the senses, in wonder but not overindulgence, so that the Zhen Jing (true essence) self solidifies and Yuan (source) Yang is self-sufficient. The true internal responds to the external, the innate true one Qi comes from the emptiness to activate the inner Jin Dan, the golden pill. Although it came from the outside, the golden pregnancy is inside. This is known as the mother's Qi embracing the son's Qi, Shen embracing Qi and Qi embracing Shen. At this point the Dantian, (the field that creates the golden pill) is warm, the three gates open, have upward and downward movement, and the upper and lower harmonize. Awakening nectar pours from the top, sweet dew sprinkles the Heart, the Heaven's magical music is frequently heard, and the treasured Xuan bead (the emptiness with substance bead) is commonly seen. This vision is so transparent that it cannot be explained. Zhen Jing, the true essence has returned to the gold room and there is a bright bead that will never leave you. This is not a falsehood.

In the absence of the postnatal, the innate cannot rescue the postnatal. How can the postnatal be transformed without the innate? This emptiness has substance and substance has created emptiness. This empty substance activates the materialization, which needs emptiness to sense and be connected to the Ling (soul). The innate and postnatal Qi domains are like sound echoing in a valley.

Chong Yang's note reads: "The innate has no form, and the postnatal is caught in the physical realm. The innate has a clear, magical bright Heart (mind); the postnatal has acquired refined shapes." The innate originally has a pure, magic, bright nature. From this moment to eternity is like a single thought; like Buddha turning the mala beads in his hand. If one does not have a body of perfect purity to recruit the Yin Ling (uncontrolled soul), the Yin Ling will be isolated. If the postnatal perfect body does not have the innate magical Yuan (source) Shen, it cannot transform and sense the Yang Ling (controlled soul). How then can it elevate from mortality into sainthood?

Xing (true self) and Ming (life) are the Shen and the life source. Qi is Heaven's Zhen Yi (true one) water, Shen is Taiyi (the infinite origin) embracing true Qi, Xing is emptiness with form, and Ming is substance with emptiness. Ming without Xing is not active; Xing without Ming cannot be established. Emptiness is the innate Xing, and Shen is the Zhen Yi Qi (true one Qi).

The postnatal Ming is the Zhen Yi Qi's Jing substance. Therefore, the apparent Yin substance comes from the invisible one drop of Yang Qi. Thus, the apparent embraces the invisible essence, which needs to refine until the clarification where the Xuan bead (the emptiness with substance bead) appears. When the Xuan bead appears, one needs to collect and return it into the furnace, the emptiness and substance mix and interact, these two Qi energies sense each other, in the manner of the shadow following the body, as sound resounding from the valley. Then naturally the Heart (mind) condenses and the body releases, bone and muscle melt, the body and Shen are both magical and unite with the truth of Tao.

The magical process toward becoming a Shen Xian immortal is to embrace the innate true Yang Qi. This is the mother of Jin Dan (golden pill) and enchants the body's Yin Qi, transforming it into a pure Yang body. Chong Yang note reads: "The Jin Dan is from the interior, the medicine is from the exterior, but the Jin Dan pregnancy is indeed internal. The Shen is created according to the body." Hence given this one drop of innate true Yang Qi substance in the human body, no one is without it; everyone carries it with them. Mortals lose their true self by following familiar the lifestyle, excess emotions transforming into greed and love, wandering into the deep and wide ocean of desire.

The study of single pointed awareness has to have a true teacher guiding the innate Qi, the medicine that comes from the exterior and is dependent on the body to create. With the collecting method one needs to forget the emotions and the body, with no intention of emptiness, without even one thought, letting you quiet into nothingness. Then suddenly with spontaneous "Heaven light one object", there is in a stage of within and out and implicitly and explicitly, the Xuan bead (emptiness that has substance bead) appears. Why is it that the Xuan bead can be seen? Because in the quiet, the Shen embraces Qi, Qi solidifies and Jing condenses to form a Jin Dan that stays in the Dantian forever.

The external Xuan (emptiness has substance) appears like a room's lighting, shining through a clear transparent window. When the Upper Dantian of sky root and the Lower Dantian of moon cave are communicating, the body's thirty six palaces are all in the spring season, until the one drop returns; then the body is turned into the spring season all the time. After warming and caring for the Ding (the three legged pot that

represents the cooking and processing of our internal
medicine and awakened awareness), the Ding will see the
light transmission as if through a tent's curtain, this what is
called "Xuan bead established", and is external medicine. The
innate true Yuan is the true Yang fire, which is created by lead
meeting Kidney water (Gui). In this moment, one has to be
quiet to collect this Xuan bead. After it is taken one will
consciously feel that the Dantian is hot, the two Kidneys are
warm, the three gates have up and down movement, and the
one Qi penetrates and harmonizes through the body. The
awakening nectar pours through from the top, and dew is
sprinkling the Heart. The infinite inner view cannot totally be
explained or written down.

Once the innate Qi is created, the one Yang's action begin to
renew the Heaven and earth, as well as the regime of Kun
(Yang) and Qian (Yin), which has the effect of regenerating
mortal bone.

In human birth, conception comes from one's parents'
copulation, the Jing forms an embryo. In ten months it has
gradually filled with the Qi to create a perfect body. The one
drop of Ling light and Yuan Yang's Qi are already included in
the body. The given body has the Yin connected to Yang and
has the five elements within. Life and death, wealth and
poverty are forms that no one can escape.

Therefore one has innate true Yang in the body, the body
imagined as a furnace and Ding (The three legged pot that
represents the cooking and processing of our internal
medicine and awakened awareness) which interacts with the
postnatal true Yin. These two types of Qi transform to
condense as Xian (the immortal) fetus and refine and reverse
the transformation of the five elements; this processing as
done as thirty thousand careful carved works, not missing
even by a hair line of optimal fire temperature, and needs ten

months to achieve the state of being in which the inner immortal fetus bursts forth and soars from the flesh. In this level, the five elements cannot halt you, Yin and Yang cannot entangle you, the whole body's turbid Yin totally transforms into pure Yang. Out of the cage, freedom and happiness will be infinite.

After the practice has been completely mastered, the innate Qi will be transformed into good fortune, and the Xuan bead will be conceived. Having the Taiyi (infinity origin) embracing the true Qi, the body and the Shen are both perfectly magical, aligned with the natural truth of the Tao. Everything occurs naturally without the slightest push. Chong Yang's note reads: "In two and six timing, practice it in reverse, not following the familiar pathway, holding to Taoist ideas, visualizing color but not meshing with them, hearing but not following the sounds, smelling but not caring about good or bad smells, tasting but not letting the tongue sense the delicious, not letting the body's feeling go into the sexual territory, and not letting the thought dwell on the familiar". Awaken yourself often with shining the quietness and stillness in the light, unlike the mortal situation, taking a period of time to dwell in nature and Heaven's purity. Refining Ji (sky stem) refining your Heart, Heart is Li (fire), Li is Ji Tu, the Spleen (earth). Refine the Heart in stillness as when the Li fire palace is stable and still, then the Qi will be harmonized. Once harmonized the body is in peace. In peace the Jing and Qi will be abundant. In this stage of fulfillment, the lead (Kidney water essence) and mercury (the Heart fire essence) will condense. The condensed form has its own self-transformation. When the Xuan (emptiness has substance) bead conceived, Taiyi (infinity origin) embracing the true Qi arrived, the golden fluid refining the body, the bone dissolved into cold-jade, the body and Shen will both be magic, aligned with the true path of the Tao. All has come naturally.

If one does not pay attention to staying on the Tao path, to enabling the descending of the Heart fire to refine the body, there will be no progress. Though this practice has to encourage and strive to forget life and death, the mortal Shen dies so that the immortal Shen will be alive. This is the way to proceed.

Chapter One: Jade Fluid

Shen cannot be without Qi, Qi has to have Shen, respiratory exchanges that come from one source. They do not have material that you can hold, and one cannot desire to use it; empty the mind into nothingness, quiet and shine inner self, body and mind into no purpose, and then the Qi and Shen will progress on their own naturally, as the sky and earth create all naturally without purpose. Chong Yang's note reads: "The one innate Qi comes from nothingness, the two Qi interact naturally; the Shen embraces the Qi; Qi embraces Shen."

If one has innate and postnatal Qi bonded and interacted, his feeling as if dreaming and drunk, all come naturally without any purpose
.

During the inhale and exhale, inhale the Qi and exhale the Shen, the Shen is exhaled and Qi is inhaled, the upper and lower contacts, reverted in origin, refining into Dan (golden pill) condensed as a fetus, physically and mentally calmed down into a solid stillness with nothingness as its purpose, while the Shen and Qi naturally make progress.

Commit oneself to no purpose, into nothingness, not visualizing, as sky and earth are quiet and still; naturally Yin and Yang go up down. All things are made by the communication of the sun and moon. After one has practiced for a long period of time, quiet creates stillness, Shen goes into the Qi, Qi unites with Shen, the five elements and four images naturally develop, Jing (essence) condenses and Qi is solid, the Kan (water) and Li (fire) copulate.

At the beginning of quiet practice is pure Yin, it requires the Yang to refine the Yin to the true Qi; the Shen brightness came automatically. Chong Yang's note reads: "Refining self into versed stage and quiet for a long period time, the Qi and Shen interact naturally." Shen is the south fire; the fire is in the Taoism's Ba Gua, represented by the trigram Li. Jing (essence) belongs to North water; represented by the trigram Kan. Hun, the Liver spirit is in the East wood, wood is in the Ba Gua, represented by the trigram Zhen. Po, the Lung spirit is in West metal; metal in the Ba Gua, represented by the trigram Dui. Yi (spleen spirit) is the central earth, earth is in the Ba Gua, represented by the trigram Kun and called center Huang Ting of the yellow palace.

Innate Xuan Guan (entering emptiness one finds substance) is represented by the trigram Qian (father of Yang), hence Shen and Qi bonded, Shen into the Qi, the five elements and four images of the four direction's Qi and Shen naturally developed; this is the achievement of the interaction of Kan (water) and Li (fire).

The pure Yin fire is used to concentrate and brighten the lower Kun (mother of Yin) palace, the Yao Ming of explicit and implicit within both clearly expressed and yet only implied quietude stage, from which is derived the true Qi and Shen brightness unsolicited; this is the one Yang found and returned.

Chapter Two: The Production of Inner Medicine

As the Shen concentrates into the Kun (the mother of the Yin) Palace, the true fire will automatically occur. The Kun palace is an internal medicine production source, and it is the region where Yin and Yang interact. Chong Yang's note reads: "The Kun palace is at the center of the body, and is called Huang Ting (yellow court); it is under the Heart, and above the Kidneys, with the Liver in the east, and the Lungs in the west, in front of the Kidneys, and behind the navel, and it is an emptiness orifice where true Qi occurs."

The human body is formed after receiving the parents' Qi and Jing, which form the fetus and the placenta. The essence of the lineage carried on from the parents' and grandparents' Jing (essence) and so on, develops from emptiness to substance. The first parts of the fetus created are the three Yuan sources of upper, middle and lower capacities and the two kidneys, and from the two kidneys, the two eyes gradually develop, then the two outside kidneys followed by the testes in a male and the ovaries in a female fetus. After the three abilities of upper Shen, middle Qi and lower Jing have been perfectly formed, the internal organs and limbs are then created.

This one orifice has original source (Yuan) Qi; it is named Kun palace. The meaning of Kun is the carrying of all things that exist; it is where the internal medicine production happens and is indeed the place of Yin and Yang interaction.

The Shen concentrates in the Kun palace and needs to be maintained all day and all night without a second of separation. The Yuan Shen, the original spirit, shines in the lower body, and in returning the light during quietness, this is reversing the transformations, switching and returning to Heaven's gate; therefore, the Kun palace is where the great medicine occurs and where the Jin Dan can be condensed and formed.

If one does not have the true fire to refine with, then the golden fluid will mixed and turbid. If one does not have dedication, then the Yang fire will be lost, and the great medicine will not complete and there is no way to have innate Qi.

While refining for a period of time, of course water meets fire naturally, transforming into one Qi, and steams up and circulates without stopping. Since the true Jing has been created, the Yuan embryo of vitality is created.

Inhale and exhale include each other; the pulse stops and Qi is paused; quietness creates stillness; the great stillness and nothingness come with the innate one Qi.

This is innate in the same manner as a mother's Qi embraces the postnatal son's Qi. Follow the natural, let whatever occurs be and do not be in haste, and the innate Qi will occur spontaneously. Chong Yang's note reads: "Fire in the Kun palace is called the true person's fire." Used often, the Shen shines and refines Yin and Yang in the Kun palace, refining the Jing to Qi. Dedicate oneself in between walking, staying, sitting, and lying down; one can keep his concentration from being random and without scattering. Over the course of time, if one is practicing without achieving any accomplishment, it is due to a scattered mind.

If one refines for long enough, Jing is refined by the fire that naturally happens when it transforms into one Qi. As days pass, there will be three sudden sounds; shocks on the Nei Wan, (the Upper Dantian where the pituitary is), is the transformation of nectar, which descends to the Zhonglou (the throat), and then coagulates into Jing (essence) and fluid, and then reverts back to the location of the Kun palace. The embryo's Yuan Qi is gradually getting stronger, the Shen exhales and Qi inhales; care for the embryo naturally and the circulation never stops. The pulse and Qi pause and in the quiet and stillness, and in this great stillness, something moves suddenly; this is the occurrence of the innate one Qi. It comes from the Kun palace, as the mother loves the child naturally, and there will be an unpredictable magical transformation.

The transformation will come in time; if left alone and not forced in haste, it will have a natural efficacy. The light of Heaven is Shen light, when one practices in long periods of silence, and the Shen light will be brighter and strong, in quiet, the Shen is agile, the interior and exterior are without obstruction, even lust cannot obstruct the body, and one is able to naturally see objects on the other side of walls, as well as finding the ability to predict the past and the future.

At the beginning of the Chaos stage, Heaven and earth had not divided, Xuan Huang, the innate stage is ready to create and mix, time passes towards transformation, stillness has vividness, and in this vivid moment of the start of development, there is one object, explicit or implicit, within or without; this is the great medicine that has started to be created; one should not hurry to adopt it; if the practitioner begins a thought, innocence is gradually lost. Chong Yang's note reads: "The sky is light at the upper and the color is Xuan, emptiness has substance, the earth is heavy and the color is Huang, the color that one may start to see. Heaven and earth did not divide yet as Chaos in one Qi, Xuan Huang did not separate, the clear and turbid are not divided yet, they remain combined as one."

Time passes towards transformation, clear Qi goes up to the sky, and turbid Qi flows down to condense as earth. In this environment, earth Qi tends to ascend and sky Qi tends to descend, two Qi are exchanging to develop everything.

Quiet practice has the same theory, innate Zhen (true) Yang with postnatal Zhen (true) Yin, as Yin and Yang are mixed in one, as sky and earth's Xuan Huang mixed. Suddenly stillness has a lively quality; transformations automatically occur; Heaven and earth dividing and establishing the regime of Qian, the father of Yang, and Kun the mother of Yin. If there is an object both explicit and implicit, it is the appearance the Xuan bead (emptiness has bead). This Xuan bead seem to be at the exterior, but when one closes his eyes, it seems to be in the interior and seen very clearly, even after opening the eyes, it has an obvious appearance, but others cannot see this image. When the self can see this non-existent image clearly, this is called the non-appearance of the Xuan bead, and is the sprout of the beginning of the great internal medicine. In this moment, it is still tender, and hence cannot be picked yet. If one has a greedy fancy, and takes this Xuan bead, then one will lose this innate treasure and be lead to the mad, maniacal devil; excess respiration and excess running around, there is no escape. Life's treasures cannot be played around with; this is my advice.

Chapter Three: Collecting Inner Medicine

The Shen concentrates in the Kun palace and the Zhen (true) Qi automatically reverts into itself. Kun palace is a source of transforming where one receives Qi at the beginning and then knowing to practice this Kun palace is considered at a sage level. Chong Yang note reads: "Kun palace belongs to earth, and as Yin, as a postnatal human body possesses a form." Qian, the father of Yang palace belongs to the sky, as postnatal human body the innate and infinite Shen. Qian palace is nothingness Xuan Guan (entering of the emptiness has substance) orifice, and it is indeed a source of transforming in the transition from none to having, and from having to transforming and creating from this emptiness one orifice.

A human creates and receives Qi from the emptiness orifice at the beginning, and eventually dies from the evaporation of his Jing (essence), illusion, and the six thieves of excessive stimulation from the external environment. Therefore, he falls in this transforming cycle, and until he comes through, he cannot enumerate the ten thousand calamity cycles in order to wake up.

At the beginning, one concentrated Shen into the Kun palace, refining the Yin Jing essence. It then transforms into Yang Qi, causing it to steam up, hauled by the He Che river vehicle into endless circulation. Next, one concentrated Shen into the Qian (the father of Yang) palace, where it refines, condenses, and gathers. Here it gradually, though solidly, forms one Xuan bead (emptiness has a bead) the size of a grain of millet, constant at the present, and afterwards gains forever. His innate emptiness true Qi returns naturally, until he has lead light flash appearance as moon light and mercury light flash as sunshine. Seeing the sun and the moon united at one spot often happens, and it appears as one drop of Ling (soul) light in a round circle; it is shiny and bright, shining up and down, this is a true internal and exterior response. Innate Qi comes from nothingness. A natural sense of the magical process of transformation is seen as the mother embraces the son's internal Qi. External medicine is not an illusion.

Chong Yang's note reads: "The human is created by receiving sky and earth, Yin and Yang, the two forms of Qi." The body's Zhen (true) Yang Qi is a combination of the characters of lead, Jing (essence) and Kan (water). The Zhen (true) Yin's Qi is in the Heart, and is a combination of the characters of mercury, Shen, and Li (fire). These are a metaphor for the human inner body's sky and earth, and the Yin and Yang environment."

The practitioner acquired great medicine in an early stage, the Xuan bead (emptiness has a bead) is appearing, while the spirit and body are strong. At this moment, the Shen's Jing (essence) descends to meet the Kan (water). Jing's Shen turns up to meet the Li (fire), Jing, and they are mingling the inner and the interaction. The Yin and Yang communicate outside, allowing the inside and outside to brighten, shining up and down and thus appearing as a brightened bead, both round and shiny, through three gates of Xiao Zhu Tian are up and down circling as a wheel which never stops. In such states, there is harmony within the Jing and Shen, while metal and wood meet and interact, and water and fire are stimulated. Yes, this is a real interior scene and reflects an external and interior balanced view. Therefore, if this is not reality, how could it be seen?

Innate Qi is the mother's Qi, and postnatal Qi is the son's Qi. They sense each other naturally, and this is a miracle of the transformation of natural mother and son Qi. At the beginning stage, the medicine is from the external of innate mother's Qi, the son's Qi is human's Qi, and if the human can always be quiet, sky and earth Qi returns unsolicited.

First, refine the Kun (the mother of Yin), then refine the Qian (the father of Yang); this is known as the exchange of the Ding (the three legged pot that represents the cooking and processing of our internal medicine and awakened awareness), and the furnace position; this is the true sign of the Jin Dan (golden pill) miracle stage and is the secret for the optimal innate fire.

At the beginning, one would be required to refine the Dan (golden pill) from the water, finally, into stubborn mind and emptiness stage. One shall use inner true Qi to sense Heaven and earth's real essence. Using the Yang to fire up the water, allowing the water and fire to resonate, leaving it automatically at peace. Chong Yang's note reads: "While beginning the refining of the Dan, first the Shen brightens the Kun (the mother of the Yin) palace, in order to set ablaze the medicine and to use the Shen to maneuver the Qi. Until the true Qi is started, it is concentrated in the Qian (the father of the Yang) palace. Suspending the immortal fetus in the Ding, it has the form of the Xuan bead; tempered into great medicine, swallowing it into the belly, it enchants the Yin Qi, turning it into pure Qian of the pure Yang body. This is emptiness of magical processing."

The public does not understand the emptiness of magical processing, and is misguided by the heresies of false teaching, practicing and refining as if blind, one demanded to refine the Dan from the water. But water is explicit and implicit, and since one forgot his thought in the body and stagnated into explicitly and implicitly. This method eventually falls on the stubborn mind of emptiness, and these false methods cannot achieve the Dan at the end, this is not the correct path.

Where the Yang fires up, the water and fire are resonating; from here, one will naturally possess the Dan. Yang firing up the fire bead is a metaphor for the fire bead acquiring fire from the sun in Tai Yang, the originating level of Yang. The water bead is like the Tai Yin of the first level of Yin's palace. This water bead is used to acquire water from the moon. The sky and earth are separated by a vast distance, but in one second, one will have fire and water. Even an animal can receive Qi and sense the sun and moon and attain water and fire instantly. Moreover, the human being has a superior soul compared to other life forms. In quiet and stillness, how one does not sense the body's magical transforming, while the Jin Dan is formed.

When one has the sun and the moon lights, those two lights gather at the moment that is innate appropriate timing. And when the Nei Wan (the upper Dantian) wind blows in the brain, the lush ocean is clear. The body is in the bottomless sea, wondering if there is water or fire, and wondering if the self exists, or there is sky or earth. During this moment while feeling drunk and caught in dream, this is the moment when the tiger and the dragon interact; metal and wood harmonize, water and fire are stimulating, an image as fast as lightning, hastily taken, in this taking, the magical processing uses a smidge on of the appropriate power to pull the bow's wire, which would actually need a thousand pounds of strength. It appears it is adopting action, though it does not really adopt it, but rather, it attains it. Chong Yang's note reads: "I do not know this medicine's moment until a feeling of drunkenness comes; this is the medicine appearing."

With the Xuan's bead imaging, the sun and moonlight gather, and it is time to collect the medicine; its innate occurs at the appropriate time. At this moment, Nei Wan (the upper Dantian) in the brain is filled with wind blowing from the sky, pouring into the Xuan Guan (entering the emptiness, one finds substance) to the eyes, and through the whole body's pathways; the orifices are all opened; it feels as if the joints and bones are broken and the body is as soft as cotton, the

Heart is cold as ice, yet the Dantian is hot as fire, physically and mentally uncomfortable. But do not be afraid, because this is the right timing; the water and fire are cooking and steaming; it is the moment when the dragon and tiger as well as metal and wood are interacting. When the Qi is full in the three palaces, and two Qi are harmonized, the mortal body's emotions are extinguished. The Shen and Qi are peaceful and stable, falling into a dreamlike and drunken stage, as ten thousand units of water and ten thousand units of wood have so much mutual appreciation of each other that they are unaware of self or sky and earth. One can hear the thousand sounds of bells and thunder, as ten thousand light beams shine in the morning. The Ling (soul) brightens both inside and outside, gems fill the space, thunder and lightning reverberate in Qian (sky) and Kun (earth). This is the advent of the internal medicine, this magical processing, as using only half an ounce of power to pull a bow a thousand times heavier than a normal bow and with just one rotation, water moves a boat as heavy as ten thousand Hu (volume measure).

The sutra says, when the inner self has started exciting, the sky and earth will turn over, and this is a really wonderful useful stage. As the sutra says, as the moon moved in the Tian Xin (Heart and center of universe), the wind came on the water's surface for a moment. It also said, as the willow's wind blows on the face, the paulownia's moon shines into the chest. As Nei Wan (upper Dantian in the brain) feels clear wind, the Jiang Gong (Lower Dantian) sees a shining moon while in the forest with an easy clear wind, and all sentences are as if they are sounds from Heaven and are all described as the innate one Qi occurring from the outside.

Chapter Four: Obtaining the Inner Medicine

The Shen is concentrated in the Xuan (emptiness has a substance) palace where the Upper Dantian is located. The Yi, which is intention, is welcomed by the Pin of Yin house of the Lower Dantian combining with the Shen. The Shen and Yi unite, which allows the innate Qi to be occurred. One is Huang Fu (awakening within quiet, one finds substance) and Yao Ming (implicit and explicit; in awakening within; both clearly expressed and yet only implied quietude, one finds substance). There is one drop of red light flashing into the Lower Yuan source, where the true Qi has been harmonized. In this combination, Yin embraces Yang, Yang stimulates the Yin, and the true Jing (essence) is found as a surge of the sea.

From Tai Xuan Guan, while entering the original emptiness, one finds substance promoted into Nei Wan (Upper Dantian) and dissolving into a golden fluid which has a sweet and refreshing taste as it is swallowed into the abdomen. The body, through its ten thousand orifices, is in spring time where the whole body is brightened. At this point, the inner selves of the Qian (sky) and the Kun (earth) copulate, gaining the inner medicine forever. But one needs to take care and firmly seal and close it, preventing leaking, to keep the inner medicine safe and warm.

Chong Yang's note reads: "Xuan palace is Xuan Guan, where the melting millet is located." It is also called hanging fetus Ding, Zhu Sha Ding, and Qian Kun Ding, which are all synonyms."

As previously mentioned, the Qian and Kun are used for refining the Dan's device (the Ding) at the beginning, First, concentrate attention into the Kun position and find quiet; in this quiet there is life; this is time to collecting Yin's Yang, where the Yang is named Tu Sui (rabbit's marrow). True Qi starts to rise up to the Qian palace; from the movement into quiet; as Yang's Yin; this Yin is named Wu Gan of (black liver). These two mix and harmonize, and are refined into a wish-come-true-bead, this is the Kan of water and the Li of fire's copulation, allowing the Gui of Kidney Jing flower to be found, and the true lead, the real Kidney water shows up. This is innate, just occurring the moment one Yang started in motion at the beginning of creation.

On the third day of the month of the lunar calendar, the moon is rising on a Geng (sky stem) appearance; this happens at the Zi (sky stem) moment. One Shi (time measure) is divided into six Hou (time measure), where two Hou will have the internal medicine, and four Hou has a different magical processing. At this moment, one will have had medicine as one Hou, and find the stillness of quiet room. Here, the transport of natural fire enters the Dui Ding (position and sky stem), a half-round moon, along with the sound of the tiger and dragon. Worrying about the lead and mercury leaking out and one needs to practice an immersion bath and clean up the Heart, wash out worry, and continue this process.

One gradually passes Qian (Yang) Jia (sky stem) in thirteen days. The full moon shines Qian (sky) and Kun (earth) in fifteen days. And the Qian (sky) and the Kun (earth) regime is fully completed, Xuan (emptiness has substance) and Pin (Yin) is established, Jin Hua (golden flower) has shown up, and the San Yang (three Yang) has been prepared. The full moon shines in the Jia (sky stem) region, which is pure Qian (Yang)'s image. Beware of seeing the moon and not the sun, as on this occasion the sun and moon fully merge in their orbits. In this moment, timing provides the medicine again at two Hou (time measure).

There is magical processing after four Hou (time measure) at the first half of the month, the interior body will make tiger and dragon sounds. We should be careful to consider and care for this magical processing.

After a developed Xian (immortal) fetus when the time of the moon's cycle is at eighteen days, one will feel one Yin Xun (Daoism's wind trigram) which protects the city; there is magical processing in the field.

Next, to refine the two Yins, while the moon is on the wane at twenty three days, Gen (Daoism's ground trigram) cleans the Heart and there will be an immersion bath of magical processing.

Refined, the front three Yins and the back three Yangs had medicine in four Hou (time measure)'s, the magical processing of the Yang Shen occurs; this is the two Hou (time measure)'s theory.

The Shen stays in the Xuan (emptiness has substance) palace and thought is welcomed at the Pin (Yin) house. This combination is a collecting medicine tactic. While in the Xuan's palace, the fine Jing (essence) and the true lead Qi occur, finding the signs of a bright moon, and true mercury's fire occurs the image of a red sun.

Between the sun and the moon there are two golden flowers, bright as a golden and red colored Dan (golden pill) and as a strong as a mountain. It is the timing of the Dan that is not too tender or old, which must be hasting seized. With this method of processing the inner medicine, thought is welcoming in Pin (Yin) house, Shen and Yi of intention bond, allowing the contentment of innate Qi.

When awakening from the Huang Fu (awakening within quiet, one finds substance) and Yao Ming (implicit and explicit in awakening within both clearly expressed and yet only implied quietude, one finds substance), and there is one drop of red light flashing into the Lower Yuan (source), here is the meeting of the true Yin, where the Yin naturally combines with and embraces the Yang. The Yang stimulates the Yin so that the Yin and Yang are excited and the practitioner feels strong waves and tides from the Tai Xuan Guan (in the perineum region) to the sacrum and Jia Ji (mid back), through the jade pillow (occipital region). Jade nectar is transformed into golden fluid, is swallowed in the abdomen, and tastes sweet and fresh, while the ears hear the sound of the drum, ten thousand thunder sounds are heard, the space has filled with magical medicine, non-Qin (a stringed musical instrument) sounded non-Se (another stringed musical instrument) sounded, non-flute sounded and non-Xiao (one of pipe musical instruments) sounded. These sounds are different than ordinary music and are magical sounds, like that of cold spring and jade, and it seems Jinqing (a stone musical instrument) sounds shake the space like the sound of a cicada releasing its emotion, or as wind blowing in the pines; all these sounds are very unusual. When the Jade's vibration rings, there is a noise of a crow's voice and the sound of birds with rhyme-harmonizing frequency, continuing until your mouth and vision have become shocked, where the mind is happy and the thought is of joy, this is surely the state of bliss; this is in Heaven's palace of wonderland. The mortal state was the equivalent of being blind and deaf.

Physical and mental purity is a feeling that there are one hundred gates in harmony and peace, ten thousand orifices are in the spring season, the whole body radiates ten thousand morning light beams, and there is a round circle of light, within which there is an image of a baby, within which the advent of the Yang Shen staying near, the awareness of the coming of possible danger. Using the method of optimal fire temperatures to care for the immortal baby is the next chapter.

Chapter Five: Warmth and Care

The Shen is concentrated into the yellow room while the golden fetus automatically forms. The yellow room is below Qian (Sky) and above Kun (Earth). One needs to keep attention on it twenty four hours a day, embracing the Shen and hiding the light into it; whether walking, staying, sitting, or lying, all of the day's activity has to be sublimated to caring for the immortal fetus, as a hen embraces her egg, and as a dragon cares for his bead.

As one embraces Yuan (source) and concentrates in one, and holds onto the innate Yuan Shen and Yuan Qi, they have a constant bond, and are gradually united into one. One only needs to concentrate and calm the Shen and the breathing, there is no need to purposely activate the fire; the fire will optimize itself.

After one hundred days, the Ling (soul) is vigorous, the immortal fetus has been fully developed and will have a perfect round appearance in ten months; the Yin Po (the uncontrolled mind) will have been self-transformed, and the Yang Shen (the self-controlled mind) will appear after one thousand days. Due to one's care and warmth created by the optimal fire temperature that will strip out every group of Yin, leaving the physical body to be changed to pure Yang, the immortal infant occurs, therefore, beyond the flesh, there is another body that takes shape as haze and beams of morning light, one's Shen matches the Taixu (Infinite space); invisible as Shen, visible as Shen with Qi, which has no shadow under the sun and the moon, which can move through metal and stone without obstacle. Warming and caring for this immortal child for three years, the immortal body will mature, but still cannot let it travel far away, and up until nine years later, the immortal body will totally match the Taixu (infinite space), and the physical body with the Shen in the magical stage in the Tao's true path.

The sky, earth, mountain and valley will all eventually collapse, my own Taoist physical body will endure disaster and last forever, I have the potential to enter the mortal world and to help the mortals gain self awareness, my Shen and Qi take over the roles of the sky and earth and Yin and Yang, and the Yin and Yang can no longer control me, this is Tian Xian (Heavenly Immortal) level.

Chong Yang's note reads: "The Huangfang (yellow room) is the Huang Ting (yellow court); therefore it is under the Qian (sky) and above the Kun (earth) and is amid the middle." The golden fetus is the Xian (Immortal) fetus as character of gold is strong and is not a perishable material and as the human's Yuan Shen cannot be damaged or perish, the Yuan Shen is the clear magically refined body, such as it is as strong as gold and sharp as steel, as clear as glass and as bright as the full moon. This innate light is usually a full brightness, as it only wanes when the Shen is illusion.

Now one has mastered this Five Ling article's strategy of returning to the Dan (golden pill) pathway, which is refining from substance to nothing, extracting the black and uniting the red to develop the Xian (immortal) fetus, and returning to the true self, matching the original magical process.

The Golden fetus magical processing strategy is to use the Shen to concentrate, keeping the thoughts in the yellow room without losing it, intending to be there the twenty four hours a day, embracing and hiding the light, reversing the vision and listening without leaving the yellow room for even a moment, as a hen cares for her egg, and as a dragon cares for his bead. Take the example of the dragon keeping a bead under his whiskers, his mind and thoughts never forgetting, his Shen affects the bead, and that bead will be brightened; when the bead's brightness shines for a period of time, and the bead will develop into a small dragon which can soar into space, back and forth, and when people see it, it is in the image of the dragon, and this is the dragon's Shen. The Shen that is fully established can be transformed to control the clouds and create rain, and regenerate his bone to soar, this is the Shen Dragon. The Shen Dragon is able to make itself large or small, it can be visible or invisible, his power can split the Tai mountain, and raise floods, create clouds and fog, command lightning and the clap of thunder, becoming quiet, it can be hidden in the springs of water, this is the Yang Ling (Soul) substance. This is the Jin Dan (golden pill) and Tian Xian (Heavenly immortal) pathway rationale.

At the beginning, one needs to embrace the Yuan and concentrate into one, caring for the innate millet, and the Yuan Shen of the magical bead. The Du Ren Jing text said "Yuanshi Tianzun (original Heavenly master) hangs a treasure bead at five Zhang (length measure) above the ground in space; there are ten thousand sages and thousands of true immortals, moving in and out from the entrance of the bead." Keeping and caring for a long period time will naturally form the Yuan Shen millet; the Yuan Shen millet can survive through the calamity circles and be gradually dissolve all of the timing, space and universe into one.

A new moon is a bright crescent, and at the next stage is a bright half moon, until the brightness of the full moon, the perfect round circle of light. There is a golden light that occurs, the moon and sun bond, lead and mercury interact to form the Xian (immortal) fetus, which needs warmth and care fro three years to raise the immortal fetus. The infant matures and grows for nine years, and fully mature, the Yin dregs have disappeared, the one Shen can be transformed into hundreds and thousands of immortal Shens; the physical body and the Shen are both magical, can be shown to be visible, and turning invisible, refining the Shen matching the Taixu (infinite space), returning to Wuji (endless) true Taoist pathway, matching the Yuanshi of the original magical stage, watching the Heaven and earth in magical mysteries, such as a millet in the infinite and as a piece of cloud in Taixu (infinite space). What is the so significant about the five elements moving and Yin and Yang changing? I am the Marshal of Heaven and Earth, and of Yin and Yang, sure never to have a beginning or an ending, endless even through all of the calamities, together with the Tao and truth. Oh, this is the Shen transforming!

Made in the USA
Lexington, KY
01 June 2013